THE
PATTERN OF
SOUND
DOCTRINE

THE
PATTERN OF
SOUND
DOCTRINE

Systematic Theology at the Westminster Seminaries

Essays in Honor of
ROBERT B. STRIMPLE

Edited by David VanDrunen

PUBLISHING
P.O. BOX 817 • PHILLIPSBURG • NEW JERSEY 08865-0817

Unless otherwise indicated, Scripture quotations are from the authors' own translations.

Scripture quotations in chapter 6, and, unless otherwise indicated, those in chapter 8, are from the HOLY BIBLE, NEW INTERNATIONAL VERSION®. NIV®. Copyright © 1973, 1978, 1984 by International Bible Society. Used by permission of Zondervan Publishing House. All rights reserved.

Italics in Scripture quotations indicate emphasis added.

Page design and typesetting by Lakeside Design Plus

Printed in the United States of America

Library of Congress Cataloging-in-Publication Data

VanDrunen, David, 1971–
    The pattern of sound doctrine : systematic theology at the Westminster seminaries / David VanDrunen.
        p. cm.
    Includes bibliographical references and index.
    ISBN 0-87552-717-5
    1. Theology, Doctrinal. 2. Reformed Church—Doctrines. 3. Westminster Theological Seminary (Philadelphia, Pa.) I. Title.

BT78.V36 2004
230′.5—dc22

                                                                2004051007

Contents

Part Three: Particular Issues in Westminster Systematics

Part Four: Westminster Systematic Theology and the Life of the Church

Acknowledgments

As editor, I wish to thank all the contributors for their willingness to participate in this project, for their hard work in getting the essays done in (relatively) timely fashion, and for sharing my enthusiasm for honoring Bob Strimple in this way.

We are grateful to Mr. Allan Fisher and his colleagues at P&R Publishing for agreeing to take on this volume and for seeing it through to publication.

Some helpful hands enabled these essays to get to the publisher in good time and contributed to making the final project better than it otherwise would have been. In particular, I am grateful to my student Aaron Denlinger for valuable editorial assistance; to James Lund, librarian and associate professor of theological bibliography at Westminster Seminary California, for providing the Strimple bibliography; and to Jennifer Redd for producing the index.

Finally, I am grateful to my wife, Katherine, for supporting my work on this project even in the midst of her struggle with leukemia. Her love and respect for her former teacher and advisor Bob Strimple are no less than mine.

A Tribute to Robert B. Strimple

David VanDrunen

I t is with great pleasure and appreciation that the contributors
present this collection of essays to our friend, colleague, and,
in many cases, mentor, Robert Benson Strimple. The presentation
of a *festschrift*, by its very nature, should not be an ordinary event,
no standard occasion that each and every retiring scholar ought
to expect. With this very much in mind, we offer these essays to a
man who has earned the respect and admiration of thousands of
students and colleagues over several decades and whose contributions to both the church and the academy have distinguished
him as an eminent minister of the gospel of Jesus Christ.

The fittingness of this *festschrift* and the form in which it
appears is evident only in light of the work of Dr. Strimple.
Dr. Strimple was born on April 18, 1935, in New Castle, Delaware.
He was raised a Methodist, though in his teenage years took a
theologically more conservative turn, a turn that landed him for
a brief time in an Orthodox Presbyterian congregation—a har-
binger of things to come. However, by the time he graduated from
the University of Delaware in 1956, he identified himself as a pre-
millennial, dispensationalist, Arminian Baptist. By a kindly act
of providence, Dr. Strimple heeded the advice of a pastor who recommended that he pursue his ministerial studies at the intellec-
tually challenging and biblically committed Westminster Seminary nearby in Philadelphia. His Arminianism and dispen-

sationalism quickly fled, and, by the time of his senior year, his premillennialism was wobbly enough to prohibit him from accepting an invitation to teach at the premillennialist FEBIAS Bible College in Manila. His Baptist convictions, however, were more persistent. Thus, after a year of teaching at a Christian high school in Paterson, New Jersey, Dr. Strimple took up duties as a professor of systematic theology at the Toronto Bible College (now Tyndale Bible College) in 1961. He ruefully recounts the time when his beloved professor John Murray invited him over from New Jersey to spend an entire day with him discussing baptism and even took him to the finest restaurant in town for lunch. Though Dr. Strimple was to complete a Th.M. under Murray in 1965, the Scotsman was not able to sway his protégé on this occasion.

Dr. Strimple taught in Toronto for eight years, during which time he began Ph.D. work in systematic theology at Trinity College of the University of Toronto (he would write his dissertation on Union Seminary theologian John Knox and receive his degree in 1972). During his later years in Toronto, at the encouragement of then Westminster Seminary president Edmund Clowney, Dr. Strimple again took up the baptism matter in earnest. After a period of wrestling with the issues, he came to paedobaptist convictions—a conversion of sorts that would prove to have great consequences for the Reformed and Presbyterian world for decades to come. For though his theological change had endangered his position at Toronto Bible College, President Clowney and the Westminster faculty wasted little time in inviting him to join them in Philadelphia. Purportedly, Dr. Strimple received his invitation without even a faculty interview—a testimony to the strength of the recommendation given him by Professor Murray, who had retired a short time before. Also, Dr. Strimple, who had been ordained in a Canadian Baptist denomination in 1964, was received by the Presbytery of Philadelphia of the Orthodox Presbyterian Church shortly after taking up duties at Westminster.

Dr. Strimple assumed his teaching responsibilities at Westminster in 1969, and it took little time before his administrative skills were also recognized. He was made dean of students a year after arrival, and in 1972 he was appointed vice president for academic affairs and dean of the faculty. In this dual capacity as teacher and administrator, Dr. Strimple became intimately involved in discussions about establishing another Westminster campus on the West Coast. In 1979, while retaining his positions at Westminster in Philadelphia, he moved his family to Escondido, California, where, with another Westminster vice president, Robert den Dulk, he began laying the foundation for what would become Westminster Theological Seminary in California. Dr. Strimple took responsibility for gathering the initial faculty and setting the curriculum, and when Westminster in California became an independent institution in 1982 with the blessing of Philadelphia, he became its first president—while retaining a full-time teaching load.

Dr. Strimple remained at Westminster in California for the rest of his career. He stepped down from the presidency after six years, in 1988, but continued his enthusiastic classroom teaching, mentoring of students, and faculty leadership for another thirteen years. And, though he retired in 2001, he continues to be a venerable presence on the Westminster California campus, dispensing solicited and wise advice to faculty, doing some writing, and occasionally making cameo appearances in the classroom. He and his wife of many years, Alice, have watched the growth of four children and now eleven grandchildren, many of whom live in Southern California and are a constant source of healthy pride to the Strimples.

Dr. Strimple is currently at work editing, for CD format, the tapes of his three required courses in systematic theology that were recorded during his last year of full-time teaching. When completed, these CDs will offer the audio of every classroom lecture plus the printed text of the lengthy course syllabus (course outline, bibliography, and essays on related topics not addressed in class). The first course to be offered will be the senior course, entitled "Salvation in Christ," 50 classroom hours on 50 CDs, and will be available from Westminster Seminary California in the fall of 2004.

This brief sketch of the work of Bob Strimple ought to give a fair indication not only of why the compilation of this volume is well deserved, but also of why this volume takes the shape that it does. Unlike many *festschriften*, this collection is not a random assortment of essays by interested parties. Rather, all the essays in this volume revolve around a single theme: the discipline of systematic theology as it has been practiced and taught at the Westminster Seminaries and, through them, as it has impacted the church of Jesus Christ. As the initiator and editor of this volume, I judged that no topic could better befit Dr. Strimple. He is, first and foremost, a teacher of systematic theology. No one who sat in his classroom could doubt his dedication and passion for the subjects he taught. But, also very importantly, he was an institutional leader and institutionally minded. His nearly 20 years in various administrative positions at both Westminster Seminaries shaped him into a teacher whose concerns did not begin and end at the classroom door, but one who always saw his task as intimately connected with the larger concerns and responsibilities of the institutions that he served. And, third, he is a man of the church. He has for many years been pleased that Westminster in California did not succumb to the common temptation to proliferate the number of programs it offered, but has continued as primarily a school training Master of Divinity students—and therefore future pastors. He knew that in the midst of the historical circumstances that made twentieth- and now twenty-first-century conservative North American Reformed and Presbyterian churches largely served by independent seminaries, the Westminsters have had a crucial part to play—and without the churches there would be no such seminaries. Dr. Strimple, who sat on the session of local congregations, devoted time to denominational study committees, and served as moderator of the OPC General Assembly in 1986, has always remained deeply committed to and active in Christ's church.

Hence, the nature of this volume: systematic theology at the Westminster Seminaries. The discipline, the institutions in which it is taught, and the churches in which their graduates minister cannot ultimately be separated. The first two essays reflect on historical issues pertinent to Westminster systematics. The next section features papers that in various ways evaluate the relationships that systematic theology has enjoyed with other theological disciplines at the Westminsters and offers proposals for subsequent work in these disciplines. The third section presents four essays on particular issues of importance for Westminster systematics. Finally, the contributors represented in the fourth section reflect upon the relationship of Westminster and its theology with the broader life of the church. We hope that these essays contribute in a helpful way to the defense and progress of Reformed theology in Reformed churches in this new century. For this is precisely the goal that Robert B. Strimple pursued in his life and work.

Given the nature of this volume, we are all the more pleased that its publication occurs on the occasion of the seventy-fifth anniversary of the founding of Westminster Theological Seminary, the twenty-fifth anniversary of the founding of Westminster Seminary California, and the thirty-fifth anniversary of Dr. Strimple's first appointment at Westminster.

Part One

Historical Studies

1

Systematic Theology at Old Princeton Seminary: Unoriginal Calvinism

D. G. Hart

Charles Hodge, of whom it was said, "No man has ever been so completely the embodiment of [Princeton Seminary],"[1] apparently took great pleasure in being dull. As Mark A. Noll observes in his anthology of the Princeton theology, at the observance of two notable anniversaries, Hodge featured his seminary's and his own teaching's conventionality. In 1870, for instance, when reflecting on editorial developments within Princeton's *Biblical Repertory and Princeton Review*, Hodge claimed that "an original idea in theology is not to be found on the pages" of the journal "from beginning until now," thus leavening the title " 'Princeton Theology' . . . without distinctive meaning."[2] Two years later, at the fiftieth anniversary of his own election as professor at Princeton, Hodge repeated that "I am not afraid to say that a new idea never origi-

1. Sydney E. Ahlstrom, *Theology in America: The Major Protestant Voices from Puritanism to Neo-Orthodoxy* (Indianapolis: Bobbs-Merrill, 1967), 252.
2. Charles Hodge, *Biblical Repertory and Princeton Review, Index Volume* (1870–71), 1:11, quoted in Mark A. Noll, ed., *The Princeton Theology: Scripture, Science and Theological Method from Archibald Alexander to Benjamin Warfield* (Grand Rapids: Baker, 1983), 38.

3

nated in this Seminary."[3] He conceded that the seminary's lack of
creativity might be grounds for reproach, and later historians have
had little trouble pointing out that what might have been an
admirable conviction was nonetheless a foolish ideal for a theological tradition trying to succeed in what was becoming one of the
most modern and innovative of nations. In assessing the Princeton
critique of liberalism, for instance, William R. Hutchison observes
that "the inspired obstinacy of the Hodges, Pattons, and Warfields,
and of John Gresham Machen, shone in marked, self-conscious contrast with all such flickering lights."[4] Even so, Princeton's theology
proved so obstinate that when the seminary celebrated its centennial in 1912, Francis Landey Patton, the school's president, stated
that Princeton "had no oddities of manner, no shibboleths, no pet
phrases, no theological labels, no trademark. She simply taught the
old Calvinistic theology without modification: and she made obstinate resistance to the modifications proposed elsewhere. . . . There
never was a distinctly Princeton Theology."[5] For theologians at Old
Princeton then, repeating the truths of the Calvinistic wing of the
Protestant Reformation, no matter how boring or predictable, was
a point of pride.

Students of American theology have found, of course, that
remaining the same is almost as difficult as being original. The
Princeton theology, in fact, may have possessed distinctive teachings, as one side in the 1970s and 1980s debates among evangelicals over inerrancy contended.[6] Even so, despite changes and
modifications within Reformed teaching that the likes of

3. Quoted in Noll, ed., *The Princeton Theology* from A. A. Hodge, *The Life of Charles Hodge* (New York: Scribner, 1880), 38.

4. William R. Hutchison, *The Modernist Impulse in American Protestantism* (Cambridge: Harvard University Press, 1976), 199.

5. Francis Landey Patton, "Princeton Seminary and the Faith," in *The Centennial Celebration of the Theological Seminary of the PCUSA at Princeton* (Princeton: Princeton Theological Seminary, 1912), 349–50.

6. See, for instance, Jack B. Rogers and Donald K. McKim, *The Authority and Interpretation of the Bible* (San Francisco: Harper & Row, 1979); and John D. Woodbridge, *Biblical Authority: A Critique of the Rogers/McKim Proposal* (Grand Rapids: Zondervan, 1982).

Archibald Alexander, Charles Hodge, Archibald Alexander Hodge, and Benjamin Breckinridge Warfield made over the course of the nineteenth century, the culture of systematics at Princeton pointed decidedly toward predictability and regularity. Conservation was the goal of the Princeton theology because novelty could very well lead to destruction.

Ironically, the conservative posture of systematic theology at Princeton turned out to be original among Calvinists in the United States. This irony became especially noticeable during nineteenth-century debates between New England Congregationalists and mid-Atlantic-states Presbyterians over Jonathan Edwards and which party could rightfully claim his theological mantle. In a valuable essay on these doctrinal contests, Mark A. Noll summarizes the arguments between Congregationalists and Presbyterians in a point that underscores the Princeton theology's dedication to unoriginality. He writes:

> New England clearly perceived the intellectual spirit of Edwards more accurately than did Princeton. Edwards had indeed been an independent inquirer. As Samuel Hopkins put it in the first biography: Edwards "took his religious principles from the Bible, and not from any human system or body of divinity. Though his principles were *Calvinistic*, yet he called no man father. He thought and judged for himself, and was truly very much an original." The New Englanders . . . were also bold and original thinkers who likewise wished to be known as Calvinists while calling no man father. The Princeton Theology, on the other hand, defined itself as a conserving effort. It was willing to say "father" to a whole host of orthodox divines.[7]

What follows is an effort to account for Princeton's congenital conservatism.[8] Several factors contributed to Hodge and com-

7. Mark A. Noll, "Jonathan Edwards and Nineteenth-Century Theology," in *Jonathan Edwards and the American Experience*, ed. Nathan O. Hatch and Harry S. Stout (New York: Oxford University Press, 1988), 268–69.

8. Although the history of theology has not been a burning topic to students of American religious history, the following assessments aside from other books cited here provide some orientation to the Princeton theology's significance: David B. Calhoun, *Princeton Seminary*,

pany's apparent pride in monotony. The one isolated in what follows is the Princeton theology's own conception of theology as a scientific enterprise through the writings of Charles Hodge, A. A. Hodge, and Benjamin B. Warfield.[9] This idea has sometimes been attacked as a form of rationalism. At other times the Princeton rhetoric of scientific theology sounds to contemporary ears like a methodological outlook at odds with the humanistic and churchly nature of theological scholarship. Yet underneath the Princeton notion of theology as a science stood an approach to systematic theology that combined a high regard for human intelligence and its capacity for precise formulations of ideas along with a keen sensitivity to the biblical witness. This combination resulted in theological stability and fidelity to Reformed orthodoxy that had no trouble identifying systematic theology as the queen of the theological disciplines. As such, the Princeton theology stood out among other schools of American theology, both for its Calvinism and for its longevity. That approach in turn informed the aims of Westminster Seminary's original faculty in whose hands the act of balancing systematic and biblical theology for the sake of unoriginality would prove harder to achieve.

The Science of Systematics

In his history of New England theology, Frank Hugh Foster said of Charles Hodge that he "showed no ability, and but lit-

2 vols. (Edinburgh: Banner of Truth, 1994–96); John W. Stewart and James H. Moorhead, eds., *Charles Hodge Revisited: A Critical Appraisal of His Life and Work* (Grand Rapids: Eerdmans, 2002); Hugh T. Kerr, ed., *Sons of the Prophets: Leaders in Protestantism from Princeton Seminary* (Princeton: Princeton University Press, 1963); Glenn T. Miller, *Piety and Intellect: The Aims and Purposes of Ante-Bellum Theological Education* (Atlanta: Scholars, 1990); W. Andrew Hoffecker, *Piety and the Princeton Theologians: Archibald Alexander, Charles Hodge, and Benjamin Warfield* (Phillipsburg, N.J.: Presbyterian and Reformed, 1981); and William K. Selden, *Princeton Theological Seminary: A Narrative History, 1812–1992* (Princeton: Privately printed, 1992).

9. I have excluded Archibald Alexander, Princeton's first professor, because of his relative silence compared to the Hodges and Warfield on systematic theology's scientific nature. Alexander's smaller output on theological method is evident in Noll, ed., *The*

tle desire, to understand the New England men." Foster added that Hodge had so constantly "misinterpreted" the New Englander's theology "that he soon lost all influence in opposing their speculations among thinking men." As such, Hodge could be "safely left by the historian of a progressive school of theology to the natural consequence of his own remark that during the many years of his predominance at Princeton that institution had never brought forward a single original thought."[10] For those like Foster, caught up in the heady advances of United States' prosperity and industry at the turn of the twentieth century, interpreting the Princeton theology as a backward school of thought made sense. But aside from questions of contemporaneity and creativity, other explanations are possible for the rift between theologians at Princeton and those in the land and shadow of Jonathan Edwards. Indeed, Foster's own use of the term "speculation" is important for understanding Princeton's posture in nineteenth- and twentieth-century theological developments. Where the New England theology and other expressions of formal religious thought in the United States were geared toward philosophy and especially rather abstract notions surrounding free will and human responsibility, Princeton's theology was concrete and scientific. For some that was a liability. But the scientific character of the Princeton theology was actually a way to preserve systematic theology's dependence on exegesis and duty to arrange biblical teaching methodically. New England theologians and the Princetonians may have indeed been talking past one another. But the reasons went deeper than being up-to-date.

Charles Hodge arguably took first place in claiming scientific method as a foundation for theology, to the embarrassment

---

Princeton Theology. For an assessment of Alexander's contribution to the Princeton theology, see Lefferts A. Loetscher, *Facing the Enlightenment and Pietism: Archibald Alexander and the Founding of Princeton Theological Seminary* (Westport, Conn.: Greenwood, 1983).

10. Frank Hugh Foster, *A Genetic History of the New England Theology* (Chicago: University of Chicago Press, 1907), 432.

of some later Calvinists.[11] In the introduction to his *Systematic Theology* (1872), a textbook on which countless American Presbyterian ministers cut their doctrinal incisors, Hodge starts with a refrain lost on many Reformed and Presbyterians after 1929. He claims that theology is a science and begins by commenting on astronomy, chemistry, and history as scientific enterprises. Every science possesses "two factors," "facts and ideas." "Science," Hodge explains, "is more than knowledge" but is also "the persuasion of what is true on adequate evidence." Consequently, "the facts of astronomy, chemistry, or history do not constitute the science of those departments of knowledge" because "in every department the man of science is assumed to understand the laws by which the facts of experience are determined."[12]

The point of Hodge's comparison was, of course, to argue for systematic theology's scientific credentials. "If . . . theology be a science," he writes, "it must include something more than a mere knowledge of facts. It must embrace an exhibition of the internal relation of those facts, one to another, and each to all." From here Hodge proceeds to the line that echoes one frequently quoted in which he likens the Bible and the theologian to nature and the scientist. "The Bible contains the truths which the theologian has to collect, authenticate, arrange, and exhibit in their internal relation to each other." Hodge adds that this is where to locate the difference between biblical and systematic theology; the former's aim is to "ascertain and state the facts of Scripture," while the purpose of the latter is to "take those facts, determine their relation to each other and to other cognate truths, as to vindicate them and show their harmony and consistency." Almost as an aside, Hodge ends this introduction with the statement that sys-

11. Mark A. Noll, "Charles Hodge as an Expositor of the Spiritual Life," in John W. Stewart and James H. Moorhead, eds., *Charles Hodge Revisited: A Critical Appraisal of His Life and Work* (Grand Rapids: Eerdmans, 2002), 181–216, offers a perceptive critique of the tension in Hodge's theological method between scientific induction and moral intuition, one that afflicted Hodge arguably more than his son or Warfield.

12. Charles Hodge, *Systematic Theology*, 3 vols. (New York: Scribner, 1872–73), 1:1–2.

tematic theology "is not an easy task, or one of slight importance."[13] No one may plausibly claim that Hodge was guilty of understatement.

The Princeton theologian's legendary statements about theological method come ten pages later and go like this: "The Bible is to the theologian what nature is to the man of science. It is his store-house of facts; and his method of ascertaining what the Bible teaches, is the same as that which the natural philosopher adopts to ascertain what nature teaches." Theological method, then, is the same as scientific method. It includes the assumption of certain "first principles" pertaining to epistemology, metaphysics, and ethics, the duty to collect facts from the Bible, and the need to do so inductively (read: objectively). "We must take the facts of the Bible," Hodge writes, "as they are, and construct our system so as to embrace them in all their integrity."[14]

Part of the legend surrounding these statements from Hodge is their apparent epistemological naivete. Dutch Calvinists from Ralph J. Danhof to John C. Vander Stelt have read the Princetonian theological method as a flawed recipe for autonomy and rebellion. Danhof claimed that the "stains of Humanism" were evident in Charles Hodge's teaching on infant salvation, original sin, election, and the means of grace.[15] Vander Stelt's criticisms went even deeper to trace the fruit of such humanism to the root of faulty theological method. The Scottish philosophy upon which Princeton relied embodied a "dualistic view of reality, a semi-autonomous understanding of man, and a reductionistic theory of knowledge and truth."[16] From the perspective of religious historians the verdict may be less polemical but no more favorable. Princeton's overly rational approach to science turned out, in the race to defend Christianity against the claims of science, to be the

13. Ibid.

14. Ibid., 10, 13.

15. Ralph J. Danhof, *Charles Hodge as a Dogmatician* (Goes, The Netherlands: Oosterbaan & Le Cointre, 1929), 192–200.

16. John C. Vander Stelt, *Philosophy and Scripture: A Study in Old Princeton and Westminster Theology* (Marlton, N.J.: Mack, 1978), 305.

also-ran. Mark A. Noll pointed out the irony of Princetonians enlisting "the procedures of the Enlightenment as apologetic means to sustain the Christian faith" while at the same time unintentionally opening "the door to the spread of naturalistic thought in America."[17] George M. Marsden added to the critique by noting the innocence by which Princetonians confidently asserted a rational basis for Christian truth. He explained that the scientific character of theology that informed the Princeton theology would, after Hodge's life, be a fight of "overwhelming odds" in which these theologians would go down "with their guns blazing." Still, it was a "hopeless . . . position."[18] It is worth observing, however, that the Dutch-Calvinist–informed assessments of Princeton's dependence on Scottish Enlightenment philosophy have of late begun to be revised themselves.[19]

As much as Princeton's theological method may have ceded too much authority to the rational autonomous mind, its scientific instincts also paid significant theological dividends. In fact, for all of the complaints about Princeton's philosophical concessions—ones assumed to produce theological novelty (read: theological liberalism)—the seminary's teaching remained much more old-fashioned (read: Reformed) than any of the other nineteenth-century schools of Calvinist theology in North America. Hodge's opening statements to *Systematic Theology* are again instructive. As naive as it would later sound to Christians once theology showed that it could not keep pace with the advances of specialized investigation of the natural world, Hodge's claims for theology's scientific method possessed a measure of common sense. By stating that the Bible is to the theologian what nature is to the scientist, he is at one level simply trying to make the point that

17. Mark A. Noll, *Princeton and the Republic, 1768–1822: The Search for a Christian Enlightenment in the Era of Samuel Stanhope Smith* (Princeton: Princeton University Press, 1989), 298.

18. George M. Marsden, *Understanding Fundamentalism and Evangelicalism* (Grand Rapids: Eerdmans, 1991), 124.

19. See, for instance, Nicholas Wolterstorff, *Thomas Reid and the Story of Epistemology* (New York: Cambridge University Press, 2001).

the Westminster Confession of Faith affirms in chapter 1 that Scripture is the basis for definite knowledge of God. "It is plain that complete havoc must be made of the whole system of revealed truth," Hodge declares, "unless we consent to derive our philosophy from the Bible, instead of explaining the Bible by our philosophy." For instance, if the Bible taught that "sin is hereditary," then the theologian needed to affirm truths in accord with "that fact." The same went for the guilt of Adam's sin, and Christ's vicarious sacrifice. Doctrine needed to conform to the material revealed in the Bible. The unexceptional aspect of this point came through clearly in the following statement about the priority of the Bible to the construction of theology, of fact to the explanation of facts:

> It would be easy to show that in every department of theology,—in regard to the nature of God, his relation to the world, the plan of salvation, the person and work of Christ, the nature of sin, the operations of divine grace—men, instead of taking the facts of the Bible, and seeing what principles they imply, what philosophy underlies them, have adopted their philosophy independently of the Bible, to which the facts of the Bible are made to bend.[20]

To read so much Scottish philosophy into such a statement is to miss the influence of the material principle of the Reformation on the Princeton theology's methodology. By the time Hodge wrote these sentences, Common Sense Realism may have been losing ground quickly to German Idealism.[21] But despite the philosophical idiom, the connection Hodge drew between the Bible and the facts of nature was also a powerful demonstration of the exegetical character of theology at Princeton. Over against the metaphysical and highly speculative orientation of New England

20. Hodge, *Systematic Theology*, 1:14.
21. On the consequences of the transition in American Protestant theology from Scottish to German philosophy, see Bruce Kuklick, *Churchmen and Philosophers: From Jonathan Edwards to John Dewey* (New Haven: Yale University Press, 1985), 117–89.

Calvinism, the Princeton theology remained firmly wedded not to intellectual consistency but to biblical precision.

The theological method of Old Princeton was more than simply exegetical, however. In his introduction to *Systematic Theology*, Hodge also devotes some space to the "need for system" in theology. He asks, for instance, "Why not take the truths as God has seen fit to reveal them, and thus save ourselves the trouble of showing their relation and harmony?" Hodge's answer is again to compare theology to science. The human mind is so constituted, he argues, so that it cannot be satisfied with "the possession of a mass of undigested facts." In addition, Hodge points out that understanding the relationships of various truths—the undergirding system—is a "higher kind of knowledge." Aside from similarities between science and theology, he also recognizes the inherently systematic character of Christian truth. "If we would discharge our duty as teachers and defenders of the truth, we must endeavor to bring all the facts of revelation into systematic order and mutual relation." Finally, Scripture itself demonstrated the need for system in theology. In the epistles of the New Testament, Hodge sees the beginnings of an attempt by teachers in the church to understand and arrange the various parts of divine revelation. These epistles function as an "authority and guide" for systematic theologians.[22]

The exegetical and systematic character of Old Princeton's theology was not only evident in Charles Hodge's long and influential career. It also marked the approach of his successors, Archibald Alexander Hodge and Benjamin B. Warfield, and so cultivated a distinct school of American theology. For instance, when Hodge's son, A. A., penned his *Outlines of Theology* (1879), he was still following in his dad's footsteps of scientific theology, and for the younger Hodge, the scientific nature of systematic theology still implied biblical exegesis and systematic thought.

The appeal to science by A. A. Hodge sounds grandiose even when remembering that the lure of the Enlightenment would take

22. Hodge, *Systematic Theology*, 1:2–3.

another century to wear off and even then only among certain sectors of the humanities.[23] Hodge begins in a vein arguably more inflated than his father when he states, "Theology is the scientific determination, interpretation, and defence, of those Scriptures, together with the history of the manner in which the truths it reveals have been understood, and the duties they impose have been performed, by all Christians in all ages."[24] This was a tall order, but one that Princetonians confidently filled. Hodge's confidence is equally brimming when he adds that "theological methodology provides for the scientific determination of the true method, general and special, of pursuing theological sciences." Systematic theology may not have been rocket science (an anachronistic comparison, to be sure), but it was not the sort of enterprise that average Christians could pursue on their own. Hodge offers the following as a reason for leaving theology to experts:

> The relations of all truths are determined by their nature, whence it follows that their nature is revealed by an exhibition of their relations. Such an exhibition will also tend to widen the mental horizon of the student, to incite him to breadth of culture, and prevent him from unduly exalting or exclusively cultivating any one special branch, and thus from perverting it by regarding it out of its natural limitations and dependencies.[25]

Still, beneath the expertise of scientific method, which also conveyed the seriousness of the enterprise, rested Princeton's firm commitment to the Bible. As much as the inductive method that science apparently required of systematic theology could exalt human rationality, Hodge, like his father, clearly believes that scientific method best preserves the Bible as the chief

23. One of the best treatments of the Enlightenment's demise is Alasdair C. MacIntyre, *Three Rival Versions of Moral Inquiry: Encyclopaedia, Genealogy, and Tradition* (Notre Dame: University of Notre Dame Press, 1990).
24. A. A. Hodge, *Outlines in Theology* (1879; Grand Rapids: Zondervan, 1972), 15.
25. Ibid., 16.

source of theological reflection. "Those who make Reason, and those who make the inspired Church, and those who make the inspired Scriptures the source and standard of all divine knowledge, must severally configure the theological sciences to the different foundations on which they are made to stand."[26] Princeton's commitment to the primacy of Scripture was evident in A. A. Hodge's arrangement of the theological sciences. These begin with those departments auxiliary to theology, proceed to apologetics, exegesis, systematic theology, and practical theology, and finish with historical theology. In this scheme the interrelatedness of exegetical and systematic theology is striking. The former seeks to determine the *"ipsissima verba"* and meaning of divine revelation. The latter develops "into an all-embracing and self-consistent system of the contents of that Revelation, and its subsequent elucidation and defence."[27] Hodge, following his father closely, adds that the method of systematic theology is inductive. "It rests upon the results of Exegesis for its foundation" and includes "the construction of all the contents of revelation into a complete system of faith and duties." In other words, exegesis was not sufficient. "The human mind," Hodge explains, "must seek unity in all its knowledge. God's truth is one, and all the contents of all revelations natural and supernatural must constitute one self-contained system. . . ."[28]

Warfield, who assumed responsibility for teaching systematic theology in 1887 after A. A. Hodge, did not write anything bordering on a manual of theological instruction. Warfield was a remarkably prolific author, and his strength as a writer was in producing a variety of articles, some popular, some scholarly, in varying lengths. This explains the books by which readers most commonly access the man who was arguably the greatest of the Princetonians; Warfield's works are a ten-volume collection of essays that cohere remarkably well in a distinct

26. Ibid.
27. Ibid., 17.
28. Ibid., 22.

number of doctrinal and historical themes,[29] and his selected shorter writings, collected in two lengthy volumes, are a testimony to his wide ranging interests and succinctness in communicating sometimes difficult teachings.[30] Even without a textbook of theology to his name, Warfield continued in the same path as the Hodges before him, still conceiving of theology as a science to argue for the exegetical and systematic character of theological studies.

One essay in particular, "The Idea of Systematic Theology" (1896), echoed the theme of theology as a science. By this time scientific theology appeared to be something of an oxymoron thanks to scientific and religious developments, and Warfield's foray into definition of terms lacked the swagger of his predecessors. But his understanding of systematic theology was no less learned and displayed the resilience of the Princeton theology's effort to be scholarly while maintaining Reformed orthodoxy. When Warfield starts with the proposition that systematic theology, "as distinguished from its sister disciplines, is a science, and is to be conceived as a science and treated as a science," the older bravado is still in evidence. But he qualifies by distinguishing scientific theology from philosophical theology, a nuance that reflects the specialization of learning that transformed the academy in the last third of the nineteenth century.[31] Philosophy is concerned with "the mass of knowledge," science with "a division of knowledge." So to speak of "Philosophical Theology" is to conceive it as "a science among the sciences" with special attention to systematic theology's "place in the universal sum of knowledge." While to talk of "Scientific Theology" is to regard it "in isolation" and in relation to "its material." Still, systematic theology "deals

29. Warfield's works came out in 1932 from Oxford University Press, edited by a committee that included Ethelbert D. Warfield, William Park Armstrong, and Caspar Wistar Hodge. Each of the ten volumes has a separate title.

30. John E. Meeter, ed., *Selected Shorter Writings of Benjamin B. Warfield* (Nutley, N.J.: Presbyterian and Reformed, 1970–73).

31. On some of these changes within American higher education, see George M. Marsden and Bradley J. Longfield, eds., *The Secularization of the Academy* (New York: Oxford University Press, 1992).

with its material as an organizable system of knowledge," and so
is "in its essential nature a science."[32]

Warfield's qualification of systematic theology's scientific
character involved greater reflection than either of the Hodges on
the apologetical task of defending the truth of Scripture. This was
only natural in a context when the reliability of the Bible could no
longer be taken for granted. It was also the product of the Princeton theology's reliance upon Scripture, as opposed to other sources
of revelation. Warfield concedes that God reveals himself in
diverse manners and that the theologian must take them into
account "when framing all our knowledge of Him into one
organic whole. . . ." But these other sources were inferior, compared to God's "written word." As such, the Bible includes "the
only authentic records of the revelation of Him" and is superior
"to all other manifestations of Him in the fullness, richness, and
clearness of its communications," and contains "the sole discovery
of much that it is most important for the soul to know as its state
and destiny. . . ." Indeed, "nothing can be a clearer indication of a
decadent theology," Warfield writes, "than a tendency to neglect the
Word in favor of some or one of all of the lesser sources of theological truth. . . ."[33] Because of the Bible's centrality, Warfield would,
like his own theology professor, Charles Hodge, liken systematic
theology to the natural sciences, in this case astronomy. But
Warfield refines the imagery not by comparing Scripture to the
stars or galaxies but rather to the observatory and telescope. "The
Word of God . . . is the instrument which so far increases the possibilities of the science as to revolutionize it and to place it upon
a height from which it can never more descend." Just as the telescope "first made a real science of astronomy," so Scriptures
"form the only sufficing source of theology."[34]

As much as systematics depends on the Bible, Warfield still
regards his own field as the "crown and head" of all theological

32. "The Idea of Systematic Theology," in Benjamin Breckinridge Warfield, *Studies in
Theology* (New York: Oxford University Press, 1932), 49–51.
33. Ibid., 59–61.
34. Ibid., 63.

disciplines. The branches of theological learning in Warfield's encyclopedia were exegetical, historical, systematic, practical, and apologetics. While systematics integrates all of these fields, for Warfield it bears a particularly close relationship to exegesis. "Scientific Theology," he writes, "rests, therefore, most directly on the results of biblical exegesis as provided in biblical theology; but avails itself likewise of all material furnished by all the preceding disciplines."[35] Because of the close relations between biblical and systematic theology, and because of a perceived rivalry between the two, Warfield clarifies the relationship. Biblical theology is not a competitor, nor is it even "a parallel product of the same body of facts, provided by exegesis. It is instead "the basis and source of Systematics." Consequently, systematic theology is not "a concatenation of the scattered theological data" furnished by exegesis but rather "the combination of the already concatenated data given to it by Biblical Theology." In sum, systematics does not use the Bible "crudely" but only after its teachings have "been worked up into Biblical Theology and have received from it their final coloring and subtlest shades of meaning."[36]

What stands out in Warfield's understanding of systematic theology's scientific character is a degree of defensiveness that is appropriate to the time. On the one hand, by the last decades of the nineteenth century the notion of scientific theology sounded increasingly at odds with the direction of specialized learning.[37] After all, advances in the natural sciences had produced warfare between science and theology. Consequently, theology did not appear to be scientific, and, in fact, the sort of theology Princeton produced looked decidedly dogmatic, not scientific. On the other hand, systematic theology itself was on the ropes among the theological disciplines. Biblical theology, the field upon which

35. Ibid., 73–74.

36. Ibid., 66–67.

37. See, for instance, James Turner, *Without God, Without Creed: The Origins of Unbelief in America* (Baltimore: Johns Hopkins University Press, 1985); and D. G. Hart, *The University Gets Religion: Religious Studies and American Higher Education* (Baltimore: Johns Hopkins University Press, 1999), pt. 1.

systematics drew most thoroughly, was beginning to assert its own academic bragging rights. In an article written the same year as "The Right of Systematic Theology," Warfield clarifies the responsibilities of the systematic theologian in relation to the other theological disciplines. He writes, "We are accustomed to regard theology as the queen of the sciences, and Systematic Theology as the queen among the theological disciplines." But no more is this the case. Not only do natural scientists sneer at systematicians but also other members of the seminary faculty. The rise of biblical theology was particularly responsible for systematics' loss of status, and the imagery that Warfield used to describe the rivalry is still apt over a century later:

> Systematic Theology may look on with an amused tolerance and a certain older-sister's pleased recognition of powers just now perhaps a little too conscious of themselves, when the new discipline of Biblical Theology, for example, tosses her fine young head and announces of her more settled sister that her day is over. But these words have a more ominous ring in them when the lips that frame them speak no longer as a sister's but as an enemy's, and the meaning injected into them threatens not merely dethronement but destruction.[38]

Warfield's defense of systematic theology's rights, then, came in a context when many theological educators and church officers possessed marked "impatience . . . with the effort to define truth and to state with precision the doctrinal presupposition and contents of Christianity."[39]

Despite systematic theology's increasingly fragile base in American learning generally and within theological education specifically, Warfield's efforts through the first two decades of the twentieth century shored up the field's position at least at Prince-

38. Benjamin Breckinridge Warfield, "The Right of Systematic Theology," in *Selected Shorter Writings of Benjamin B. Warfield*, ed. John E. Meeter (Nutley, N.J.: Presbyterian and Reformed, 1973), 2:220.
39. Ibid., 221.

ton Seminary. One sign of the strength and vitality of the Princeton approach to systematic theology came in 1929 at the opening of Westminster Seminary. J. Gresham Machen was the leader of the effort to found a new seminary in Philadelphia, and the reasons for beginning the school had to do directly with Old Princeton and its theology. Owing to administrative restructuring that brought Princeton into conformity with the inclusive policies of the Presbyterian Church U.S.A.'s denominational officials, Machen and other conservatives in the church believed a new seminary was needed to perpetuate Princeton's unoriginal theology. As he put it in his 1929 convocation address:

> [T]hough Princeton Seminary is dead, the noble tradition of Princeton Seminary is alive. Westminster Seminary will endeavor by God's grace to continue that tradition unimpaired; it will endeavor, not on a foundation of equivocation and compromise, but on an honest foundation of devotion to God's Word, to maintain the same principles that Old Princeton maintained.[40]

The principles for which Old Princeton stood, in Machen's estimation, were three. First, Christianity as set forth in the Westminster Standards is true; second, it is "capable of scholarly defense"; and third, the gospel should be proclaimed "without fear or favor" as the only way of salvation.[41] But when Machen described the course of instruction at the new seminary, he also followed in the well-worn paths of the Hodges and Warfield by conceiving of systematic theology as the queen of the theological sciences and the center of the Westminster curriculum. Biblical theology would be a vital part of Westminster's teaching and would be interwoven in the Old and New Testament departments. But systematic theology would be "at the very center of the Seminary's

40. J. Gresham Machen, "Westminster Theological Seminary: Its Purpose and Plan," in *What Is Christianity? And Other Addresses*, ed. Ned Bernard Stonehouse (Grand Rapids: Eerdmans, 1951), 232–33.
41. Ibid., 233.

course." Machen explained the relationship between biblical and systematic theology in a manner that showed the unmistakable influence of Old Princeton. He asserted:

> [A]n error should be avoided: it must not be thought that systematic theology is one whit less Biblical than Biblical theology is. But it differs from Biblical theology in that, standing on the foundation of Biblical theology, it seeks to set forth, no longer in the order of the time when it was revealed, but in the order of logical relationships, the grand sum of what God has told us in his Word. . . . God has spoken to us in his Word, and . . . he has given us not merely theology but a system of theology, a great logically consistent body of truth.[42]

That understanding of systematic theology and its relationship to biblical and exegetical theology was characteristic of the Princeton theology. To liberal theologians, Princeton's approach was stuffy, and to biblicist fundamentalists, Princeton's system appeared an imposition on Scripture. But it generated a reliable and learned theological tradition that, in the words of Mark A. Noll, was "pithy and profound on the cardinal tenets of the faith, expanding provocatively to encompass both recondite academic discussions and the practical problems of the church, manifesting a consistent synthesis of learning charged with piety and piety infused with learning."[43]

The Princeton Tradition and Theological Creativity

That the Princeton theologians conceived of systematic theology in scientific categories is beyond dispute. What is not so clear is why this conception of theology would nurture a commitment to unoriginality. Science has not typically been the stuff from which to create uniformity or constancy, since it thrives upon new discoveries and challenges to received truth. So was Princeton's stress

42. Ibid., 228–29.
43. Mark A. Noll, "The *Princeton Review*," *Westminster Theological Journal* 50 (1988): 302.

on science at all responsible for its theology's conservatism? One way to answer is to note how the scientific character of Princeton's theology stood out in nineteenth-century American Protestant theology. Unlike the New England theology that followed in Jonathan Edwards's speculative trajectory, the Princetonians recognized a responsibility to do justice to the whole range of disciplines in the theological encyclopedia. As such, Princeton worked out of a fuller range of theological scholarship that, even if not thoroughly up-to-date with German trends, was not as susceptible to break down when confronted by certain difficulties. Princeton's scientific theology was truly systematic and forced its practitioners to dialogue with a breadth of material and not pursue doctrinal, exegetical, or philosophical rabbit trails. Moreover, unlike some of the confessional theologies to emerge among nineteenth-century Lutherans and Reformed, the ideal of scientific method gave to the Princeton theology a measure of exegetical sophistication that dogmatic theology could fail to provide. This is not to say that the Princetonians were less confessional than their Lutheran and Reformed counterparts. But thanks to the lure of science and induction, Princeton's theology does manifest both a defense of special revelation in theological method and a reliance upon biblical exegesis not evident in other conservative Protestant theologies.[44]

Another way to discern the influence of the scientific ideal upon the Princeton theology's conservatism is to look at what became of the Princeton paradigm in subsequent formulations at the daughter institution, Westminster Theological Seminary. As much as Machen's formulation of systematic theology as the center of the new seminary's curriculum perpetuated the older Princeton theological method, the scientific character of systematics became harder to maintain in the twentieth century. For instance,

---

44. These comparisons are based upon the following useful overviews: Ahlstrom, *Theology in America*; Kuklick, *From Churchmen to Philosophers*; Walter H. Conser Jr., *Church and Confession: Conservative Theologians in Germany, England, and America. 1815–1866* (Macon, Ga.: Mercer University Press, 1984); and Claude Welch, *Protestant Thought in the Nineteenth Century, Volume 1: 1799–1870* (New Haven: Yale University Press, 1972).

John Murray, whose own practice of exegetical theology replicated Warfield's essays on biblical topics, wrote on systematic theology in the early 1960s without explaining much about systematics' relationship to the other theological disciplines or its scientific aspects. He begins in an unmistakable Princetonian cadence: "The task of systematic theology is to set forth in orderly and coherent manner the truth respecting God and his relations to men and the world. This truth is derived from the data of revelation, and revelation comprises all those media by which God makes himself and his will known to us men."[45] Even so, Murray makes no appeal to scientific method. More interesting is how much time he devotes to biblical theology. After explaining Scripture's necessity for systematics, he observes the development of theology throughout church history, and this progression of doctrine provides the opening for Murray to explore systematic theology's dependence on biblical theology. From there he spends the rest of the essay (half) discussing the defects of biblical theology as practiced by his contemporaries— this in an essay devoted to the task of systematic theology.[46]

If the Princeton pattern of scientific theology suffered from Murray's high regard for biblical theology, it also encountered difficulty in Cornelius Van Til's apologetical interests. In his *Introduction to Systematic Theology*, the apologist starts with words that reinforce Princeton's high regard for systematics. "It is sometimes contended," he writes, "that ministers need not be trained in systematic theology if they know their Bibles." But, he adds, " 'Bible-trained' instead of systematically trained preachers frequently preach error." As such, the study of systematics helps pastors preach "theologically"; "it will help to make men proclaim the whole counsel of God."[47] Like the Hodges and Warfield, Van Til also demonstrates a sense of the wider theological encyclopedia. "Systematic theology," he explains, "uses the fruits of

45. John Murray, "Systematic Theology," in *The Collected Writings of John Murray* (Carlisle, Pa.: Banner of Truth, 1982), 4:1.

46. Ibid., 9–21.

47. Cornelius Van Til, *In Defense of the Faith, Volume V: An Introduction to Systematic Theology* (Nutley, N.J.: Presbyterian and Reformed, 1974), 5–6.

the labors of exegetical and biblical theology and brings them into a concatenated system."[48] Where Van Til neglects the science of systematics is in his discussion of methodology. Here he begins with a lengthy foray into epistemology, and specifically a Christian method, that leads to a critique of Princeton's commitment to science as induction. In particular, Van Til argues against the intellectual neutrality implied in Hodge's estimate of the intellect's primacy in faith.[49] Of course, Van Til is simply setting the stage for the importance of presuppositions and the need for a comprehensive apologetic. Yet, one consequence of these criticisms, perhaps unintended, is to call into question the whole enterprise of systematic theology as a science. If the epistemology that informed Princeton's methods was off, maybe the Hodges' and Warfield's understanding of theology as a science was also wrongheaded.

Whatever the consequence, by the next generation Westminster Seminary theologians would be hard pressed to summon up the language of science once Murray and Van Til had begun to dissent from it. For instance, in his inaugural address as professor of New Testament, Richard B. Gaffin Jr., who would follow in the path of Charles Hodge and Warfield to move from biblical studies to systematic theology, made the "not entirely modest proposal" of discontinuing the designation of "systematic theology." Instead, he suggests using "biblical theology" to refer to "the comprehensive statement of what Scripture teaches (dogmatics), always insuring that its topical divisions remain sufficiently broad and flexible to accommodate the results of the redemptive-historically regulated exegesis on which it is based."[50] The ascen-

48. Ibid., 2.
49. Ibid., 40–42.
50. Richard B. Gaffin Jr., "Systematic Theology and Biblical Theology," *Westminster Theological Journal* 38 (1976): 298. For a more recent iteration with greater nuance by Gaffin of the relationship between biblical and systematic theology, readers should consult Richard B. Gaffin Jr., "The Vitality of Reformed Dogmatics," in J. M. Batteau, J. W. Maris, and K. Veling, eds., *The Vitality of Reformed Theology* (Kampen: Uitgeverij Kok, 1994), 16–50; and Richard B. Gaffin Jr., "Biblical Theology and the Westminster Standards," *Westminster Theological Journal* 65 (2003): 165–79.

dancy of biblical theology continued at Westminster in the equally "not entirely modest" case by John M. Frame for biblicism. In a critique of historical theology, Frame sensibly called for the primacy of Scripture in relation to "history, sociology, or any other science." "It is Scripture that supplies the norms of these sciences," he added, "and which governs their proper starting points, methods, and conclusions."[51] Yet while Frame defends the formal principle of the Protestant Reformation, he also implicitly dissolves the status of systematic theology as the queen of the sciences. His understanding of the sufficiency of Scripture is so broad as to question any part of theological methodology that does not stem directly from the Bible. The impression he leaves is that theology is not like other sciences but instead is the model for all of life.[52]

What is interesting to note is how the shift away from Princeton's scientific conception of theology in the Westminster tradition also occasioned a change in rhetoric. Where the Princetonians were proud of their unoriginality, subsequent theologians at Westminster took delight in theological creativity. In fact, in his piece defending something approximating biblicism, Frame lauds his education at Westminster for its originality. "We often associate orthodoxy with stagnancy and traditionalism," he writes, "but at Westminster, the commitment to *sola Scriptura* propelled it in the opposite direction." He goes on to walk through the curriculum and faculty of his student days during the 1960s and concludes that the school's "combination of freedom and orthodoxy" generated a "flourishing of original and impressive theological thought."[53] More recently, Tim T. R. Trumper, who taught systematics at Westminster (Philadelphia), also highlights the seminary's theological creativity. Toward the end of a review essay of

51. John M. Frame, "In Defense of Something Close to Biblicism: Reflections on *Sola Scriptura* and History in Theological Method," *Westminster Theological Journal* 59 (1997): 291.

52. See, for instance, Frame's review of Richard Muller's *The Study of Theology* (1991), John M. Frame, "Muller on Theology," *Westminster Theological Journal* 56 (1994) 133–51.

53. Frame, "In Defense of Something Close to Biblicism," 277, 279–80.

a book on the John Murray-Meredith Kline debate about the law and covenant theology, Trumper observes two significant parties within the Westminster Seminary theological tradition, the "orthodox" and the "constructive" Calvinists. According to Trumper, the former are "faithful to the form and content" of the Westminster Standards, while the latter are in sympathy with seventeenth-century Reformed orthodoxy "yet wish to see the moderate scholastic form of Westminster [Assembly] Calvinism recast in the biblical-theological approach to theology of Scripture and, in the Reformed tradition, of Calvin most notably."[54] As such, constructive Calvinists differ from their orthodox peers on issues of theological method.

Trumper's assessment is particularly germane to the relationship between Princeton's conventionality and its theological descendants' creativity at Westminster Seminary. One obvious difference is the matter that Trumper identifies as the factor dividing orthodox and constructive Calvinists, namely, theological method. For Princetonians, systematics was a science exalted high above the other realms of learning and the theological discipline, whose task was to give coherence to the rest of the theological curriculum. This conception, to be sure, rested upon an older appreciation for the theological encyclopedia that twentieth-century learning, both religious and secular, was ill-equipped to preserve. Still, the method of science yielded an approach to theology that was orderly, precise, and routine. In sum, Princeton's method bred a pride in unoriginality because its purpose was to preserve the system, not just of systematics, but also of systematic theology's relationship to the other theological disciplines. At Westminster, in contrast, systematics lost its regal standing and has vied especially with biblical theology for supremacy. The methods of systematics no longer provide the coherence they once did at Old Princeton. Hence, creativity and constructive Calvin-

54. Tim J. R. Trumper, "Covenant Theology and Constructive Calvinism," [a review of Jeong Koo Jeon, *Covenant Theology: John Murray's and Meredith Kline's Response to the Historical Development of Federal Theology in Reformed Thought* (1999)] *Westminster Theological Journal* 63 (2002): 403.

ism have become virtues in the Westminster tradition in the way that unoriginality was the hallmark of the Princeton theology.

Of course, the scientific character of systematic theology alone cannot explain the difference between Old Princeton and Westminster. Other factors also include the ecclesiastical ties of a seminary, the nature of subscription, and the relative place of a theological tradition to the surrounding institutions of religious and academic culture. But the different attitudes toward theological creativity are striking and appear to correspond directly to the way in which systematic theologians regard their craft and discipline. Because of their high regard for the Enlightenment and the progress of human knowledge, the Princeton theologians took pride in conceiving of their own studies as scientific and sought methods to bolster that conception. As much as that understanding of systematics was susceptible to a disproportionate regard for human reason, it also established an idea of theological learning that valued systematic thinking, precise formulation, and the historic debates that had produced such meticulousness. Princeton proved that inflexibility—pride in unoriginality—was often the product of such scientifically informed theology. At a time when in the words of Carl Trueman, the churches need "clear teaching," "confidence in the substantial unity of God's revelation," and a sense of an orthodox theology "to be defended in a coherent fashion," Princeton's idea of systematic theology could be especially welcome. Its methods may have produced theological stodginess, but that unoriginality turned out to be remarkably adept at preserving the character and content of Reformed orthodoxy.[55]

---

55. Carl Trueman, "Editorial: A Revolutionary Balancing Act," *Themelios* 27 (Spring 2002): 3.

2

Professor John Murray at Westminster Theological Seminary

Edmund P. Clowney

Westminster Seminary opened its doors for students in 1929 under the leadership of J. Gresham Machen, who had been a professor at Princeton Theological Seminary. At that time Princeton Seminary was the banner institution for Reformed orthodoxy in the Presbyterian Church U.S.A. Novelist and missionary Pearl Buck represented the liberalism that had been supported by the Foreign Missions Board of the denomination. Machen had been in touch with her, and both recognized the rift between what she regarded as fundamentalism and Machen as Christian orthodoxy. When Machen brought charges of unbelief evident on denominational boards in such matters as miracles worked by Jesus and the inerrancy of Scripture, his complaints were dismissed by the courts of Presbytery and the Synod, and finally by the General Assembly, which ruled that it was as necessary to support the boards and agencies of the church as to come to the communion table of the Lord.

Machen responded by leading in the organization of the Independent Board for Presbyterian Foreign Missions. Although there were many independent agencies for foreign missions, Machen was disciplined by church authorities for refusing to resign from the Independent Board. When new appointments to the Princeton Seminary Board included liberals—one was a signer of the liberal Auburn Affirmation—four professors resigned from the Princeton faculty: Dr. Robert Dick Wilson, Dr. Oswald T. Allis, Dr. Machen, and Dr. Cornelius Van Til. These men formed the core of the faculty of Westminster Theological Seminary.

John Murray, born in Bonar Bridge, Scotland, in 1898, had received the Th.B. and Th.M. degrees from Princeton Seminary in 1927. He taught systematic theology there as an instructor until he left to join the new faculty in Philadelphia in 1930. (Because of his contract obligation at Princeton, Murray was not part of the faculty in the first year of Westminster's history.) He passed through the series of appointments from instructor to full professor of systematic theology. For forty-two years he taught at Westminster, until 1972, when he became emeritus. His death on May 8, 1975 was a great loss, but his formative influence continues to shape the ministry of the seminary into the twenty-first century. Dr. Cornelius Van Til became the best-known teacher at Westminster. He argued that you cannot begin with rationalism and proceed to establish Christian theism. Van Til showed the need of a *pou sto*, a place to stand. We cannot begin without assuming God's existence, and reason our way to the self-existent God of the Scriptures. The living, triune God reveals himself in his works and words. John Murray held the apologetics of Van Til in high esteem, but his concern was not with Christian philosophy, but with biblical theology. He began with God's witness to his Word, in the Scriptures, and in his Son, the Word Incarnate. If we consider the influence that John Murray had on the development of Westminster Seminary, we must recognize his burning zeal for what the Scriptures teach.

Murray as Teacher of Scripture

My own acquaintance with John Murray began as a student in his classroom at Westminster. Before studying systematic theology with Professor Murray, we had spent a year with apologetics, the biblical languages, church history, and preaching. Following the Westminster curriculum, we needed Greek and Hebrew first. Murray taught the topics of theology by exegeting the principal biblical passages in Hebrew or Greek from which these doctrines were drawn. He would regularly call on a student to translate the assigned passage.

John Murray saw himself as a workman in the Word, who prepared future preachers to be careful expositors of revealed truth. He wrote out his lectures in full, for he knew that he worked in the God-breathed Scripture texts. He constantly revised his lectures to clarify and sharpen his exposition. He did not welcome discussion till the marrow of the text had been expounded, but he then warmed to well-considered and brief comments from class members. Nothing pleased him more than a comment from a student that advanced the doctrine taught in the text. I treasured a comment he wrote on a test paper I had submitted. He was not simply grading papers, but preparing workmen in Scripture.

Professor Murray followed the outline of the heads of doctrine as formulated in the documents of the Westminster Assembly. He spoke of the views of commissioners to the Assembly, with particular attention to the Scottish divines. Yet his lectures used historical backgrounds sparingly, for he was teaching the Bible, not church history. His biblical teaching was enriched by his attention to biblical theology. I took a course from him that followed the structure of biblical theology rather than that of dogmatics. He first distinguished the periods of biblical history, then examined the systematic theology of each period: from Creation to the Fall of Adam and Eve; from the Fall to the Flood, from the Flood to the call of Abraham, then on to the patriarchal period and the history of Israel. His treatment of the period from the Fall to the Flood included God's revelation about sin and judgment, and his promise of the Seed to come. Students gained an understanding not only of the history of redemption but also of how systematic theology summarized biblical revelation within each era of redemptive history. Systematic theology is often presented historically, from the works of the church fathers, the Scholastics, Reformers, then modern and postmodern writers. John Murray's focus was not on church history, but on the biblical history of redemption.

Murray's meticulous faithfulness to the theology of God's Word did not mean that his lectures were pedantic and predictable. To the contrary, his lecture style was often dramatic. He began with nearly a whisper in an opening prayer. (That prayer was not to be recorded, although he permitted the audio recording of his lecture.) From the hushed reverence of the start of his words, he moved to a climax in thought and volume. He never shouted, but there was memorable power at the end of most of his class lectures. I still remember one of his summaries: "No known or predicted eschatological era separates us from our hope!" That remembered quote shows the aim of his teaching. He was not simply instructing students who had paid tuition. He was nurturing disciples like Timothy, who could preach the Word to others. Only the Spirit can change men's hearts, but it is the Word of the Lord that is the sword of the Spirit.

John walked for exercise, following a habitual route, known by students as the "Murray Mile." I remember times when John suggested that I join him on his walk. On one such walk he said to me, "The Son that was given, according to John 3:16, was not just the incarnate Son, but the eternal Son, given from all eternity in the plan of God." On another occasion, I remarked that the more insight the Lord gave us in the surrounding mystery of the gospel, the greater was the fuller mystery we encounter from the circumference of that new understanding. John appreciated that observation.

John Murray's teaching was not Socratic, but Apostolic. He stimulated reflection in the riches of revelation in Jesus Christ.

Murray as Churchman

Professor Murray, the workman in the Word, was also a leader in the church. Westminster Seminary served the Orthodox

Presbyterian Church, the Christian Reformed Church, and, later, the Presbyterian Church in America. Many Baptists were also students. Professor Murray long labored on church committee assignments. My recollection is that I served with him for 25 years on the committee revising the Book of Church Order. Ned Stonehouse, John Galbraith, and Robert Marsden were also members of this committee. At one point John Murray joined in preparing a revised set of proof-texts for the Westminster Standards.

Far beyond his committee work, John Murray led the church from the depths of his theological understanding. His commentary on Romans continues to be mined for treasures of insight. C. E. B. Cranfield, in his two-volume study of Romans, has 47 citations of Murray on Romans.[1] On a rare occasion when Cranfield disagrees with Professor Murray, he brings compelling evidence to support his interpretation. I believe that Romans 2:14 is often misunderstood because the Greek word *physei* "by nature" is taken with what follows rather than with what precedes. Paul is speaking of Gentiles. Taken with what follows, the sense is, "Gentiles, who do not have the law, do by nature the things of the law." Taken with what precedes, the sense is, "Gentiles, who by nature do not have the law, do the things of the law." Verse 27 supports this second reading of the passage, for there Paul speaks of uncircumcision by nature: that is, as Gentiles they belong to the class of the uncircumcised. This understanding is supported by Paul's language in Galatians 2:15 and Ephesians 2:3. In his commentary, John Murray, however, interprets the law as the "things of the law" in the sense of things practiced by pagans as "natural virtues which are required by the law."[2]

By taking the word with what follows, the passage has been used to develop a natural theology. Unbelieving Gentiles may then be recognized as doers of the law. On the other hand, the passage here may (and should) be seen as describing *believing* Gentiles. Paul

---

1. C. E. B. Cranfield, *A Critical and Exegetical Commentary on the Epistle to the Romans*, 2 vols., 6th ed. (Edinburgh: T&T Clark, 1975).

2. John Murray, *The Epistle to the Romans*, 2 vols. (Grand Rapids: Eerdmans, 1959–65), 1:72–74.

is speaking of the true Israel, whose hearts are circumcised by the Spirit. They keep the law, though Gentiles, and therefore judge Jews who are circumcised in the flesh, but not in spirit. Those whom God recognizes as circumcised are not the Jews who boast of circumcision yet do not keep the law, but those, Jews and Gentiles, who are doers of the law with circumcised hearts, and therefore pleasing to God. Paul's theology here is consistent with the whole message of the Book of Romans. Those who walk in the Spirit, Jews and Gentiles, are those who have the Spirit of Christ (Rom. 8).

In agreeing with the exegesis of Romans 2:14 by Cranfield, I do not feel that I am betraying John Murray, but rather seeking to heed his admonitions to seek the meaning of the text in its context, and not simply to follow a tradition of interpretation, no matter how venerable or accepted. In this as in other respects I certainly stand in the sphere of his influence. In Westminster Seminary (Philadelphia) today, DeWitt Jayne's portrait of John Murray hung there does not mark an era from the past, but rather the present commitment of Westminster to the supremacy of the Word of God. We do not stand over it, but sit under it—both the written and living Word. The intensity of John Murray's labors in interpreting the Bible appears in his commentary on Romans. It continues to undergird generations of teachers and preachers who share his awe before the Word of God. John Murray's devotion to faithful exposition has shaped the impact of leaders from every part of the world who come to Westminster to be discipled in the Scriptures.

John Murray's teaching still has continuing influence at Westminster Seminary in the training of pastors to be workmen in the Word. The construction of a whole new wing to the library is an architectural tribute to John Murray's diligence as a workman in Scripture. In his classroom, the use of the Hebrew Bible was required, and students were called on to translate key texts from the Old Testament, those that provide a principal source of the doctrine being considered. The top floor of the new library is now given to Old Testament study. Beside a collection of books for research, a classroom is provided, together with study carrels. The area is not reserved for Old Testament specialists, but made readily accessible to all students who are working in the original languages of Scripture.

Murray's Piety

Murray's continuing influence in the development of Westminster draws also from the aroma of godliness that is at the heart of his heritage. Professor, he was, but pastor as well. His faithfulness to his tasks did not compete with his practice of devotion. When I had contact with pastors in Scotland who served the "wee free" Church of Scotland, I found the atmosphere of deep piety in which John Murray was nurtured. I discovered that he was not alone in the passion and eloquence of his intercession at the throne of grace. Here were men whose prayers, like John's, were symphonies of praise and intercession. They, too, had nurtured their life of prayer in the closet and were immersed in the Scripture's language of praise, adoration, confession, thanksgiving, and petition. They drew water from the wells of salvation—or, more strongly, their prayers flowed like streams from the fountain of God's love and glory. Yes, no doubt, they had a tradition of prayer, but with a living, burning awareness of the presence of the Lord who leans over to hear our cries. These were men of prayer who were deeply respected for their walk with the Lord, but whose genuine humility John Murray also showed.

Iain Murray, who knows the Puritan piety that these men displayed, has written about John Murray in the context of his ministry in Scotland. (Iain Murray had little firsthand knowledge of John Murray's years in Philadelphia.) While I esteemed Professor Murray as a teacher, and respected his evident learning and defense of the faith, I am sure I often presumed on his humility. During the summer when few students were present, he and I had sandwiches together in a side room of Machen Hall. I had little understanding of the recognition that Iain Murray and others had for him. John talked freely of his croft in the highlands, where he

would breathe again the air of the hills of Scotland and get in
shape by digging ditches and working with his hands.

I will never forget John Murray's prayers for me on the death
of my mother. John knew the Lord, and he brought the comfort
of the Lord's presence to the faculty room where we prayed.

Professor Murray loved the Psalms. He believed that, in the
worship of God, inspired psalms should be used exclusively. When
students protested that Ephesians 5:19 and Colossians 3:16 speak
of Psalms and hymns and spiritual songs, they were reminded
that these terms are used in the superscriptions to the Psalms. He
was unmoved by the argument that the Colossians passage speaks
of the richly indwelling Word of Christ as the source of the singing
that we do in the name of Jesus. Although John would remain
silent while others sang New Testament praises, he nevertheless
did not abstain from praise. He participated, consciously or
unconsciously, by keeping time with his body to the meter of the
song. His commitment to exclusive psalmody was no doubt part
of his close friendship with the Freeman family, who shared these
convictions. Calvin Freeman has written of his memories of Sunday afternoons when John Murray was a guest in their home on
the Sabbath. Calvin's memories go back to his early childhood
when he was initiated to the circle of John Murray's hugs!

We had thought of John Murray as a confirmed bachelor and
were pleased and delighted to see him walking hand in hand with
Dr. Valerie Knowlton. She had come to Westminster to study theology, having already earned a degree in microbiology. They were
married in 1967 and had two children, a son, Logan, and a daughter, Anne-Margaret. Their daughter died in Scotland, after Valerie
had driven many miles from their cottage in the highlands to seek
medical help. Logan is a ruling elder in an Orthodox Presbyterian church in Bangor, Maine.

Murray and the Distinctiveness of Reformed Theology

As a leader in the Westminster Seminary movement, John
Murray participated in the controversies of the time. In contrast

to the growing liberalism of the mainline Presbyterian church, the Orthodox Presbyterian Church maintained the orthodoxy of the Westminster Confession of Faith and Catechisms. Articles by John Murray in the *Presbyterian Guardian* made clear that the Confessions of the church were Reformed, not merely fundamentalist. The church battle was seen by many as a struggle between modernists, who denied the authority of Scripture as the Word of God written, and the fundamentalists, who accepted the fundamentals as set forth in a series of pamphlets defining these doctrines. Murray's articles disturbed some in the OPC, whose theology was fundamentalist and not specifically Reformed. John Murray's articles in the *Guardian* urgently reminded the Orthodox Presbyterian Church of its heritage of Reformed doctrine. A Murray memorial issue, following his death in 1975, contained the heart of Murray's teaching on the central place in Christian theology of the doctrine of union with Christ. The fountain of salvation is the eternal election of the Father "in Christ." We were chosen in him before the foundation of the world (Eph. 1:3–4). Murray's article showed that we cannot think of the past, present, or future apart from union with Christ. He wrote, "By union with Christ the whole complexion of time and eternity is changed and the people of God may rejoice with joy unspeakable and full of glory."[3]

John Murray's conviction about union with Christ unfolded in the system of Reformed doctrine that he believed and taught. Many fundamentalists were Arminian in their theology. They believed that Christ's atoning death only made possible the salvation of all men, and denied at least one of the five points of Calvinism. These points from the Canons of Dort are often stated in summary form with the mnemonic device "tulip": **T**otal depravity, **U**nconditional election, **L**imited atonement, **I**rresistible grace, and **P**erseverance of the saints. Most fundamentalists made decisive the sinner's choice of Christ rather than God's choice of the sinner. Fundamentalist apologetes opposed Calvinism on the

---

3. John Murray, "Union with Christ," *The Presbyterian Guardian* 44 (June 1975): 87.

ground that it undermined the free offer of the gospel. How could a Calvinist be an evangelist? Dean Wallace Emerson, in a chapel talk at Wheaton College when I was a student there, argued against Calvinism on the ground that if God's election were sovereign, the reprobate could say on judgment day that they had done God's will.

That struck a chord in my memory. I climbed the fire escape to my room on the fourth floor of Blanchard Hall and looked in the Book of Romans. Sure enough, there it was in my American Standard Version: "So then he hath mercy on whom he will, and whom he will he hardeneth. Thou wilt say then unto me, Why doth he still find fault? For who withstandeth his will?" (Rom. 9:18–19). The apostle Paul had anticipated the dean's objection to his doctrine. For a Wheaton student, to choose between the administration and the apostle was not difficult.

But how did the apostle support his teaching of God's sovereign election? His first reply is a rebuke. What right has any creature to dispute the will of the Creator? He is the potter, we are the clay. "What if God, willing to show his wrath, and to make his power known, endured with much longsuffering vessels of wrath fitted unto destruction: and that he might make known the riches of his glory upon vessels of mercy, which he afore prepared unto glory, even us, whom he also called, not from the Jews only, but also from the Gentiles?" (vv. 22–24 ASV). Paul, a Hebrew of the Hebrews, had learned the folly of trusting in his own self-righteousness, and was amazed at the choosing of the Lord, whose election brought not only Jews but Gentiles to salvation by grace.

John Murray, in an article in the *Torch and Trumpet*, showed the harmony of John 3:16 with the free offer of the gospel and the definite extent of the atonement.[4] If the word *world* in John 3:16 had a distributive force to include all humanity, then all humanity would be included in God's judgment that they are all saved in the Son (John 3:17). The point of "world" in this passage is not

---

4. John Murray, "The Free Offer of the Gospel and the Extent of the Atonement," *Torch and Trumpet* 15 (May-June, 1965): 14–16.

how big the world is, but how bad it is. The love of God embraces rebellious sinners, his enemies. John Murray turned to chapter 10 of John's Gospel to show the distinction between those who are the sheep of the Good Shepherd, and those who are thieves climbing the wall or wolves devouring the flock.

Christian liberty was another point of controversy flowing from the fundamentalist background of many who stood with Machen against the liberals. The student code for Wheaton College banned drinking, smoking, and dancing as worldly habits to be avoided. The issue, however, was not the right of a Christian college to maintain such a code, but the danger of regarding as sinful actions that the Bible does not regard as sinful. John's Gospel tells us that Jesus turned into wine six large waterpots that held a total of about 120 gallons. The point of the miracle includes both the quantity and the quality of the wine. The wedding feast became a sign of the glory and grace of Christ, the true bridegroom. The water of purification had become the wine of Messiah's feast.

John Murray had not been raised in the culture of American fundamentalism reflected at Wheaton College. Dr. Evan Runner, who had been a boyhood friend at a fundamentalist Presbyterian church, did try to enlighten me on the principles of Christian liberty. John Murray understood my background and never suggested that I join him when he ordered a little whiskey on a plane trip. John Murray was rightly indignant that fundamentalists would regard as sinful the provision of Jesus for a wedding feast. To be consistent, they had to adjust the interpretation of the miracle and transform the wine into grape juice. Attending a movie theater was another practice forbidden at Wheaton College, but this eroded with the spread of television.

Again, partly due to John Murray's birthplace in Scotland, he warned against the American fundamentalist misunderstanding of Christian liberty. He also appreciated, however, the apostle's warning against the use of Christian liberty in a way that would create a stumbling block for a weaker brother. John Murray surely had a pervasive influence in the development of Westminster Seminary by distinguishing the seminary from American fundamentalism as it was represented at that time by Wheaton College.

Another controversy that influenced that development was the debate that emerged between the faculty members of Westminster and Dr. Gordon Haddon Clark. Here the division was less between John Murray and Clark and more between Cornelius Van Til and Clark. While a student at Wheaton College (I graduated in 1939), I took all the courses that Dr. Clark offered. While still teaching at the University of Pennsylvania, he had published *Thales to Dewey: A History of Philosophy*.[5] Dr. Clark's history of philosophy presented it as a continuing chess game in which one master after another would pass from the scene, but the game would go on. We kept waiting for the philosopher who would bring the checkmate. In the sequence of his courses, everything pointed toward a contemporary Christian philosopher. Dr. Clark presented Cornelius Van Til as the philosopher to be studied, and referred to a copy of his syllabus. Dr. Van Til, however, concluded that Dr. Clark was a rationalist rather than a presuppositionalist. Van Til pronounced a plague upon both rationalism and irrationalism as positions that made human reason supreme. Instead, we must begin by presupposing the existence of the living and true God, the Creator and Redeemer, the Alpha and Omega of our faith. Both Van Til and Murray emphasized the history of redemption. In chapel talks at Westminster, both showed the influence of Geerhardus Vos's biblical theology.

The Enduring Legacy of John Murray

John Murray's influence has certainly remained at Westminster. He was the principal advocate of the biblical theology of Geerhardus Vos. That understanding remained a distinguishing mark of Westminster instruction; it also equipped the

5. Gordon Clark, *Thales to Dewey: a History of Philosophy* (Boston: Houghton Mifflin, 1957).

seminary to meet radical changes in contemporary thought and culture. When Tim Keller addresses the "post-everything" young people of New York City, he is grounded in the biblical theology of Geerhardus Vos, John Murray, Cornelius Van Til, and Harvie Conn. Because biblical theology takes seriously the history of redemption, it does put theology in context. The contextualizing power of biblical revelation provides understanding in our era, the "end of the ages." Through the work of the Spirit, the person of Christ Jesus also opens eternal truth for the age to come.

Further, and it may seem a contradictory way, John Murray's concern for an accurate grasp of the Westminster Confession of Faith and Catechisms has been part of his continuing influence. A recent General Assembly of the Presbyterian Church in America (June 2003) considered the form of confessional subscription and adopted an amendment to the Book of Church Order. The revised form requires candidates for ordination to teaching and ruling office to state the specific instances in which they may differ with any statements or propositions in the Westminster Standards. This form of subscription is now spoken of as consistent with "good faith" subscription. My own subscription and that advocated when I subscribed in 1942 was to the "biblical system of doctrine summarized in the Westminster Confession of Faith and Catechisms." The concern in the PCA for guarding the form of subscription to these Standards owes much to the teaching of John Murray and of those who studied with him.

John Murray was fond of the symbolism of the Psalms. He was involved in the discussions that led to the establishment of the Banner of Truth publications. He loved the passage, "Thou hast given a banner to them that fear thee, that it may be displayed because of the truth" (Ps. 60:4 KJV). Another favorite of his was Psalm 48, especially verses 12–14: "Walk about Zion, and go round about her: tell the towers thereof. Mark ye well her bulwarks, consider her palaces; that ye may tell it to the generation following. For this God is our God for ever and ever: he will be our guide even unto death" (KJV). He surely prayed for the Orthodox Presbyterian Church and the "wee" Free Church in Scotland with the same vision, but he also bore the burden on his heart for the need of the church universal.

His memory summons me to rejoice in the growth of the church in the Southern Hemisphere of our planet, and to intercede for the Presbyterian Church in America and other sister churches. We would be amazed to discover the place John Murray still has in the hearts of those he taught, and those who now read his writings. As we walk about Zion, we may see John's hand in towers and palaces, and praise God for his servant.

Part Two

Systematic Theology Among Other Disciplines

3

What God Hath Joined Together: Westminster and the Uneasy Union of Biblical and Systematic Theology

Michael S. Horton

It is difficult to keep marriages together these days, especially when the union in view concerns biblical and systematic theology. Preeminent Old Testament specialist Walter Brueggemann speaks for many biblical scholars more generally when he concludes,

> There can, in my judgment, be no final resolution of the tension between the systematizing task of theology and the disruptive work of biblical interpretation. Thus I propose that the Old Testament lives with systematic theology with as much uneasiness as it does with historical criticism. . . . Neither is an enemy of Old Testament theology, but in quite parallel ways, neither is a permanent partner nor an easy ally of Old Testament theology.[1]

Our goal is to engage briefly in crisis counseling for the reconciliation of biblical and systematic theology by (a) asking our-

---

1. Walter Brueggemann, *Theology of the Old Testament: Testimony, Dispute, Advocacy* (Minneapolis: Fortress, 1997), 107.

selves where the relationship deteriorated and (b) what can be
done to encourage more fruitful conversation and to lead to a
reintegration of these sub-disciplines. These goals are in the spirit
of the Westminster Seminaries, whose theologians have advocated the closest of relationships between biblical and systematic
theology. Toward the end of this chapter we will specifically
address this issue in the Westminster context.

First, by *systematic* theology we refer to that task of har-
vesting the results of exegesis in order to display the logical connections and canonical coherence of biblical teaching. To do this,
systematic theology often follows a *loci communes* method,
whereby harvested exegesis is organized topically. By *biblical* theology we refer not merely to exegesis *per se*, but to the attempt
to follow the unfolding drama of redemptive revelation in its historical aspect. Today, chairs in biblical theology are rare; it is
ordinarily Old Testament or New Testament scholars who write
biblical theologies of their respective part of the canon. In rare
cases today (e.g., Brevard Childs), bold attempts are made to
approach the whole Bible canonically as providing a broader
"biblical theology."[2]

A Fruitful Marriage

While hardly representing biblical theology in full flower, the
Reformation at the very least can be said to have sown the seeds.
At the most basic level—concern for exegesis—the Reformers
applied their Renaissance-humanist training to the study of Scripture and, secondarily but significantly, the ancient Christian writers. Questions may well be raised concerning their success in specific instances, of course, but it cannot be denied that they brought
to their work a humanistic concern for perspective, context, history, and language that had been lacking in the commentaries and
theologizing of medieval scholasticism.

2. Brevard Childs, *A Biblical Theology of the Old and New Testaments* (Minneapolis:
Fortress, 1992).

That their vernacular translations of the original texts is often credited with having a formative influence on modern German, French, and English languages is an indication of the breadth and depth of their philological-lexical competence, awareness of extant textual sources, as well as the history of source-criticism. One could also point to the Reformation's renewed concentration on the *sensus literalis* and the corollary assumption of the basic perspicuity of Scripture, the priority of exegesis over dogmatics (sufficiency of Scripture), and the *analogia fidei* (the hermeneutical circle in embryo).

Furthermore, many of the paragons of "systematic theology" were also exegetes, masters of philology, antiquity, and textual criticism in addition to being as competent in Old and New Testament studies as many specialists. In fact, it is anachronistic to draw tidy lines of specialization that emerged in the modern academy. Although his commentaries are consulted by more people in more parts of the world today than in his own time and place, Calvin was not only flanked by peers, but in terms of technical training, he was surpassed by a fair number of Reformed colleagues whose names are largely forgotten today.

Catholic, Lutheran, and Reformed scholastics, despite what one might think of the style and method of their dogmatics (and even there a wide diversity exists), were ordinarily as adept in preaching, liturgy, and pastoral care. They recognized that different tasks called for different methods, but their diverse corpus was united by their ecclesiastical *vocatio* and accountability. Beza, Calvin's successor in Geneva and a formative scholastic, is perhaps more widely known today for his contributions to New Testament scholarship than for his theological *Tabula*. Despite the tendency of some to contrast the pastoral spirit of the Heidelberg Catechism with an ostensibly "dogmatic" (understood perjoratively) scholasticism, the Catechism's authors (Ursinus and Olevianus) were among the most precise of the scholastic federal theologians. As Richard Muller has argued, all of the major sixteenth- and seventeenth-century Protestant systems engaged in this double movement of analysis and synthesis, exegesis and system. One may criticize a given system or tradition for its results, but one cannot fairly conclude that the most representative efforts reflect superficial proof-texting or that they simply imposed a ready-made system on the text.[3]

Even if one finds material disagreements with these writers (as indeed they found among themselves), Reformed scholasticism represents our tradition's most sophisticated attempt at (a) learned exegesis, (b) catholic breadth (incorporating the best insights of the pre-Reformation—even medieval—Christian tradition), and (c) a passion for simultaneously solidifying the gains of the Reformation and exploring still greater territory in the interest of being "reformed and always reforming according to the Word of God." Even Paul Tillich could describe this project more sympathetically than many who claim nearer affinity with this tradition in terms of content:

> Protestant Orthodoxy was constructive. It did not have anything like the pietistic or revivalistic background of American fundamentalism. . . . One of the great achievements of classical orthodoxy in the late sixteenth and early seventeenth centuries was the fact that it remained in continual discussion with all the centuries of Christian thought. . . . These orthodox theologians knew the history of philosophy as well as the theology of the Reformation. . . . All this makes classical orthodoxy one of the great events in the history of Christian thought.[4]

Tillich found the American ignorance of the Protestant scholastics a constant source of surprise:

> We could also call it Protestant scholasticism, with all the refinements and methods which the word "scholastic" includes.

3. See Richard Muller, *After Calvin: Studies in the Development of a Theological Tradition* (New York: Oxford University Press, 2003), 63–102; *Post-Reformation Reformed Dogmatics*, vol. 1: *Prolegomenon*, 2d. ed. (Grand Rapids: Baker, 2003), 27–84.

4. Paul Tillich, *A History of Christian Thought*, ed. Carl Braaten (New York: Simon and Schuster, 1968), 276–77.

Thus, when I speak of Orthodoxy, I refer to the way in which the Reformation established itself as an ecclesiastical form of life and thought after the dynamic movement of the Reformation came to an end. It is the systematization and consolidation of the ideas of the Reformation. . . . Hence, we should deal with this period in a much more serious way than is usually done in America. In Germany, and generally in European theological faculties—France, Switzerland, Sweden, etc.—every student of theology was supposed to learn by heart the doctrines of at least one classical theologian of the post-Reformation period of Orthodoxy, be it Lutheran or Calvinist, and in Latin at that. Even if we should forget about the Latin today, we should know these doctrines, because they form the classical system of Protestant thought. It is an unheard-of state of things when Protestant churches of today do not even know the classical expression of their own foundations in the dogmatics of Orthodoxy. . . . All theology of today is dependent in some way on the classical systems of Orthodoxy.[5]

The Tie That Binds

Federal (covenant) theology was an essential link, historically, between traditional loci (i.e., "systematics") and an incipient biblical theology. Contrary to what is sometimes asserted, Johannes Cocceius, regarded as a founding father of biblical theology, does not represent an attempt to break from "scholasticism," but was himself a fairly typical representative of this circle of writers.[6] The growing significance of "covenant" as a *leitmotif* was not developed as an alternative to the ostensibly sterile, timeless, and speculative categories of scholastic method but

5. Ibid.

6. See Willem J. van Asselt, *The Federal Theology of Johannes Cocceius* (1603–69), trans. Ramond A. Blacketer (Leiden: E. J. Brill, 2001) and especially his essay, "Johannes Cocceius Anti-Scholasticus?" in *Reformation and Scholasticism: An Ecumenical Enterprise*, ed. W. van Asselt and E. Dekker (Grand Rapids: Baker, 2001), 227–51; see also Brian Lee, "Biblical Exegesis, Johannes Cocceius and Federal Thought: Development in the Interpretation of Hebrews 7:1–10:18," Ph.D. dissertation, Calvin Theological Seminary (2003).

was *generated from within* the Reformed scholastic project, a fact that has been underscored by such contemporary theologians as Jurgen Moltmann and Wolfhart Pannenberg, and represents a challenge to the caricature of post-Reformation theology as engaged in mere ahistorical abstraction.[7]

None of this is to be slavishly imitated or merely repristinated. This cannot be done, even if it should. For instance, advances in biblical studies—including the prominence of biblical theology as a distinct sub-discipline—necessarily reconfigure the process of discovery and refinement. But such discoveries can also add further data in support of previous consensus. Despite

7. See especially Cocceius, *Summa doctrinae de foedere et testamento Dei* (1660), most notably chapter 16. Pannenberg traces the interest of the Roman Catholic Tubingen school in the kingdom of God to Cocceius, *Systematic Theology*, trans. G. W. Bromiley (Grand Rapids: Eerdmans; Edinburgh: T&T Clark, 1998), 3:26. Further, "Only in the federal theology of Johannes Cocceius does the kingdom of God come into view again as a dominant theme of salvation history and eschatology. . . ." (3:530). Similarly, Moltmann, in *The Coming of God: Christian Eschatology* (Minneapolis: Fortress Press, 1996), says that the "initial form" of the "transposition of eschatology into time . . . can be found in the 'prophetic theology' of the seventeenth century. . . . Prophetic theology tacitly assumes that history and eschatology, experienced present and predicted future, lie along one and the same temporal line," a position that Moltmann rejects (7). Nevertheless, he does appreciate this movement's "rebirth of messianic eschatology," although Moltmann exaggerates both the anti-apocalypticism of the confessional writings and the chiliasm of the "prophetic theology" (157). In *Theology of Hope* (Minneapolis: Fortress, 1993), he notes that the ideas of "progressive revelation" in history and of redemptive history as eschatological "go back to late federal theology (J. Cocceius). . . . In contrast to Orthodoxy's supranaturalistic and doctrinaire view of revelation, the Bible was here read as a history book, as the divine commentary upon the divine acts in world history. . . . It was the start of a new, eschatological way of thinking, which called to life the feeling for history" (70). Despite the unwarranted contrast with orthodoxy (Cocceius was a leading Reformed scholastic), Moltmann is certainly accurate in his account of where things went wrong, when, especially in pietism and a renewed millenarianism of a certain type, "eschatological progressiveness of salvation history" was no longer read off of the cross and resurrection, "but from other 'signs of the times,' " which led to either optimism or despair, depending largely on world and ecclesiastical conditions (71). M. Douglas Meeks, in *Origins of the Theology of Hope* (Philadelphia: Fortress, 1974), observes the influence of Otto Weber on Moltmann's thought: "Weber was a representative of the Reformed tradition and its emphasis on covenant, theocracy, election, and continuity in history. . . . In large part the theology of hope is a contemporary exegesis of Calvin's view of the faith-hope dialectic" (20–21).

gains since their day, the massive achievements and balance of the older systems do represent the realities that once obtained in integrating exegesis and system in a never-ending dialectic that yielded considerable fruit not only for the academy but for the church and not only for faith but for practice as well. However similar the Reformed scholastics appeared to be to their medieval ancestors in terms of method, sources, and terminology, their breadth of learning helped them not merely to criticize the older systems at predictable points but to do so with nuance and constructive insight for generating alternative accounts.

It may well be that post-Reformation orthodox systems are less animated than the preaching and popular polemics of the Reformers themselves, just as the sermons and popular pamphlets of these scholastics themselves differed in style from their theological writings. Nevertheless, in its growing appreciation for the federal model of Christ the Mediator, the "second Adam" in a history of redemption, these systems turned away from the dualisms that not only preoccupied the medieval synthesis but also have haunted modern criticism and apologetics. In so doing, they turned away from the model of timeless ideas, approaching the object of theology more as one might approach another person than an experiment or an instrument. By drawing on the covenant theology that they were convinced rose organically from the text, theology had a structural commitment to a historical-eschatological hermeneutic centering on Christ. One may disagree with the conclusions of a Peter Vermigli or a Herman Witsius, but only with insufficient familiarity could one say that they substituted a speculative method for exegesis and imposed an abstract system upon the biblical text.

The Separation

With the rise of rationalism, criticism displaced authority, whether ecclesial or textual. Instead of beginning with faith (Anselm), one was to begin with doubt (Descartes) and establish

universal foundations for understanding that transcended particular texts and traditions. Aided by the pietist polemic against
dogmatics, the Enlightenment established as the criterion for
"truth" that which was accessible to an allegedly universal
autonomous reason. It is the Enlightenment, not Protestant
scholasticism, that treated the Scriptures as a source to be plun-
dered by criticism until the historical particularities of redemptive revelation were separated from the timeless truths of reason
and morality. When the Romantics added experience as a foundation, pietism and rationalism converged in Protestant liberalism, and the particular, historical, dynamic shape of revelation
was regarded as at least less authentic than the universal, abstract,
static gnosis available to anyone with the correct method.
J. P. Gabler's *oratio* in 1787 set out to mark the boundaries of biblical theology and dogmatics, contrasting them in terms of the
historical versus the didactic, anticipating the now widespread
opposition between "dynamic" and "static" approaches.

Two centuries after the Reformed scholastic enterprise had
reached its climax, Abraham Kuyper, along with Herman Bavinck
and others, sought also to reintegrate exegesis and system, biblical and systematic theology, after both disciplines had languished
under the pietism and criticism that followed the demise of orthodoxy. And long before it was fashionable to emphasize the eschatological and historical shape of theology, a growing ad hoc circle of biblical theologians was developing in the Netherlands and
in the United States.[8]

Nevertheless, while the Dutch school was drawing upon its
Reformed resources, mainline American theology developed its
own version of biblical theology that was more closely attuned to

8. With this group one ordinarily associates the likes of Herman Bavinck, J. A. C. Van
Leeuwen, Klaas Schilder, Herman Ridderbos, and Princeton's Geerhardus Vos, the rank-
ing representative of this impressive school. Declining Abraham Kuyper's invitation to
occupy the first chair in biblical theology at the Free University of Amsterdam, Vos taught
at Calvin Seminary (which he had also attended, fresh from The Netherlands) until he
finally accepted Princeton's offer to become professor of biblical theology in 1893, remaining there until his retirement in 1932.

the critical school in Germany. Scornfully referred to by some as the *so-called* biblical theology movement, associated in the United States with the name of G. Ernest Wright, this mid-twentieth-century project helped to shape even evangelical and Reformed attitudes toward systematic and confessional theology. Wright's comments reflect a bias that is shared by what appears to be the great majority of biblical scholars more generally. According to Wright, classical systematic theologies and confessions of faith "lack the colour, the flexibility, the movement of the Bible" and "attempt to freeze into definite, prosaic rationality that which was never intended by the Bible to be so frozen." Referring to the confession that he had promised to defend, Wright says of the Westminster Confession, "By its cold, abstract and tight nature such a definition of God somehow separates us from his living, active and warm Presence which we come to know by contemplation of what he has done and by seeing ourselves as the recipients of his gracious work." Furthermore, "theology must always beware of the scholastic tendency to become unhistorical."[9] What is perhaps surprising is how frequently such sentiments are expressed today even in confessional (even Westminster Seminary) circles.

In some ways, the biblical theology movement in mainline circles today is experiencing its own internal debate between those who insist on a churchly theology (e.g., Yale's Brevard Childs) and those who regard biblical theology and biblical studies as relatively autonomous academic disciplines suspicious of confessions and systems (e.g., Columbia Seminary's Walter Brueggemann). Childs has insisted that the Old and New Testaments are not mere *sources* but *Scripture*, and that for all their diversity they nevertheless constitute a single canon and ought not to be approached with the prejudice that they are nothing but historical documents of dubious credibility, lacking any theological unity or organic composition. Biblical theologians ought to be rigorous scholars and faithful church members simultaneously.

9. G. E. Wright, *God Who Acts: Biblical Theology as Recital* (London: SCM Press, 1952), 110–11.

Childs appeals to the examples of Irenaeus, Augustine, Luther, and Calvin:

> Ebeling (*Lutherstudien* I, 2) has stressed repeatedly that it is a basic misunderstanding to view Luther as an exegete whose biblical work was then supplemented by a separate theological system. Rather, his entire corpus is characterized by an indissoluble union of his theological reflection and biblical exegesis. Lotz ("Sola Scriptura," 258) goes so far as to state that "the Lutheran Reformation was . . . the work of a professor of biblical theology."[10]

In his carefully nuanced treatment of the relation between the two testaments, Calvin also established himself as a first-rank pioneer of what would become biblical theology.[11] While the medieval tendency was to engage in exegesis in service to theology, Calvin reversed the priority: "The role of theology was to aid in interpreting the Bible."[12] Childs calls for a correlation of exegesis not with higher criticism, but with church theology and practice, while Brueggemann and James Barr represent the older guard, demanding autonomy for biblical scholarship.[13]

The Effect of Biblicism

But why does this tension exist? Is there something about the respective natures of biblical and systematic theology that was bound to end in separation or even divorce? Doubtless, there are many reasons that could be put forth. In the next sections, I

---

10. Childs, "A Biblical Theology," 43.

11. Ibid., 48.

12. Ibid., 49. At the same time, Childs still works within the customary Barthian disjunction between "Calvin and the Calvinists": "It is not by chance that scholars like Cocceius appealed to an unfolding sequence of Israel's covenants in an effort to break out of the static categories of scholastic orthodoxy" (16). As we have seen, Cocceius himself was a scholastic orthodox theologian.

13. It should be pointed out that Childs himself still regards higher criticism an important aid in biblical theology.

suggest some possible reasons why the current tensions between biblical and systematic theology exist.

The first is *biblicism*, which is here understood as including everything from a popular to an academic suspicion that systematic theology acts as an alien (usually "Greek") framework imposed upon the naked ("Hebrew") text. One finds this suspicion in "inductive Bible studies," where participants are encouraged to put their particular church theologies on the shelf and simply read the Bible according to a fail-proof method, as if one were merely diagramming sentences. But one also finds it among biblical scholars who, though willing to point out the reductionism in the method (viz., simplistic word studies, insufficient linguistic training, etc.), exhibit a similar naïvete. Happily, no biblical scholar today discounts the importance of the hermeneutical circle: interpreting the parts in the light of the whole, and vice versa, in an unresolved dialectic. And what biblical scholar today subscribes knowingly to "the view from nowhere," failing to do adequate homage to the situated character of all interpretation? Nevertheless, many of these same biblical scholars fail to locate *their* situatedness and explicitly *articulate* their view of the "whole" in terms of their belonging to a specific church body in which they have made certain ethical commitments to uphold its faith and practice.

Walter Brueggemann, who provides an excellent survey of these developments, leaves no doubt as to where he stands in the current debate:

> The rise of modern criticism was aimed against that coherent system of church belief in two ways. First, a fixed system of doctrinal theology has a great propensity toward reductionism about variation and diversity in the text. Conventional systematic theology cannot tolerate the unsettled, polyphonic character of the text. This is evident in terms of *any doctrinal claim of the church*. Thus, for example, if theology, in its metaphysical propensity, holds to an affirmation of God's omnipotence, an interpreter *must* disregard texts to the contrary. . . . If it is claimed that God is morally perfect,

> the rather devious ways of the God of the Old Testament must
> either be disregarded or explained away. In truth, some of
> the most interesting and most poignant aspects of the Old
> Testament do not conform to or are not easily subsumed
> under church theology. . . . Thus Old Testament scholarship
> has sought to maintain some interpretive freedom, and there-
> fore some interpretive distance from systematic theology and
> from church authority. (emphasis added)

Most of the time in our day, it is not the threat of inquisitions
against Hebrew professors as much as it is "the long-established
and uncritical reflexes of church communities, who have known
only a reductionist Bible for so long that they neither know nor
can tolerate what is actually said in the Bible."[14]

While one may sympathize with the frustration that often
attends reactionary traditionalism, what is the implication of
brandishing the sweeping generalization that these "church communities" are essentially brainwashed so that "they neither know
nor can tolerate what is actually said in the Bible"? The implication, of course, is that one cannot really know what the Bible says
without the appropriate authority—that is, the biblical scholar
or, in its popular version, the leading Bible study guru or method.
Thus, biblicism—whether in its popular or academic varieties—
finally gets us no closer to the "naked text" than the traditionalism against which it oftentimes lodges a legitimate protest.

Brueggemann continues:

> It is the work of a serious theological interpreter of the Bible
> to pay close and careful attention to what is in the text, *regard-
> less of how it coheres with the theological habit of the church*.
> This is particularly true of the churches of the Reformation
> that stand roughly in the tradition of *sola scriptura*. The truth
> of the matter, on any careful reading and without any ten-
> dentiousness, is that *the Old Testament theological articula-
> tion does not conform to established church faith*, either in its
> official declaration or in its more popular propensities. . . . It

14. Brueggemann, *Theology of the Old Testament*, 106.

is clear on my reading that the Old Testament is not a witness to Jesus Christ, in any primary or direct sense, as Childs
proposes, unless one is prepared to sacrifice more of the text
than is credible. . . . There can, in my judgment, be no final
resolution of the tension between the *systematizing* task of
theology and the *disruptive* work of biblical interpretation.
Thus I propose that the Old Testament lives with systematic
theology with as much uneasiness as it does with historical
criticism. . . . Neither is an enemy of Old Testament theology,
but in quite parallel ways, *neither is a permanent partner* nor
an easy ally of Old Testament theology. (emphasis added)[15]

Across the theological spectrum, from evangelicalism to radical theologies, one observes a sometimes visceral reaction against
doctrine and especially against systems. Note even Brueggemann's
appeal to *sola Scriptura*, as if the formal principle of the Reformation set the Bible *against* the church rather than *above* it. The
cumulative consensus of an ecclesial community Brueggemann,
as worthily as any *Aufklärer*, consigns to the dustbin in one sweep.
One either accepts the hopelessly inaccurate view of God that one
encounters in the church theologies and confessions, or allows
the Bible to have its say. And yet can we be bold enough to identify our interpretation so simply with "what the Bible says" in
opposition to what a great cloud of witnesses has said the Bible
says? The choice that biblical scholars often put to their students,
though presented as a decision between stifling church systems
and the obvious interpretation of Scripture, is often nothing more
than a choice between the church's consensual interpretation of
Scripture versus the interpretation offered by a current consensus of the academic guild or individual scholar. Evidently, only
traditional theologies are captive to the alien thought-forms of
their time and place: Brueggemann can read the Bible "from
nowhere"—in fact, with the *presupposition* that the church's interpretation of Scripture is probably far from what the Scriptures
really say.

15. Ibid., 107.

However, lest we become too contemptuous of Brueggemann's reaction, after deconstructing the totalizing claims of individual biblical scholars against the (ostensibly) totalizing claims
of the past, let us recall that individual biblical scholars *did* successfully challenge the consensual interpretation of the medieval
church. Yet these exegetes who challenged some traditional interpretations were also servants of the church who drafted confessions and catechisms in order to express a common faith. The
Reformers did not start from scratch, determined to clean the
slate and begin afresh with the Trinity, the two natures of Christ,
and other wide areas of agreement. Such self-confidence would
have to wait for the Enlightenment. Still, we do well to applaud
Childs's program only as we are attentive to the warnings of
Brueggemann and others not to allow biblical scholarship in general and biblical theology specifically to be muted in their distinctive contribution by placing our confessions above Scripture.
A genuinely "confessional" approach, at least for the Reformed,
has insisted that the only basis for subscription is that these dec-
larations faithfully express the principal teachings of Scripture.
Reading the Bible faithfully with the church is the only salutary
way forward, but exegesis must continue to remind us that our
"system" is never finished even if our confessional statements
remain faithful summaries of Scripture.

The assumption not only of pious laypeople but also of biblical scholars seems to be that the very suggestion of a system is
to do violence to the text, a task regarded as both impious and
unscholarly. Whether it is the scholar lobbying for the autonomy
of biblical studies or the average layperson "just reading the Bible"
without any explicit theological formation, it is not simply a lack
of *familiarity* with theology, but a *suspicion bordering on fear*. Francis Watson has suggested that this phenomenon is connected to
a certain evangelical pietism in which many biblical scholars were
reared. In addition to other considerations, "it is believed that
theological concerns have an inevitable tendency to distort the
autonomous processes of biblical exegesis—a prejudice so strong
that to identify a theological motivation underlying an exegetical

position is often held to be sufficient refutation." There is "an unwillingness to accept the existence and the significance of theology as a discipline in its own right."[16] Further,

> When one has the Bible, what need is there for subtleties and sophistries of theology? In evangelical Christianity, the Bible is typically read with scant regard for the long and intricate dialogue with the Bible that is the history of Christian theology. Many (most?) Protestant biblical scholars are attracted to the field in the first place by an evangelical piety of this kind, and—whatever else is abandoned under the notoriously destructive impact of the so-called "historical critical method"—the abstraction of the biblical texts from their theological *Wikungsgeschichte* is tenaciously maintained.[17]

Watson surmises that there is also a bias among many academic theologians against relating their scholarship to a particular confessional stance to which they are themselves committed:

> The lines of demarcation between systematic theology and Old and New Testament scholarship represent more than a mere division of labour; they are ideologically motivated. They represent the collective decision of biblical scholarship that the biblical texts are to be construed as something other than Christian scripture.[18]

Is it advisable, much less possible, then, to maintain as the dominant "church theologies" have always done that a particular confession of faith "contains the system of doctrine taught in scripture"? And is it then still possible to formulate and articulate the details of such a system?

On one hand, I think that it is good that we have to ask ourselves that question. For too long this was taken for granted, and

---

16. Francis Watson, *Text and Truth: Redefining Biblical Theology* (Grand Rapids: Eerdmans; Edinburgh: T&T Clark, 1997), 4.

17. Ibid.

18. Ibid., 6.

in that environment it became increasingly easy for systematicians to lord it over the text and to engage in (sometimes dubious) exegesis only to endorse a position that may not arise organically, either directly or by good and necessary consequence from
clear passages. In some cases, especially among the manuals of
the eighteenth and nineteenth centuries, there appeared derivative systems, imitations of imitations, summaries of summaries.
It is as possible for Protestants as anyone else to forfeit the surprise of wrestling with a text and to rely on textbook formulations. Just as the Reformers complained that if one wanted to
investigate the Scriptures it was almost always done by digging
through several layers of commentaries, too much theology has
been received (and even done) secondhand in the circles of orthodoxy. (By the way, this danger is just as apparent when we rely on
biblical commentaries as when we rely on summaries of doctrine.)

   In this regard, it would be worthwhile perhaps, with more
space, to pursue a comparison of recent systematic and biblical
theologies. While mainline theologians and biblical scholars seem
to be somewhat more aware of one another than is often the case
among evangelicals, there is often sufficient justice for biblical
scholars to worry that their systematic colleagues raise a central
dogma ("Theology of . . .") to such a hermeneutical status that
exegesis is rendered servant rather than lord. In evangelical circles, my general impression is that the rare recent examples of
systematic theology in conservative circles tend to be wooden and
formulaic elaborations not even of a church tradition, but of a
post-war evangelical movement. Lacking the breadth and depth
of classic systems, this formulaic approach tends to render such
presentations thin and predictable. Often, seminal theologians
are taken into account, but interaction with paradigmatic proposals in biblical studies, historical, and even important systematic theologies from other traditions are few and far between. Furthermore, a certain commitment to modern foundationalist
assumptions prejudices much of conservative evangelical theology toward univocal propositions of a timeless character,
abstracted from the history of redemption. None of this bears

resemblance to at least the better examples of patristic or early Protestant systems and the more recent ones situated in that stream (both of the Amsterdam and Old Princeton schools). Clearly, a reunion of these two partners is required no less for the health of systematic than of biblical theology.

The Rejection of System

A second reason I suspect for the biblical scholar's wariness of systematic theology is "the system"—in other words, *the critique of systematics as a (Greek) discourse alien to the (Hebraic) domain.* One is reminded of the rival sentiments of Descartes and Hegel on one side (despite their own differences), and Kierkegaard and Pascal (despite their less substantial ones). Siding with the latter (and, sometimes with reason, suspecting that systematicians side with the former), biblical scholars vote in favor of "existence" over the "rational objectivity" of *the system*. Theirs is the God of Abraham, Isaac, and Jacob, over against the god of the philosophers. While the former is a living Subject who acts in history and in the concrete life of a historical community, the latter is an Object who is "known" as the *causa sui*, the *supreme* being in the chain of Being. Exchanging a personal relationship with a Thou who is truly "other" and beyond comprehension, for an impersonal, abstract, and scientific concept of "divinity," systematic theology (or ontotheology, as it is now known) lives and moves and has its being in someone or something other than Yahweh.

As with the concern to ensure the possibility of exegesis to always surprise and revise our systematic paradigms, the suspicion that systematic theology subjects its discourse to questions and sometimes even answers that are irrelevant and at points even inimical to biblical faith is well-founded. It is a critical challenge that I have begun to take up in a serial project.[19] However, if post-

---

19. I am referring to my first volume, *Covenant and Eschatology: The Divine Drama* (Louisville: Westminster John Knox, 2002), to be followed by *Lord and Servant* and *People and Place*.

modern critics of the "onto-theological" project can themselves appeal to such premodern sources as Augustine, Thomas, Luther, and Calvin, perhaps biblical scholars will patiently allow that this epithet is less appropriate to some approaches in the past than to others and allow time for contemporary systematics to catch up with the critique.

It was not Martin Heidegger or Emmanuel Levinas, after all, but the Reformed scholastic Francis Turretin who, echoing the Reformers, demanded that theology "treats of God not after the manner of metaphysics inasmuch as he is Being (*Ens*)," adding that "theology deals with creatures not as they are things of nature (*res naturae*) but as they are things of God (*res Dei*)."[20] In fact, Richard Muller directs us to the similarities of Calvin and Turretin on this point. Calvin writes,

> When faith is discussed in the schools, they call God simply the object of faith, and by fleeting speculations, as we have elsewhere stated, lead miserable souls astray rather than direct them to a definite goal. For since "God dwells in inaccessible light" (1 Tim. 6:16), Christ must become our intermediary. . . . Indeed, it is true that faith looks to one God. But this must also be added, "to know Jesus Christ whom he has sent" (Jn. 17:3).[21]

Now Turretin:

> But when God is set forth as the object of theology, he is not to be regarded simply as God in himself (for thus he is incomprehensible [*akataléptos*] to us), but as revealed and as he has been pleased to manifest himself to us in his word. . . . Nor is he to be considered exclusively under the relation of deity (according to the opinion of Thomas Aquinas and many Scholastics after him, for in this manner the knowledge of

20. Francis Turretin, *Institutes of Elenctic Theology*, 3 vols., trans. G. M. Giger, ed. J. T. Dennison Jr. (Phillipsburg, N.J.: P&R, 1992–97), 1:16.

21. John Calvin, *Institutes of the Christian Religion*, 3.2.1. Muller's own comparison is found in his *Post-Reformation Reformed Dogmatics*, 202–3.

him could not be saving but deadly to sinners), but *as he is our God (i.e., covenanted in Christ as he has revealed himself to us in his word not only as the object of knowledge, but also of worship)*.[22]

In fact, Turretin goes on to elaborate the differences between various medieval approaches and that of Reformed orthodoxy:

> Thus although theology treats of the same things with meta-physics, physics and ethics, yet the mode of considering is far different. It treats of God not like metaphysics as a being or as he can be known from the light of nature, but as the Creator and Redeemer made known by revelation. . . . This mode of considering, the other sciences either do not know or do not assume. . . . For theology treats of God and his infinite perfections, not as knowing them in an infinite but in a finite manner; nor absolutely as much as they can be known in themselves, but as much as he has been pleased to reveal them.[23]

These theologians insisted that theological prolegomena are related to the doctrinal system itself in an *a posteriori* rather than *a priori* fashion.[24] By following the Reformers in turning away from "the god of the philosophers" to "the God of Abraham, Isaac, and Jacob," and from the knowledge of God's essence to the knowl-edge of God's self-revelation in covenantal, historical relatedness to the people chosen, redeemed, and called by God, they can help us to recover a distinctly biblical narrative from its platonizing distortions, medieval and modern. Christ as the Mediator of the covenant of redemption is the *fundamentum* of all fundamentals, including prolegomena. The formula of "God, not as he is in him-

---

22. Turretin, *Institutes*, 1:16. Emphasis added.

23. Ibid., 1:17.

24. Richard Muller: "We note, again, that theological prolegomena are never *vordog-matisch* [for these scholastics]: they are in integral part of dogmatic system that develops in dialogue with basic dogmatic conclusions after the system as a whole has been set forth," *Post-Reformation Reformed Dogmatics*, 1:81.

self, but as he has covenanted in Christ . . . ," is more than pious platitude for these systematicians, and it stands as an antidote to both Thomas and Tillich. Conscious of their departure from medieval system at important points, they were articulating a new method with a distinct aim: ontology was to take a backseat to redemptive action and revelation.

We can concur wholeheartedly with the insistence upon the concrete particulars of the Christian narrative determining the shape of theology. At the same time, even approaching the theological task in this manner, one must engage in metaphysical propositions. Even to identify the characters and the plot—to say, for example, that "God is one" or to assert the Trinity, the hypostatic union, or divine immutability—is to practice metaphysics. (It should be added that to *deny* divine immutability is just as metaphysical a claim as it was for the Arians, who appealed to philosophical notions of unity to deny the *homoousion*.) Diffidence to any kind of metaphysical assertion is to suggest that we cannot even attribute love to God. At stake, of course, is not only the possibility of theology, but the possibility of faith and piety. Prayer would be meaningless or at least arbitrary, and worship would be denied a referent beyond individual or communal experience, constructing a god on the basis of our projected needs or transcendental deductions.

As with the other false dilemmas, what is required here is a distinctively Christian metaphysics that is suspicious of *speculation*, not *precision*. If all of theology is analogical, the alternative to univocal rationalism need not be equivocal agnosticism. By reintegrating exegesis and system, Christian theology can not only cease being intimidated by the assault on metaphysics (inevitably by engaging in it), but can begin to wean itself from the false metaphysics (caught between Heraclitus and Parmenides) that critics have every reason to deconstruct. Needless to say in the present volume, the approach to theological method taken by Cornelius Van Til, which he inherited from this earlier Reformed orthodoxy, offers a model of how a genuinely Christian metaphysics can challenge the modern and postmodern orthodoxies of our day.

Beginning with the revelation of the divine name (in each case a lodestar of metaphysical predication), leading to the *Shema* and other confessional statements, God authorized Israel to ascribe distinct attributes and to form succinct propositions concerning the divine being and God's relation to the world. In as much as it is a fuller revelation, especially given the decisive revelation of God in Christ, it is not surprising that the New Testament would add exponentially to this repertoire. While this is not the place to make the case, the consensus of the first five centuries concerning the two natures of Christ, for example, is inconceivable apart from the already-systematized and significantly articulated formulations that one finds in the Gospels and Epistles, as in the sermons in Acts. If the biblical writers had not been inculcated in the systematic theology of the Hebrew Scriptures, they would hardly have been valuable human organs of new covenant revelation, with Christ as the puzzle-piece that made the whole canonical picture fall together.

There is a time for every purpose under heaven and different methods as well. Systematic theology is not merely edifying literature, as important as that is. Nor is it evangelistic or practical, although the same systematician may also engage in writing those sorts of books. I think that we are quite right to anchor the Christian kerygma in the history of redemption (i.e., biblical theology). Nevertheless, at some point challenges to even the simplest assertions naturally arising from the narrative itself will call for comparison of particular passages with others. Each time this occurs, greater refinement will result and, one may hope, a greater sense of the connectedness not only of canon and covenant, but of Christology and ecclesiology, of our understanding of the relation of the kingdom of God to election, and of the sacraments to faith. Genuine worship and piety will flourish.

Further, clashes between interpretations will, depending on their magnitude, continue to excite this refinement. This is why biblical-theological critics of systematics must beware of ignoring their colleagues who have taken account of these clashes. Rather than being the product of steady exegetical refinement, much in the way of theological advance has been due to the crisis in which exegetical conclusions confronted extratextual challenges (philosophy, science, history, etc.) and had to rethink its exegetical formulations. The doctrine of the Trinity, for instance, is hardly the product of Hellenization, but is rather largely the result of being forced by non-Trinitarian groups who were motivated by Hellenistic *a prioris* to formulate a cumulative body of exegesis and reflection with greater consistency. James Barr was quite correct to criticize the oversimplifying tendency of the biblical theology movement, especially its obsession with categorizing whatever it did not appreciate as "Hellenistic" as opposed to "Hebraic."[25] Characteristically, the former becomes the umbrella for metaphysics and systematic reflection, while the latter encompasses biblical theology. Often, genuine contrasts of this nature are undermined because of the tendency to oversimplify, a perennial danger to *both* biblical and systematic theologians.

Modern theology's apparent fear of the *fides quae creditur* (which encounter theology largely rejects as objectifying God—I-It rather than I-Thou) rests on an Enlightenment (especially Kantian) suspicion of referential religious assertions, authority and assent, as well as idealist metaphysics. But the environment today is more open to a greater range of possibilities. As Michael Polanyi and Thomas Kuhn have shown regarding scientific revolutions, periods of "prophetic" and revolutionary insight are followed by systematization. It is simply wrong-headed to pit the Cappadocian Fathers and Augustine (or Paul!) against the simple-minded fishermen at Jesus's side, or the Protestant scholastics against the Reformers. Nevertheless, to every method there is a time and place.

25. James Barr, "The Old Testament and the New Crisis of Biblical Authority," *Interpretation* 25 (January 1971): 24–40, especially 26: "The purging of this Greek thought and a rethinking in Hebrew categories would, it was supposed, revivify the whole corpus of Christian thinking and enable its content to be made relevant for the modern world; for—it was, rather vaguely, supposed—the Hebrew way of thinking had much in common with modern trends in science, in psychology, and in history; and it was the presence of Greek elements in traditional Christianity which had caused blockages of communication."

Our time seems to parallel those impoverished periods into which the free course of the gospel seems impeded by its "Babylonian captivity" to godless ideologies and forms of life. It may be chiefly a time requiring fresh proclamation and confession of Christ, not a time *chiefly* of systematization and new scholastic enterprises. Closer to the periods of the apostolic church and the magisterial Reformation than to the remarkable ages of medieval and Protestant scholasticism, our own moment calls for a new commitment to kerygmatic tasks. Thus, a doctrine of God in our day will be best presented not only by repeating or reformulating classical formulae, but by announcing and explicating the sense of God's relation to history as "the God of Abraham, Isaac, and Jacob," which is to say, "the God and Father of our Lord Jesus Christ." New proposals in dogmatic and biblical theology should be encouraged, but it does not follow that new confessions are required for this task. New challenges to classic formulations cannot simply be dismissed as "old heresies," but such challenges will nevertheless have to be tested by the wise reflection of the church on Scripture, as that is reflected in its creeds, confessions, and catechisms. Theology serves the church: reconciling sinners to God through Christ in the power of the Spirit through Word and sacrament, giving rise to a new people who bring good news to the world and whose lives are lived *coram deo*. Although it will not shrink from making metaphysical assertions and even engaging in apologetics, it will seek primarily to announce God's saving activity in history as its greatest apologetic strategy.

As an aside, it may also be worth observing that biblical scholarship is hardly immune to philosophical captivity. For instance, while Brueggemann's *Theology of the Old Testament* is vastly illuminating in its exegetical rigor, his approving footnotes attest to his own acknowledged debt to certain contemporary philosophers. Surely few well-informed biblical scholars today would wish that they had never heard of semiotics, rhetorical analysis, speech-act theory, narrative theology, and a vast array of emerging approaches that enrich their exegesis. The critical question to ask, whether concerning Anselm's ontological argument or Paul Ricoeur's analysis of testimony, is not whether philosophical concepts are being employed, but how they are being appropriated and whether that appropriation renders the most faithful exegesis of the biblical text.

Toward a Renewing of Vows

The sort of marital advice we often hear in conservative Reformed circles today for the health of biblical and systematic theology too frequently sides with one partner over the other in the supposed dispute. Could it be that a solution is under our nose and that the old covenant theologians had it reasonably right when they treated "covenant"—itself a historical concept tethered to a concrete history of God's relationship with creatures—as the dramatic structure for the integration of both logical relations and descriptive analysis with the dynamic play of the narrative? Even outside of our own tradition, no less a biblical theologian than Walther Eichrodt saw the covenantal motif in this way. But have the implications been jointly pursued in our biblical and systematic theologies? Can there be an integrationist approach that does not simply repristinate past efforts but build on them in the light of current exegesis as well as appropriate useful conceptual and rhetorical insights from recent thought? To be sure, reductionism is possible, but is it inevitable?

"Covenant" could be elaborated in a biblical-theological manner by tracing the specific arrangements throughout redemptive history, and it could be developed systematically by organizing the material in their thematic relations. Thus, for instance, this federal union with Christ could become the paradigm within which one could relate election, justification, sanctification, adoption, and glorification. In this way, the covenant becomes an integrative structure rather than a central dogma, and in so doing, it keeps each of these other key elements in the *ordo salutis* from displacing or obscuring the other. In both biblical and systematic theology, there is the dialectic of whole and parts, never resting on one or the other, but always generating greater refinement as well as scope. In light of the more recent work that has been done on the covenant, both within biblical and systematic theology, it is at least imaginable that a reinvigorated and revised covenant theology could not only provide an exemplary exercise but offer a rich paradigm for the reintegration of these sub-disciplines and their implications for praxis. The covenant is not just a concept, it is a praxis—not just a theoretical basis for praxis, but a praxis in progress. How might we enrich our understanding of and appreciation for the nature of worship, the church, the sacraments, and our mission in the world by reflecting on its covenantal shape, especially in view of our immersion in a culture of individualism and consumerism?

While relief maps (biblical theologies) are helpful for some tasks, one-dimensional freeway and street maps (systematic theologies) are helpful for others. Biblical and systematic theology keep each other in check, in the all-important effort to avoid either enthusiasm or dogmatism. Far then from the model that George Lindbeck has identified as cognitive-propositionalist, Vos argues, "The Bible is not a dogmatic handbook but a historical book full of dramatic interest." At the same time, "Biblical Theology can counteract the anti-doctrinal tendency of the present time. Too much stress proportionately is being laid on the voluntary and emotional sides of religion. Biblical Theology bears witness to the indispensability of the doctrinal groundwork of our religious fabric."[26] And while only a certain modern philosophical prejudice will reduce truth to propositional assertions, the task of making such assertions, in both biblical and systematic theology, not only is an ineluctable fact of writing essays but is legitimized by the example of Scripture itself.

An Appeal to the Westminster Community

This contribution to a *festschrift* honoring a mentor of so many of us in the Westminster tradition could hardly be complete

26. Geerhardus Vos, *Redemptive History and Biblical Interpretation: The Selected Shorter Writings of Geerhardus Vos*, ed. Richard Gaffin Jr. (Phillipsburg, N.J.: Presbyterian and Reformed, 1980), 23.

without a special plea to our own community to pursue the reintegration of systematic and biblical theology. Like his own mentor, John Murray, and in some ways more broadly than his distinguished predecessor, Professor Strimple was determined to
demonstrate how the Reformed system of doctrine arose piece
by piece out of the close study of Scripture rather than being
imposed upon it from without. Through his patient exegetical
arguments many who came to the school from non-Reformed
backgrounds became convinced that Reformed theology simply
made the most sense of the texts. Whatever contributions from
historical theology and renewed attention to the tradition may
yield, the awe of being introduced to the system through the Scriptures themselves is an indispensable Westminster hallmark. Further, although he has dedicated enormous energies and resources
to his church over the years, Professor Strimple himself has never
been parochial in the pejorative sense. His "Christianity and Modern Atheism" course was perhaps the most memorable of my seminary days, and his learned lectures on contemporary Roman
Catholic thought usually included guest lecturers from the nearby
Roman Catholic school, the University of San Diego.

In our wider circles, however, there appears to be something
like a crisis of confidence in the marriage between biblical and
systematic theology. On the one hand, some suspect that an
emphasis on the dynamism of redemptive-history and the eschatological dimension of revealed truth will undermine the stability and constancy of God's eternal decree. On the other hand, some
in our wider circles invite the end of systematic theology. The *his-
toria salutis* and the *ordo salutis* are in irresolvable conflict, we
are sometimes told. One is Hebrew (i.e., biblical), while the other
is Greek (i.e., pagan). Accordingly, the Westminster Standards
themselves, it is sometimes said, accommodate a "scholastic" theological program that is no longer ours in key respects.[27] Its sum-

27. For a superb analysis of this problem in relation to a specific proposal, see Richard
Gaffin's review of Gordon J. Spykman's *Reformational Theology* (Eerdmans, 1992), in the
Westminster Theological Journal 56 (1994): 379–90. Further, recent criticisms of tradi-
tional evangelical formulations of justification by some conservative Reformed and Pres-

maries of the divine attributes, the law, justification, and its relation to sanctification and the final judgment are naïve and at odds with what we have learned from the more eschatologically sensitive and biblical-theologically oriented exegesis that has finally unlocked the true meaning, especially of Pauline thought. Still others in our circles invoke "something close to biblicism" as a critique of accumulated ecclesial wisdom, forgetting that the choice is never between a confessional view and a biblical view, but a consensus interpretation of Scripture and one's own.[28]

---

byterian ministers and elders have typically employed the increasingly discredited contrast between Calvin and the Calvinists both in terms of method (biblical versus scholastic) and content. Such easy reductionism as one finds in neo-orthodox (e.g., James Torrance and Jack Rogers) and evangelical (e.g., Daniel Fuller and R. T. Kendall) circles are now abundant in Westminster circles, although there are encouraging signs of serious engagement with historical theology (e.g., Carl Trueman in Philadelphia, R. S. Clark and the historical theology program at Westminster Seminary California).

28. See for instance John Frame, "Something Close to Biblicism," *Westminster Theological Journal* 59 (1997): 269–91; see also the responses by David Wells and Richard Muller in that same issue, 293–318. Frame recalls a Westminster alumnus who "regretted that Westminster did not have any 'real systematic theology.' In his view, Murray's courses were not true systematics courses, but mere courses in exegesis. I disagree radically with that alumnus's evaluation of Murray, but I grant that that alumnus observed a genuine and important difference between Murray's teaching and other systematic theologians" (277). Professor Frame appeals to "Norman Shepherd's rethinking of the doctrine of justification" as evidence that "students of the early Westminster faculty were moved to reconsider traditional ideas by going back to Scripture" (278). It is not clear whether "traditional ideas" refers simply to long-assumed dogmatic formulations or to that which is confessed as the teaching of Scripture in the form of subscription. It would be tragic if the assumption were that "traditional ideas" and "Scripture" are in fundamental tension, and that a denial of the view subscribed by Professors Shepherd and Frame (i.e., in the Westminster Standards and Three Forms) reflects creative advance via *sola Scriptura*. Despite enormous differences on the higher-critical questions, John Frame's sympathies would certainly seem to lie with Brueggemann over Childs. No wonder Frame, commenting on "the relative absence at Westminster" in the early '60s "of a confessional or traditional focus," recalls, "I felt as a student that we were being stimulated to originality more than we were being indoctrinated into a tradition." Thus he recalls, "During my student years, I was never asked to read any of the Reformed confessions, or Calvin's *Institutes*, except in small bits. I never read any official standards of church government or discipline, not to mention Robert's Rules of Order. We used Hodge and Berkhof in our systematics classes, but for the most part we were graded not on our reading, but on our knowledge of Murray's lectures. After graduation I became ordained in the Orthodox Presbyterian Church, and I confess I was rather surprised at the seriousness with which my

That our tradition is prone to consume its energies in conserving its legacy with endless debates should not be denied. In fact, there is a certain respect of individuals and party lines that should be overcome with greater charity and input from both older sources and fresher insights. Yet squandering its inheritance by separating what, in its relatively modest history, has been divinely joined together is no adequate counter-measure. New initiatives in systematic theology are certainly called for in our day, with greater attention to biblical-theological and exegetical developments. However, as we pursue a constructive course, we should hear the reminder of philosopher Hans-Georg Gadamer: "We welcome just the guest who promises something new to our curiosity. But how do we know the guest whom we admit is one who has something new to say to us? Is not our expectation and our readiness to hear the new also necessarily determined by the old that has already taken possession of us?"[29]

In briefly surveying the story of the crisis of biblical and systematic theology in mainline Protestant theology, we have hopefully seen glimpses of our own fate if we should feel pressed into a false choice. To subjugate systematic to biblical theology, as if only the latter actually engaged in genuine exegesis, much less to send the former away with a letter of divorce, is to echo a moribund biblical-theological movement that is far removed from that of Geerhardus Vos. It is fitting, then, that we close with Vos's own plea for the deepest matrimonial union of these partners in service to her who is the ultimate bride of her unrivaled groom:

fellow ministers took the confessional standards and Presbyterian traditions" (279). While it is perhaps forgivable that a Presbyterian seminary would fail to familiarize students in "Presbyterian traditions," assuming that Professor Frame's memory accurately reflects his student days, how could one explain, much less justify, the failure to familiarize candidates for the Presbyterian and Reformed ministry in their standard theological resources? Is it possible that a seminary culture could be so out of touch with the ecclesial community it ostensibly serves?

29. Hans-Georg Gadamer, "The Hermeneutical Problem," in *The Continental Philosophy Reader*, ed. Richard Kearney and Mara Rainwater (London: Routledge, 1996), 115.

Biblical Theology is of the greatest importance and value for the study of Systematic Theology. It were useless to deny that it has been often cultivated in a spirit more or less hostile to the world in which Systematic Theology is engaged. The very name *Biblical* Theology is frequently vaunted so as to imply a protest against the alleged un-Biblical character of Dogmatics. I desire to state most emphatically here, that there is nothing in the nature and aims of Biblical Theology to justify such an implication. For anything pretending to supplant Dogmatics there is no place in the circle of Christian Theology. . . . Dogmatic Theology is, when rightly cultivated, as truly a Biblical and as truly an inductive science as its younger sister. And the latter needs a constructive principle for arranging her facts as well as the former. The only difference is, that in the one case this constructive principle is systematic and logical, whereas in the other case it is purely historical. In other words, Systematic Theology endeavors to construct a circle, Biblical Theology seeks to reproduce a line. . . . The line of revelation is like the stem of those trees that grow in rings. Each successive ring has grown out of the preceding one. But out of the sap and vigor that is in this stem there springs a crown with branches and leaves and flowers and fruit. Such is the true relation between Biblical and Systematic Theology.[30]

30. Vos, *Redemptive History*, 23–24.

4

Systematic Theology and Apologetics at the Westminster Seminaries

John M. Frame

Systematic theology and apologetics are closely related disciplines, for systematics formulates the biblical truth that the apologist defends. I have defined theology as "the application of the Bible by persons to all areas of human life."[1] Among the various theological disciplines, systematic theology "seeks to apply Scripture *as a whole*."[2] Apologetics, then, is "the application of Scripture to unbelief,"[3] which makes it a subdivision of systematic theology.[4] In this chapter, I shall reflect on the relation of systematics to apologetics in the history of the Westminster Seminaries.

1. For defense of this definition, see my *Doctrine of the Knowledge of God* (Phillipsburg, N.J.: Presbyterian and Reformed, 1987), especially 81–85.
2. Ibid., 212. Emphasis in the original.
3. Ibid., 87.
4. Other definitions, of course, are also legitimate. In *Apologetics to the Glory of God* (Phillipsburg, N.J.: P&R, 1994), I define it as "the discipline that teaches Christians how to give a reason for their hope," 1, alluding to 1 Peter 3:15.

Van Til, the Systematic Theologian

Apologetics has probably never been related as closely to systematic theology as it was in the writings of Cornelius Van Til (1895–1987), who taught apologetics at Westminster from its founding in 1929.[5]

Defending Christianity as a Unit

Van Til's interest in systematic theology is reflected in his frequent emphasis that Christian theism should be defended "as a unit."[6] As Van Til often put it, we should not try to prove *that* God exists without considering *what kind* of God we are proving. And that means, in turn, that such proof defines God in terms of all the doctrines of Scripture.

Van Til did not mean to say that every apologetic discussion must prove the whole body of biblical doctrine. Rather, (1) the apologist must "presuppose" the full revelation of the Bible in defending the faith.[7] (2) He must not tone down any biblical distinctives in order to make the faith credible. (3) His goal should be to defend (by one argument or many) the whole of biblical theism, including the authority of Scripture, Trinity, predestination, incarnation, blood atonement, resurrection, and consummation. And (4) the apologist should seek to show that compromise in any

5. He retired officially in 1972, but taught courses occasionally until around 1979.

6. Cornelius Van Til, *Apologetics* (n.p., n.d.), 72. This is one of Van Til's favorite phrases. A search of "unit" on the Van Til CD-ROM *The Works of Cornelius Van Til* (Labels Army Corp., for the Logos Library System) yielded 88 hits. This CD-ROM contains all the writings of Van Til, plus many audio lectures. It is the easiest place to find the writings of Van Til that I cite in this article.

7. That we must presuppose the Bible in order to prove the Bible raises the most standard objection to Van Til's apologetic, namely that it is circular. In reply, Van Til insists (1) that all systems of thought are circular when it comes to establishing their most basic principles: e.g., rationalists must assume reason in order to prove reason. (2) Unless one presupposes biblical theism, all human thinking, including non-Christian thought, becomes incoherent. For more discussion, see my *Knowledge of God*, 130–33, *Apologetics*, 9–14, *Cornelius Van Til: An Analysis of His Thought* (Phillipsburg, N.J.: P&R, 1995), 299–309.

of these doctrines leads to incoherence in all human knowledge. These principles make apologetics heavily dependent on the content of biblical doctrine. Thus, for Van Til systematic theology was especially important.

Van Til's Writings

The importance of systematics for Van Til appears in his basic classroom text, *Apologetics*, which spends two of its five chapters expounding loci of systematics:[8] 37 out of its 99 pages. Van Til taught systematic theology, as well as apologetics, at Westminster Seminary through much of his career.[9] He taught the required courses in the doctrine of revelation, the doctrine of God, and ethics. His other writings also comment on many theological issues. In my judgment, he made important contributions to theological method (the concept of a theological system, analogy, paradox, the role of Scripture), the Trinity, divine sovereignty, election and reprobation, revelation, and common grace.[10] He also wrote voluminously on modern theologians: Barth, Brunner, Whitehead, the "new hermeneutic" group, and many more.[11] Clearly much of his apologetic work had theological targets.

8. Van Til, *Apologetics*, 1–22. Much of this material is included also in Van Til's first published work, *The Defense of the Faith* (Philadelphia: Presbyterian and Reformed, 1955; abridged edition, 1963).

9. Beginning in the 1960s, the seminary assigned these courses to junior members of the systematics department: Edwin H. Palmer, Norman Shepherd, and the present writer, who all made substantial use of Van Til's writings.

10. For a critical exposition of his distinctive teachings in these areas, see my *Cornelius Van Til*, 51–230. My book spends far more pages on Van Til's theological contributions than on his apologetics as such, reflecting my own estimate of the importance of these contributions.

11. See his *Christ and the Jews* (1968) (dealing with Buber and others), *Christianity and Barthianism* (1962), *Christianity in Modern Theology* (1955), *The Confession of 1967* (1967), *The Great Debate Today* (1971), *Is God Dead?* (1966) (on "Christian atheism"), *The New Hermeneutic* (1974), *The New Modernism* (1946), *The New Synthesis Theology of the Netherlands* (1975), *The Reformed Pastor and Modern Thought* (1971), *The Triumph of Grace* (1958). All titles are published by Presbyterian and Reformed and can be found on the above-cited CD-ROM.

Van Til and Murray

Van Til greatly respected John Murray, who taught systematics at Westminster from 1930 to 1966, and considered him a close friend. The two men went on walks together. In "The First Forty Years: A Tribute to My Colleagues," he says, "As for John Murray, who of us did not suffer healing through his seemingly impeccable holiness of conversation?"[12] He quoted Murray a number of times in his writings, always with approval.[13]

The two men were very different: Murray the detailed exegete, Van Til the philosopher who discussed biblical doctrines in the big picture of the Christian theistic worldview. But there was little if any tension between the two men. Murray did find fault with Van Til's view of an "old man" within the unbeliever who clings to the truth of general revelation that he has not managed to repress. Murray disagreed with Van Til's understanding of the "old man" in Romans 6,[14] and he thought that the phrase "old man" was inappropriate to refer to the unbeliever's suppressed knowledge of God. In one class I had with him, Van Til began to talk about the unbeliever's old man, then retracted it, saying something like "John Murray doesn't like that way of putting it, and I guess I don't either."

Van Til, Berkouwer, and the Primacy of Exegesis

G. C. Berkouwer, author of many volumes of dogmatics, devoted some criticism to Van Til, both in *The Triumph of Grace in the Theology of Karl Barth*[15] and in his article "The Authority of Scripture (A Responsible Confession)" in the 1971 Van Til

12. This tribute can be found on the *Works* CD-ROM.

13. For example, in *Apologetics*, 41, *Defense* (1955 ed.), 413, *The Protestant Doctrine of Scripture*, (n.p., n.d.: 1967), 45–46.

14. He pointed out that the old man in Rom. 6:6 was *dead* and therefore not a continuing influence, though he did recognize the continuing need of believers to mortify the flesh.

15. Grand Rapids: Eerdmans, 1956.

festschrift.[16] In the latter piece, Berkouwer complains against Van Til's lack of biblical exegesis in his polemics against other theologians, including Berkouwer. In reply, Van Til says, "I agree that my little book on *The Sovereignty of Grace* should have had much more exegesis in it than it has. This is a defect. The lack of detailed scriptural exegesis is a lack in all my writings. I have no excuse for this."[17] But Van Til then adds that he is familiar with the commentary literature. In the point of dispute, the doctrine of election in Romans 9, Van Til says that he agrees with Murray, over against Herman Ridderbos and Berkouwer.

From this exchange, we can understand that Van Til agreed with Murray that exegesis is the foundation of systematic theology, and indeed of apologetics as well. In fact, no apologist has given as much attention as Van Til to the biblical foundations of his apologetic and theological method. Nevertheless, although Van Til did not seek to justify his lack of exegesis, he made that fault understandable: he felt a freedom to focus on philosophical issues because of his confidence in Murray and in other Reformed exegetes.

At Westminster, Van Til trusted his colleagues. When he was criticized for failure to emphasize historical evidences for the Bible's reliability, he pointed to the work of his colleagues in the "other departments of the seminary," saying that they "are doing it better than I could do it."[18] There was a unity of conviction on the early faculty of Westminster that gave to each professor the freedom to specialize.

Although I agree with both Van Til and Murray as to the primacy of exegesis in theology, I think Van Til was too hard on himself in his response to Berkouwer. The Spirit of God has given many different gifts to members of his body, and ideally each of

---

16. E. R. Geehan, ed., *Jerusalem and Athens* (Nutley, N.J.: Presbyterian and Reformed, 1971), 197–203.

17. Ibid., 203.

18. Cornelius Van Til, *A Christian Theory of Knowledge* (Nutley, N.J.: Presbyterian and Reformed, 1969), 293. This quote and many others refute the common complaint that Van Til allowed no role for historical evidences in his apologetic.

us should have the liberty to do what he does best. God called Van Til to do systematic theology and apologetics from a broad, philosophical, worldview perspective, and it was good that he focused on that. It was also good that he recognized the primacy of exegesis and was willing to learn from those who were gifted differently from himself. If Van Til had tried to re-do the work of Ned Stonehouse and Murray, most likely he would have wasted his time and God's.

John Murray, the Apologist

A Seminary of Apologists

John Murray was less of an apologist than Van Til was a systematic theologian. But he was an apologist, at least in the sense that the whole early faculty of Westminster were apologists. Westminster, born in the struggle with theological liberalism, took an apologetic stance against it in all its departments. Its founder, J. Gresham Machen, a New Testament scholar, was primarily known for his polemics against liberal biblical scholars, and in that sense was an apologist.[19] Like Van Til, Murray joined in that apologetic effort.

Apologetics in Murray's Writings

Of all the early faculty, John Murray was probably the least inclined toward apologetics. Yet he taught courses dealing with Schleiermacher, Ritschl, and other liberal theologians.[20] In 1936

19. Machen was appointed to the chair of apologetics at Princeton in 1928, but that appointment was rejected by the Board, which wanted to encourage, rather than discourage, the liberal movement. This rejection was one of a series of events that led to the founding of Westminster. Greg Bahnsen thus spoke of Machen and Van Til as two distinct, but compatible, strains in the "apologetical tradition of the Orthodox Presbyterian Church." Greg Bahnsen, "Machen, Van Til, and the Apologetical Tradition of the OPC," in *Pressing Toward the Mark*, ed. Charles Dennison and Richard C. Gamble (Philadelphia: The Committee for the Historian of the Orthodox Presbyterian Church, 1986), 259–94.

20. He did not teach such courses when I was a student, presumably because that was such a strong focus of Van Til's teaching.

he published a series of articles in the *Presbyterian Guardian* on "The Reformed Faith and Modern Substitutes," which dealt with liberalism, as well as Arminianism and "modern dispensationalism."[21] Murray did not often reflect on questions of apologetic method. The late Dr. John Gerstner, who graduated from Westminster around 1940, once asked me whether I thought John Murray was a Van Tillian. Gerstner remarked to me, "You know, those old Scots ate up natural theology with their oatmeal."

There are two documents that give us something of an answer to that question. One is a set of student notes from Murray's lectures on the doctrine of God, or "Theology Proper." The other is a paragraph from his article, "The Attestation of Scripture."

Murray's Lectures on Theology Proper

Murray rarely taught the seminary course in the doctrine of God. I assume, however, that he taught it once or twice when Van Til was on leave, prompting one student to take very detailed notes and make mimeographed copies of them for others. I assume the lectures were given in the late 1940s or the 1950s. They are not as polished as the lectures in Murray's other courses. They were not included in the volumes of Murray's *Collected Writings*.[22] But they do reflect Murray's customary high quality of thought. I shall discuss the epistemological section of these lectures.

Murray on the Knowability of God

In these student notes, the first 29 of 93 pages deal with the knowability and incomprehensibility of God, indicating that Mur-

21. It is interesting to see how Machen's associates in the 1930s began to attack other evangelicals with the same passion with which they had earlier attacked liberalism. Eventually, that same passion would be devoted to attacks against other Reformed believers, in the Clark controversy, the debate over apologetic method, and (by my count) in nineteen other intra-Reformed controversies. See my "Machen's Warrior Children," in *Alister McGrath and Evangelical Theology*, ed. Sung Wook Chung (Grand Rapids: Baker, 2003).

22. John Murray, *Collected Writings of John Murray*, 4 vols. (Edinburgh: Banner of Truth, 1976–82).

ray, like Van Til, placed great emphasis on religious epistemology. He begins with the biblical teaching that all people know God (Rom. 1:21) (also a very strong emphasis in Van Til).[23] Then he explores "the character of this knowledge." He points out that Calvin's statement "we do not know God as he is in himself" can be taken in a proper or an improper sense. The proper sense is that "we are entirely dependent for our knowledge of God on the revelation that He has given to us."[24] The improper sense is "that we do not know God as he really and truly is."[25] The former proposition, Murray says, is biblical. The latter "leads to skepticism."[26]

Murray on Analogy

On the question of analogy, Murray makes another distinction. Our knowledge of God is analogical, in the sense that our knowledge is "after the likeness of" God's own knowledge of himself. But what we know, the object of our knowledge, according to Murray, is not an analogy, but the truth: "Our knowledge of the truth is analogical, but what we know is not analogical; e.g., our knowledge of that Truth is analogical, but it is not an analogy of the truth that we know. What we know is the Truth."[27] Murray says that if what we know, the object of our knowledge, is a mere analogy, then we do not know the truth at all.

These statements address issues that were raised in the 1940s controversy between Van Til and Gordon H. Clark. Van Til emphasized that our knowledge of God was analogous to God's own, but not identical with it, seeking to protect the Creator-creature distinction. Clark emphasized that our knowledge was the same as God's own, seeking to prevent skepticism. Murray's formulation adds a valuable clarification of this debate: our method of knowing is different from God's, though "analogous"

---

23. John Murray, "Theology Proper" (anonymous mimeographed student notes, n.d.), 1–2.
24. Ibid., 4.
25. Ibid.
26. Ibid., 5.
27. Ibid.

to it; but the object of our knowledge, what we know, is not an analogy, but the truth itself.

The Clark party was willing to say that our *way* of knowing (they called it the "mode") is different from God's. But they wanted to insist that God and human beings could know the same propositions (such as "Jesus rose from the dead"). Van Til too was willing to say that God and man know the same propositions. In his *Introduction to Systematic Theology*, he says, "That two times two are four is a well-known fact. God knows it. Man knows it."[28] But he wanted to insist that our way of knowing is different from God's. On these matters, the most heatedly debated of the controversy, Van Til and Clark actually agreed.[29] One imagines that if John Murray had urged his distinction on the parties during the debate, and if the parties had listened to him with a teachable spirit, much of the battle could have been avoided.[30]

I should say too that in my judgment Murray's concept of analogy here is quite compatible with Van Til's. For Van Til, to speak of God "analogously" does not mean to speak of him in nonliteral language, as with Thomas Aquinas.[31] Rather, he meant, as Murray says, that our knowing images God's, that we think God's thoughts after him. So Van Til did not deny the point that Mur-

---

28. Cornelius Van Til, *Introduction to Systematic Theology* (Phillipsburg, N.J.: P&R, 1974), 172.

29. Van Til's party insisted that Clark's references to the "mode" of God's knowledge were insufficient. Rather, for them, the difference between divine and human thought had to be described as a difference in "content." But they never made clear what they meant by a "difference in content" beyond what Clark described as a "difference in mode." Certainly, they did not mean to say that God and man had no propositional beliefs in common. I think what they meant is more like this: Even when God and man believe the same proposition, what is "in God's mind" is different from what is in man's. For God's thought, like God himself, is infinite, eternal, and unchangeable, etc. and man's is not. Yet I cannot imagine that the Clark party would have objected to this view if the Van Til party had explained it clearly.

30. I do not know when Murray arrived at this formulation, or whether he tried to urge it during the controversy. I wish that he had and that he had been heard. For a more detailed analysis of the controversy, see my *Cornelius Van Til*, 97–113.

31. Thomas Aquinas, *Summa Theologiae*, 1a.13.5. More precisely, Thomas denies that we can use language about God that is univocal or literal "according to its mode of signification." (*Summa Theologiae*, 1a.13.3)

ray makes here, that "it is not an analogy of the truth that we know. What we know is the Truth." Van Til's interpreters, both friendly and unfriendly, have often misunderstood him on this matter.[32]

Murray on the Incomprehensibility of God

Murray's lectures on theology proper continue by discussing directly the nature of the incomprehensibility of God.[33] Murray does not here use Van Til's rather novel definition of "incomprehensibility," namely the lack of any "point of identity" between a divine thought and a human one, but rather the more traditional definition: that human beings cannot know God exhaustively, or as God knows himself. Murray then makes various traditional distinctions. For example, he affirms that incomprehensibility denies inapprehensibility (unknowability). He also emphasizes helpfully that God is incomprehensible not only in those things that are unrevealed (Deut. 29:29) but also in the things that are revealed (Rom. 11:33–36).

Murray on Revelation

Then Murray discusses "The Sources of Our Knowledge of God."[34] As in Van Til's *Introduction to Systematic Theology*, Murray distinguishes between the revelation of God in "Man himself," in "the external world," and through "special revelation." Under "Man himself," he discusses Romans 2:12–15 and Romans 1:32 in some detail but emphasizes also, as Van Til also does, that concretely this revelation always works together with revelation in the external world and with God's special revelation.

Under "Revelation given in the external world," Murray, like Van Til, focuses on Romans 1:18–20. He reads *katechon* in verse 18 to mean "holding back" rather than "holding down," but he doesn't explain the significance of that distinction. Van Til usu-

---

32. Van Til, *Introduction to* "Systematic Theology," 89–95, 161–75.
33. Murray, "Theology Proper," 6–12.
34. Ibid., 12–22.

ally translated the term "suppressing." It is not clear here whether Murray is supporting Van Til's interpretation or suggesting an alternative.

Under "special revelation," he makes several points, not in this order: (1) Though it is chiefly redemptive in content, it is not exclusively so. Like Van Til, Murray describes God's pre-Fall speech to Adam as special revelation. (2) Special revelation is necessary to remove our sinful blindness. Therefore, it enables us to use other forms of revelation rightly. (3) Special revelation is more direct, intimate, rich, and more diversified than general revelation. (4) Christian theology is not

> simply the super-structure of the theology derived from special revelation erected upon a foundation provided by unenlightened human reason as it deals with data of general revelation. There is a place for natural theology in Christian theology, but it is not the unaided, unenlightened human inquiry; natural theology properly conceived of is simply the knowledge of God derived from general revelation, as general or natural revelation is wrought upon by the enlightened human understanding, derived from special revelation.[35]

To answer Dr. Gerstner's question, this passage shows what kind of natural theology John Murray ate up with his oatmeal. It is a natural theology that presupposes special revelation. Here Murray's formulation is just as Van Tillian as Van Til's own, though in different language.

Murray on Theistic Proofs

Then Murray goes on to discuss "Theistic Proofs,"[36] emphasizing as above that "we may never think of this argumentation as conducted in abstraction from the light derived from special revelation."[37] He begins with an important distinction between

35. Ibid., 22.
36. Ibid., 23–29.
37. Ibid., 25.

evidence and argument. The evidence is God's self-manifestation in the world. Argument is our formulation of the evidence. I do not believe that Van Til ever noted this distinction. He seemed to think, for example, that because the evidence of God's general revelation is clear, a sound apologetic argument must yield certainty, not mere probability. Van Til did not consider that although the evidence (God's revelation) is certain, our argumentative formulation of that evidence is fallible and sometimes only probable.[38] Murray's distinction here adds a necessary clarification to Van Til's formulation.

Murray says that theistic proofs, in their proper context of general and special revelation, are valid. Van Til is often supposed to have rejected theistic proofs, but in fact he endorsed them, as long as they are used in a way that presupposes the truth of special revelation.[39] Van Til proposed that they be reformulated in a way consistent with biblical presuppositions, but he said little about how that could be done. Murray, however, outlines positive reconstructions of the proofs.

The ontological argument traditionally argues from our idea of God as the greatest possible being to the actual existence of God. The argument says that if God does not exist, it would be possible to conceive of a being greater than he, namely one who does exist. So if God is the greatest possible being, he must exist. Murray describes this as an argument based on man's *sensus divinitatis*, God's witness in human consciousness. That divine witness brings about an *idea* in our minds of a being "than which no greater can exist" (Anselm's phrase). Murray agrees that that phrase is a true description of the biblical God, and he agrees with Anselm that "if we believe in God there is implicit in the conception [of God] the conception of His reality."[40]

Murray disagrees, however, with Anselm's "method." Anselm argues from an idea of God produced by God's revelation, rather

38. For more discussion of this issue, see my *Cornelius Van Til*, 275–79.
39. Van Til, *Introduction to Systematic Theology*, 102–4, 196. Compare my *Cornelius Van Til*, 177–84.
40. Murray, "Theology Proper," 29.

than from the revelation itself. Murray considers this procedure inadequate. I confess that I do not follow Murray's argument here. We cannot refer to, or argue from, God's revelation apart from our own ideas of that revelation. I believe that here Murray has forgotten the important distinction he made earlier between evidence and argument. God's revelation is the evidence. But the argument is always one step removed from the evidence, a formulation in human language and ideas. So we should not hold it against Anselm that he argues from his idea of God.

Murray then discusses the "historical argument,"[41] that the nearly universal belief in God through centuries of history can be explained only by God's real existence. Murray sees this as an extension of the ontological argument. As the ontological argument reasons from one person's idea of God to God's reality, so the historical argument reasons from the ideas of God held by people universally to God's existence. The two arguments work from the *sensus deitatis*: individual and universal respectively. In the "moral argument," Murray says, there is recognition of the fact that without a personal Creator "the concept of responsible creaturehood is meaningless."[42] The teleological argument says that the universe displays "the imprint of God's wisdom," certainly a biblical theme.[43] And the cosmological argument turns on the point of Romans 1:19–20, "that the phenomenal world finds its only adequate explanation in the fact of creation, and creation by the God whose eternal power and divinity is imprinted upon it."[44]

Murray's remarks on these arguments are very brief paragraphs, but they sum up (in my view better than Van Til ever did it) a strategy for formulating the traditional arguments in a Reformed and biblical way, though his comments on the ontological argument require clarification.

41. Ibid., 28.
42. Ibid.
43. Ibid.
44. Ibid., 28–29.

Murray's "The Attestation of Scripture"

The second evidence of Murray's apologetic position is his article "The Attestation of Scripture" in the Westminster Seminary symposium on Scripture, *The Infallible Word*.[45] In the original version of this article, Murray says,

> We do not elicit the doctrine of Scripture from an inductive study of what we suppose determines its character. We derive our doctrine of Scripture from what the Scripture teaches with respect to its own character—in a word, from the testimony it bears to itself.
>
> This might seem to be arguing in a circle. It might seem analogous to the case of a judge who accepts the witness of the accused in his own defence rather than the evidence derived from all the relevant facts in the case. We should, however, be little disturbed by this type of criticism. It contains an inherent fallacy. It is fully admitted that normally it would be absurd and a miscarriage of justice for a judge to accept the testimony of the accused rather than the verdict required by all the relevant evidence. But the two cases are not analogous. There is one sphere where self-testimony must be accepted as absolute and final. This is the sphere of our relation to God. God alone is adequate witness to himself. And our discussion with respect to the character of Scripture belongs to this category. Our discussion is premised upon the proposition that the Bible is the Word of God and therefore premised upon the presupposition that it is unique and belongs to the realm of the divine. For this reason, the argument from self-testimony is in order and perfectly consistent. Indeed, it is the only procedure that is consistent with the uniqueness of the question with which we are dealing.[46]

This is the most explicitly Van Tillian passage in Murray's writings. Here he emphasizes the theme that Scripture is self-attesting

45. John Murray, "The Attestation of Scripture," in *The Infallible Word*, ed. Ned B. Stonehouse and Paul Woolley (Grand Rapids: Eerdmans, 1946).
46. Ibid., 9–10.

and that discussions of the Bible must be based on the "presupposition" that it is God's Word, themes familiar to readers of Van Til. He even implies, as Van Til, that such presupposing is a kind of circular argument.

However, I confess to having been surprised and a little disappointed that in the Third Revised Printing of the volume[47] the paragraph beginning "This might seem to be arguing in a circle" is missing. So in 1973 I wrote to Professor Murray, who was then retired and living in Scotland, bringing greetings and asking him the reasons for the omission of that paragraph. I asked him if perhaps the omission was an accident. He replied on June 20, 1973, as follows:

> The omission you refer to was revision on my part. I am not sure that I can recollect all the considerations that prompted me years ago. However, this I can say. The argument of the context is not affected by the omission nor is the underlying apologetic. I think the main reason was that some people who would be quite amenable to the argument propounded would be likely to be repelled by the expression "arguing in a circle," not because they are unwilling to accede to the method exemplified, but because "arguing in a circle" as description is for them a bogey that arouses unfavorable reaction even though in reality the argument involved is not alien to their thinking.

Van Til, of course, was not as squeamish about the phrase "arguing in a circle." But we should take Murray at his word here that his revision to the article represents no change in his apologetic method, that the change is terminological rather than conceptual.

Murray and Van Til

The evidence of Murray's writings, therefore, is that he and Van Til were united in their apologetic method. I should also men-

---

47. Philadelphia: Presbyterian and Reformed. No date given for the revision. I would guess it was around 1965.

tion Murray's article, "Common Grace,"[48] which provided exegetical support to a doctrine that Van Til also defended in controversy, and his "The Free Offer of the Gospel,"[49] written in the heat of the Clark controversy, which supported Van Til's view of the gospel offer rather than Clark's. It is possible that Murray's apologetic position was not clearly formulated during Dr. Gerstner's student years. Most likely the attacks on Westminster Seminary from various quarters, particularly the Clark controversy of the 1940s, moved the professors at the seminary to greater unity and mutual support. Certainly during the Clark controversy the Westminster faculty was united behind Van Til.[50] I would assume that under such pressure they came to express themselves in more explicitly Van Tillian ways than they had before.

The relation between Van Til and Murray established the pattern for later generations of Westminster apologists and systematic theologians. I can therefore be briefer on the later teachers. I do have more to say, especially about the Westminster apologists. I will say less about the members of the systematic theology departments because other essays in this volume deal with their work in some detail.

Robert D. Knudsen

Robert Knudsen (1924–2000) taught apologetics at Westminster from 1955–95. On apologetic matters he followed Van Til's thought closely. His emphases and style of thought can be discerned in his paper, "The Transcendental Perspective of Westminster's Apologetics."[51]

48. Murray, *Collected Writings of John Murray*, 2:93–119.

49. Ibid., 4:113–32.

50. One professor, now deceased, told me that the faculty feared the Clark party was seeking to take over the seminary, replace Van Til with Clark, and change the character of the institution. Whether or not his perception was accurate, it was a perception held by a number of faculty members.

51. Robert Knudson, "The Transcendental Perspective of Westminster's Apologetics," *Westminster Theological Journal* 48 (1986): 223–39. Also posted at http://www.reformed. org/apologetics/knudsen_westapol.html.

At Van Til's suggestion, Knudsen studied the school of philosophy founded in the Netherlands by Herman Dooyeweerd and D. H. Th. Vollenhoven, known as "The Philosophy of the Idea of Law." But by 1960, Van Til was beginning to lose confidence in these Dutch thinkers. They did not clearly affirm the inerrancy of Scripture, and they recommended a form of dialogue with secular philosophers that in Van Til's view did injustice to the antithesis between belief and unbelief.[52] Knudsen agreed with Van Til that the Dooyeweerdian thinkers held inadequate views of Scripture, but he did not accept Van Til's criticisms of their dialogue-strategy, and in general he sought to promote the Dooyeweerdian approach at Westminster. There was tension between Van Til and Knudsen over this issue.

The Dooyeweerd group also raised questions about the methods and assumptions of traditional Reformed systematic theology, accusing it of "dualism" and dependence on Greek philosophy.[53] Knudsen to some extent agreed with these accusations, though he thought they were often overdrawn. I can remember him questioning the reference in the Westminster Confession of Faith, 1.1, to the "light of nature," suggesting that the Confession at that point was making a concession to rationalism.

Knudsen continued Van Til's practice of criticizing modern theologians, focusing on post-Barthian developments: Tillich, Bultmann, the New Hermeneutic. He also dealt with modern philosophy, especially existentialism and Marxism.

Though Knudsen did teach at least one systematics course in the mid-1950s when John Murray was on leave, he did not regularly teach required courses in the systematics department, as Van Til did. Although he had some objections to the categories and methods by which the traditional Reformed doctrines were formulated, he did not spend much time reflecting on how to

52. I discuss Van Til's concerns about Dooyeweerd in my *Cornelius Van Til*, 371–86.
53. For an example of these criticisms and an exhibit of an alternative style of systematic theology, see Gordon J. Spykman, *Reformational Theology* (Grand Rapids: Eerdmans, 1992).

reformulate them. He rather focused on the more narrowly apologetic task of refuting the opponents of these doctrines.

Harvie M. Conn

Harvie Conn (1933–99) became a missionary to Korea after his studies at Westminster. In 1972 he returned to Westminster to teach. Van Til formally retired that year, and Conn took over his introductory apologetics course. Conn added nothing new to Van Til's theory of apologetics, or to the formulations of Reformed systematics, but he applied Van Til's apologetics to missions, evangelism, and modern culture, especially film. He asked students to produce multimedia presentations dealing with apologetic issues. Conn maintained the close relation between apologetics and systematics at Westminster. It is interesting at this point to note the variety of gifts that can be brought to bear on the work of apologetics: biblical studies (Machen), philosophy (Van Til, Knudsen), systematic theology (Murray), evangelism, missions, and knowledge of culture (Conn). Apologetics brings together all the theological disciplines as it seeks to prove Christianity "as a unit."

In 1975 Conn asked to be relieved of the apologetics course to focus more on missions, in which he made many distinguished contributions. The next section will describe his successor.

Autobiographical Interlude

With some reluctance I now inject myself into the narrative, for I am part of the story, for better or worse, and very much a bridge between apologetics and systematics at Westminster. I majored in philosophy as an undergraduate, took electives at Westminster from Van Til, and studied philosophical theology at the graduate level. So I figured that if I were ever invited to teach at Westminster, that invitation would come from the apologetics department. That did not happen, because in the late 1960s there were no openings in Westminster's apologetics department, and,

I suspect, because Van Til had some doubts as to my full allegiance to his approach. We had some problems communicating: his philosophical language was from the idealist tradition, mine from Anglo-American language analysis. He was steeped in the Dutch theological and philosophical literature; I was not. I also had some disagreements with Van Til—on details, as I saw it, rather than matters of major emphasis. Van Til preferred to work with people who did not disagree with him, even on details.

So I did not expect to be asked to return to teach at Westminster. But, to my surprise, I received in 1967 a communication from Norman Shepherd about teaching in the Westminster systematics department. Murray had retired in 1966 and returned to Scotland. So I became a systematic theologian, teaching the courses Van Til had taught for many years: Doctrine of the Word, Doctrine of God, and Ethics. Van Til did welcome me to the faculty and asked me also to teach Th.M. electives in the apologetics department. There I taught courses in contemporary analytic philosophy, an area that had not been covered by Van Til or Knudsen.

I was committed to Van Til's apologetic method and to Murray's exegetical emphasis. I sought to integrate these as much as possible: detailed exegesis with worldview consciousness. In Ethics, Van Til's distinction between goal, motive, and standard provided a course structure. In the Doctrine of the Word, I took special note of Van Til's emphasis on the interrelation of different forms of revelation: revelation from God, from the world, and from the self. In the Doctrine of God, I first structured the course using the traditional distinction between God's transcendence and immanence. But eventually I saw that "transcendence" is somewhat ambiguous. The term can evoke the idea that God is so far away from us that we cannot know him or speak truly of him. That idea, characteristic of neoplatonism, mysticism, and much modern liberal theology, is not biblical.[54] If we are to use

54. The unbiblical norm of "transcendence," together with unbiblical forms of "immanence" (i.e., when God enters time he becomes less than himself or divinizes the world) correspond respectively to Van Til's "irrationalism" and "rationalism," in the epistemological sphere.

the word *transcendence*, I thought, we should use it to represent the biblical language of God's exaltation: the exaltation of royal dignity rather than distance from us. But even that concept of transcendence has some ambiguity. As king, God is exalted both in the *control* he exercises over creation and in his *authority* to command rational creatures. So I structured the Doctrine of God course in terms of God's control, authority (these constituting his transcendence), and presence (his immanence).

Three courses, three threefold distinctions: In Ethics, *goal*, *standard*, and *motive*. In Doctrine of the Word, revelation from *nature*, *God*, and *the self*. In Doctrine of God, *control*, *authority*, and *presence*. These three triads came together in my mind: (1) *Goal* seemed to fit together with *nature* and *control*; for God's control of nature and history determines what means are conducive to what ends, (2) *standard* with *God* and *authority*, and (3) *motive* with *self* and *presence*, for we are motivated to good only by God's Spirit in our inmost being.

So we can look at ethics and other theological disciplines "situationally" (focusing on the nature of the created world), "normatively" (focusing on the authority of God's revelation) or "existentially" (focusing on God's presence with his people). I defined these as three "perspectives" on theology, for they are interdependent. One cannot understand the situation without the light of revelation and our personal involvement. One cannot understand revelation without understanding its history, and without being able to apply it to the world and the self. And one cannot understand himself without understanding revelation and the world, his environment.[55] The theologian can begin at any of these three points, but in seeking to understand one of them, he will be forced to gain an understanding of the other two.

Such is my "multi-perspectivalism,"[56] an exegetically based epistemology. Even apart from these triads, however, the idea of

55. Compare Calvin's statement that we cannot know ourselves without knowing God, and vice versa. John Calvin, *Institutes of the Christian Religion*, 1.1.1.

56. For a thorough exposition, see my *Doctrine of the Knowledge of God*. For briefer treatments, see my *Medical Ethics* (Phillipsburg, N.J.: Presbyterian and Reformed, 1988)

perspectives is important: We are finite beings, so we cannot see everything at once. To know something, we must seek to look at it from different angles and to benefit from the perspectives of others. It is thus that I have tried to enrich my teaching of Reformed theology with insights developed out of Van Til's philosophical apologetic.

I taught mostly systematics courses until 1975, when Harvie Conn vacated the introductory apologetics course. I was asked to teach it then, with Van Til's blessing. I combined that course with the first semester systematics course, The Doctrine of the Word of God. In that combined course I developed a unit on biblical epistemology, important to both apologetics and systematics. This led to my *Doctrine of the Knowledge of God*, published in 1987, a close integration of theology and philosophy: traditional philosophical questions answered by biblical exegesis.

Despite my philosophical background, I have been more of a systematic theologian than an apologist. My main strengths have been in the integration of the two disciplines, in the spirit of Van Til and Murray.

In 1980 I left Westminster in Philadelphia to become one of the founding faculty of Westminster in California. I taught there for twenty years, in both apologetics and systematics. In 2000 I left Westminster to accept a position at Reformed Theological Seminary, Orlando, Florida, where I continue to teach in these same areas. RTS continues the close integration of apologetics and systematics characteristic of Westminster. The predominant apologetic position at RTS is Van Tillian, the emphasis of its systematic theology department exegetical. Nine former students of mine teach on the faculty of RTS, and others have been very sympathetic to a multi-perspectival approach. In this way as in others, Westminster has had an influence beyond its own campuses.

---

and *Perspectives on the Word of God* (Eugene, Ore.: Wipf and Stock, 1999). I defend a threefold understanding of God's lordship in *Doctrine of God* (Phillipsburg, N.J.: P&R, 2002), 21–115.

Vern S. Poythress

It might seem strange to refer to the work of a New Testament scholar in a chapter on the relationship of systematics to apologetics. But Vern S. Poythress, who joined the Westminster faculty in the late 1970s, is as much a systematician as he is a biblical scholar, and he has been deeply interested in apologetics as well. His *Philosophy, Science, and the Sovereignty of God*[57] is a brilliant integration between Van Til's apologetics, Reformed systematics, my multi-perspectivalism, and the linguistic system of Kenneth Pike, with whom Poythress studied. Poythress applied this approach to theological method in *Symphonic Theology: the Validity of Multiple Perspectives in Theology*,[58] and to hermeneutics in *God-Centered Biblical Interpretation*.[59] Besides his teaching in New Testament, he has taught systematics courses on the Doctrine of God and the Doctrine of Man. Although Poythress is a former student of mine, I have certainly learned more from him than he has from me. His work has profoundly reinforced the integration of systematics and apologetics at Westminster.

Recent Westminster Theologians

I will say little about other members of Westminster's systematics departments, since other articles in this volume discuss their contributions. Norman Shepherd joined the systematics department in the mid 1960s. He was very much like Murray in the clarity and preciseness of his thinking, his Reformed convictions, his theological emphases, even his manner of speech. He was self-consciously Van Tillian in his apologetic and philosophical orientation. Of the faculty in the early 1970s, he would have been, in my judgment, the least likely to be the center of theological controversy.

57. Vern S. Poythress, *Philosophy, Science, and the Sovereignty of God* (Nutley, N.J.: Presbyterian and Reformed, 1976).
58. Vern S. Poythress, *Symphonic Theology: The Validity of Multiple Perspectives in Theology* (1987; reprint, Phillipsburg, N.J.: P&R, 2001).
59. Vern S. Poythress, *God-Centered Biblical Interpretation* (Phillipsburg, N.J.: P&R, 1999).

In 1974, however, concern arose on the campus about Shepherd's view of justification by faith alone. The controversy is not relevant to the subject of the present article. But I should mention that Van Til, though retired during this period, considered Shepherd to be orthodox and vocally supported him in faculty discussions.

Robert B. Strimple, whom we honor in this volume, joined the systematics department in 1969, one year after I did. He had been teaching in Baptist circles for several years. But when President Edmund Clowney of Westminster heard that Strimple had come to a Presbyterian view of baptism, he jumped at the opportunity to invite him to join the faculty, even though a three-man systematics department[60] was something of a luxury for us in those days. Strimple was an erudite and eloquent teacher of Reformed theology, with excellent administrative gifts, which he displayed as Academic Dean at the Philadelphia campus and later as President of Westminster in California. Strimple was quite committed to Van Til's approach in apologetics. Alongside his standard courses in systematics, he taught courses in Roman Catholic thought, developing critiques through direct exegesis and through Van Til's apologetic method. One of Strimple's most popular electives was an apologetics course, "The Christian Confronts Modern Atheism," which explored such atheist writers as Nietzsche and Camus. Strimple and I enjoyed an excellent professional and friendly relationship at Westminster in California, supporting each other's work without reservation. The faculty enjoyed deep doctrinal unity and collegiality under his presidency.

Following Strimple's recent retirement, David VanDrunen has joined the faculty, committed, I believe, to the same principles as Van Til, Murray, and Strimple.

Westminster in Philadelphia faced the need to rebuild completely its systematics department in the early 1980s. The relatively young department of Shepherd, Strimple, and Frame suddenly vanished, with Shepherd leaving the faculty and Strimple and Frame moving to California. Later appointments included Sinclair Fergu-

---

60. Actually a two-and-a-half, since part of my teaching load was in apologetics.

son, Richard B. Gaffin, and Timothy Trumper. These were all convinced Van Tillians. Ferguson has been known for his profound applications of the Reformed faith to the Christian life. Gaffin and Trumper, especially, have sought to bring biblical theology, or redemptive history, into systematics. This emphasis would have delighted Van Til, who was a close friend and admirer of Geerhardus Vos, who brought the redemptive historical emphasis to Princeton and Westminster. These teachers, with additional contributions from Vern Poythress and historian D. Clair Davis, have continued to demonstrate the unity of systematics and apologetics.

Recent Westminster Apologists

The additions to the apologetics departments after 1980 continue the Van Tillian tradition and hence Westminster's traditional integration of apologetics and systematics. David W. Clowney, son of Westminster's first president Edmund Clowney, replaced me when I went to California in 1980. He left in 1988, when he came to the conviction that Scripture allowed the ordination of women. He made ample use of Van Til's work and of my multi-perspectival approach.

William Edgar has taught apologetics at Westminster from 1989 until the present. Before he studied with Van Til, Edgar was influenced by Francis Schaeffer, a former student of Van Til with whom Van Til had some disagreements. In an article, "Two Christian Warriors,"[61] Edgar compares Van Til and Schaeffer, agreeing with Van Til's substantive points, but lamenting the lack of good communication between the two men. Edgar's apologetic, then, is fully Van Tillian, but he has focused on issues that were more characteristic of Schaeffer: music, art, general culture. In his short books *Reasons of the Heart*[62] and *The Face of Truth*[63] he has put Westminster's apologetic within the reach of thoughtful laypeople.

61. William Edgar, "Two Christian Warriors," *Westminster Theological Journal* 57.1 (Spring, 1995): 57–80.
    62. William Edgar, *Reasons of the Heart* (1996; reprint, Phillipsburg, N.J.: P&R, 2003).
    63. William Edgar, *The Face of Truth* (Phillipsburg, N.J.: P&R, 2001).

With Knudsen's retirement, Scott Oliphint joined the faculty. Edgar reports that Oliphint "is really THE Van Til expert here, and while well trained in philosophy, understands the theological thrust of CVT. . . ."[64]

In 2000 Michael S. Horton replaced me in the apologetics department of Westminster in California. Horton's background is in historical theology. As I said earlier, God has formed Westminster's apologetic using many different kinds of human gifts: philosophy, systematic theology, missions and evangelism, biblical studies, linguistics, the arts and culture. We can see that this apologetic can be viewed from many "perspectives." It will be interesting to see what Van Tillian apologetics looks like through the lens of historical theology.

I should mention also Peter Jones, who has taught New Testament at Westminster in California beginning in 1989. Jones has studied intensively the literature of ancient Gnosticism and discovered significant parallels between Gnosticism and modern thought, particularly the "New Age" movement of the eighties and nineties and the "new spiritualities" of our own time. Jones has therefore become as much of an apologist as a biblical scholar, as he has developed an extensive ministry of confronting neo-Gnostic thinking in present day philosophy, theology, politics, and culture. To this task he brings a strong Van Tillian sense of antithesis and the resources of Reformed systematic theology.[65]

Conclusion

We have seen that there has been a deep unity and interdependence between Westminster's apologetics and her systematics. I believe that this degree of unity has never been achieved before. The pioneering work of Van Til and Murray has been faith-

64. E-mail from William Edgar, Feb. 17, 2003.
65. His main publications on this subject are *The Gnostic Empire Strikes Back* (Phillipsburg, N.J.: P&R, 1992), *Spirit Wars* (Escondido, Calif.: Main Entry, 1997), and *Gospel Truth/Pagan Lies* (Escondido, Calif.: Main Entry, 1999).

fully honored in their successors. This work has led to a remarkably consistent and cogent presentation of the gospel to the seminary's students and to the world. There has been no war between
philosophers and theologians on the Westminster campuses. Biblical studies too has been well integrated into this general framework, while serving as its exegetical foundation. This integration
is worthy of export to other Reformed institutions, as it has been
successfully exported to RTS.

5

On Practical Theology
as Systematic Theology

Dennis E. Johnson

In God's kind providence Robert Strimple has played a decisive role in my service to Christ's church for over thirty years. When I was about to graduate from Westminster Seminary in 1973, he encouraged me in my acceptance of a pastoral call and in my desire to continue theological studies with a view toward eventually educating other pastors. His example of *exegetically grounded* theologizing (in the tradition of John Murray) later influenced my decision to supplement a Th.M. in New Testament with a Ph.D. concentration on systematic theology. At Bob's initiative I was invited to join the founding faculty of Westminster Seminary in California; and, as he assumed the presidency, it was my privilege to assist him as academic dean. I thank our Lord for Bob's and Alice's example, encouragement, friendship, and courage.

In both his administrative leadership and his scholarship, Bob personifies Westminster's history of maintaining the unity of theological insight and ministerial practice. From the early years of Westminster Seminary (Pennsylvania), Dr. R. B. Kuiper placed a decidedly systematic-theological cast on the department of practical theology. It has been written of Kuiper:

Of first importance was the point that Practical Theology,
is *theology*. He did not think of his work at the seminary as
anything like a glorified assembly line turning out kits con-
taining ten simple tools for becoming a successful preacher.
His teaching in no way resembled a popular image of a
department of Practical Theology as being little more than
a place for learning the techniques of effective pastoral public relations. . . .[1]

Edmund Clowney, who was first president of Westminster Seminary Pennsylvania and California and taught practical theology
at both schools, reports that Kuiper sternly charged him to remain
robustly *theological* in all his teaching and writing on preaching
and every other aspect of pastoral ministry. Clowney's rich biblical-theological insights in homiletics, ecclesiology, Christian nurture, and missions benefited generations of ministerial students
and, through them, countless churches throughout the world.
When Westminster Seminary California was begun in the 1980s,
Derke Bergsma brought the same theological focus to his role as
professor of practical theology. One indicator of the close affinity between systematic and practical theology in the Westminster
tradition is the fact that, from Kuiper's days onward, the required
course on ecclesiology, traditionally a systematic-theological
locus, has been taught by members of the department of practical theology. The study of the church's identity and design,
revealed in Scripture and progressively clarified since the age of
the apostles, cannot be isolated from its mission.

What, precisely, is entailed in Westminster's commitment to
shape ministry praxis in line with the contours of Reformed theology—to insist that the message mold the medium, not vice
versa? My hope is that this essay, offered in appreciation for a
respected, beloved colleague and mentor, may cast light on this
question.

1. Edward Heerema, *R. B.: A Prophet in the Land* (Jordan Station, Ontario: Paideia,
1986), 131.

Practical Theology in Identity Crisis

Practical theology is the adolescent of the theological encyclopedia, brought to birth as a recognized discipline long after its siblings: exegetical, historical, and systematic theology.[2] Although subjects now taught by faculties of practical theology—preaching and the sacraments, worship in general, the cure of souls, church polity, and the like—were discussed by the church's great theologian-shepherds before such subjects were grouped and labeled "practical theology,"[3] scholars typically credit the seventeenth-century Reformed theologian Gisbertus Voetius[4] or the nineteenth-century "father" of liberalism, Friedrich Schleiermacher,[5] with

2. See Geerhardus Vos, *Biblical Theology: Old and New Testaments* (Grand Rapids: Eerdmans, 1948), 12: "The usual treatment of Theology distinguishes four departments, which are named Exegetical Theology, Historical Theology, Systematic Theology, and Practical Theology." Abraham Kuyper, *Encyclopedia of Sacred Theology: Its Principles*, trans. J. H. de Vries (New York: Scribner, 1898), 630, had previously recognized this fourfold division, but objected that the traditional terms were oriented toward man rather than toward the Word as the *principium* of theology. He proposed that the disciplines that examine "the Word of God, first *as such*, then in its *working* [in church history], after that according to its *content*, and finally in its *propaganda* [i.e., propagation]," and be called bibliological, ecclesiological, dogmatological, and diaconiological theology, respectively (emphasis original). Some distinguish *dogmatic* theology, the history of the church's progressive clarification of its faith, from *systematic* theology, the articulation of the system of interrelated truths revealed in Scripture. Others use these terms synonymously.

3. See, e.g., Augustine, *On Christian Teaching*, trans. R. P. H. Green (Oxford: Oxford University Press, 1997), book 4, which applies classical rhetoric to Christian preaching. John Calvin, *Institutes of the Christian Religion*, ed. John T. McNeill, trans. F. L. Battles (Philadelphia: Westminster, 1960), book 4, discusses the church's marks, officers, authority, discipline, and sacraments. See also Thomas C. Oden, *Christian Pastoral Care* (4 vols. 1986–89; reprint, Grand Rapids: Baker, 1994), a distillation of Patristic pastoral wisdom.

4. Gisbertus Voetius, *Selectae Disputationes Theologicae* (5 vols. Utrecht, 1648–69). Selections in English appear in John W. Beardslee III, ed. and trans., *Reformed Dogmatics* (New York: Oxford University Press, 1965), 265–316. Voetius's discussion of "practical theology" concentrated on moral theology but also included church polity.

5. Friedrich Schleiermacher, *Brief Outline on the Study of Theology*, trans. Terrence N. Tice (1830; Richmond: John Knox, 1966), 91–114. Because Schleiermacher's "encyclopedia" reflected his conception of Christianity as an evolving movement, he identified three categories of theology: philosophical (defining the religious essence of Christianity), historical (exegetical theology [§103–48], church history [§149–94], and dogmatic theology [§195–231] with church "statistics" [§232–50]), and practical theology (church

bringing together into a distinct discipline the topics pertaining to ministry practice.[6] The church has interpreted its Scriptures from its inception, narrated its history from the days of Luke, and systematized its understanding of revealed truth from the time of the christological-Trinitarian controversies; but only in the last few centuries has the *practice* of theology in ministry become a distinct focus of theological reflection.

Like adolescents generally, practical theology is experiencing an identity crisis. Part of the confusion is attributable to its semi-alienated relationship to the other, older disciplines. Following the Enlightenment, specialization in European universities produced a dissociation of theory from practice that led, in turn, to practical theology's reduction to second-class status as derivative, "applied" science, in contrast to the "pure" theological sciences. Recent literature from various viewpoints bemoans the effects of this disjunction between theory and practice.[7] Thomas Ogletree observed that when we isolate "what we are wont to call academic and practical aspects of theological study" from each other,

> we impoverish and distort them both. . . . On the one hand, we tend to subject our academic activities almost exclusively to considerations internal to the unfolding logic of the sub-specialties of theological study. . . . We lose a sense of connection between critical thought and vital life concerns. On the other hand, we tend in our practical thinking to become preoccupied with technique.[8]

---

service [§277–308: worship, homiletics, catechetics, evangelism, missions, pastoral care] and church government [§309–34: polity, church discipline, church and state]).

6. See Edward Farley, "Theology and Practice Outside the Clerical Paradigm," in Don S. Browning, ed., *Practical Theology: The Emerging Field in Theology, Church, and World* (San Francisco: Harper & Row, 1983), 25–28; John E. Burkhart, "Schleiermacher's Vision for Theology," in Browning, *Practical Theology*, 42–57.

7. Farley, "Theology and Practice," 29–34; Ray S. Anderson, *The Shape of Practical Theology: Empowering Ministry with Theological Praxis* (Downers Grove, Ill.: InterVarsity, 2001), 7–8; Dorothy C. Bass, "Introduction," in Miroslav Volf and Dorothy C. Bass, ed., *Practicing Theology: Beliefs and Practices in Christian Life* (Grand Rapids: Eerdmans, 2002), 1–2, 6.

8. Thomas W. Ogletree, "Dimensions of Practical Theology: Meaning, Action, Self," in Browning, *Practical Theology*, 83.

Nevertheless, this segregation of the "practical" from the "academic" maintains a tenacious grip on seminary curricula.

Another factor clouding practical theology's identity is the variety of cognate disciplines with which it must interact. Its calling to explore how the truth revealed in Scripture should be implemented in the lives of specific people and churches, embedded in concrete cultural settings, requires practical theology to integrate insights from disparate intellectual disciplines—not only its companions in the theological encyclopedia but also investigations into human personality, social relationships, and communication principles and processes. The borders it shares with other disciplines seem to invite identifying practical theology as an adjunct to one of its more clearly defined "neighbors." This may lead, on the one hand, to approaches to pastoral care that are little more than baptized versions of secular psychological theories and practices. On the other hand, reaction against the behavioral sciences may produce an approach that tacitly assumes that earlier precedents in one's own ecclesiastical tradition supply straightforward, definitive answers to contemporary issues in ministry.

Although practical theology can learn both from research into human behavior and from church history, each of these related disciplines provides only a fragmentary perspective on the whole panorama that practical theology must take into account as it constructs and refines a theoretical framework for Christian ministry. When practical theology is annexed to psychology, sociology, anthropology, or demographics, the connection between *theological* reflection and obedient response is jeopardized or even severed. Subordinating practical theology to historical theology devalues history by underestimating the unique contexts, past and present, in which the church lives its faith. It also devalues Scripture, replacing the normative authority of God's Word with the church's historically conditioned response to the Word at some past moment.

My contention is that practical theology must be pursued as a form of systematic theology[9]—specifically, as *the*

9. See Thomas Oden, *Pastoral Theology: Essentials of Ministry* (New York: Harper and Row, 1982), x: "Pastoral theology is a special form of practical theology because it focuses

theology of the means established by God and revealed in Scrip-
ture for communicating and implementing biblical truth and
norms in the church's life and mission throughout the world.
This thesis entails four corollaries: First, like the systematic
exposition of the classic theological *loci*, practical theology
must be grounded in exegetical theology, the contextually sensitive interpretation of Scripture. Good theology is always a
reflective reading of the Bible, hearing each text and truth in
the literary, redemptive-historical, and conceptual contexts
of the whole. Second, in exploring the unity and diversity of
the system of revealed truth, practical theology must be
catholic, listening respectfully to the debates and conclusions
of the church's shepherds in earlier ages and in other places.
Third, while grounding itself in special revelation, practical
theology must also take account of general revelation—not
only the ways in which the universe unveils its Creator, but
also the sobering realities of human fallenness and the complex cultural contexts in which the church pursues its calling. Fourth, the *content* of biblical truth and norms determines the *methods* by which it is to be implemented in the
church's life and mission. The message molds the medium.
God's Spirit applies the redemption accomplished by Christ
through means that reflect the gospel message itself: the
power of Christ's resurrection comes through the weakness
of Christ's death.

I will first discuss two definitions of practical theology in
terms of cognate disciplines—behavioral sciences and historical
theology—noting their contributions and their inadequacy as
bases for a theology of ministry. Then I will unfold more fully
what is entailed in pursuing practical theology as the systematic
theology of ministry practice.

---

on the practice of ministry. . . . Pastoral theology is also a form of systematic theology,
because it attempts a systematic, consistent reflection on the offices and gifts of ministry,
and their integral relationship with the tasks of ministry."

Fragmentary Approaches to Practical Theology

Practical Theology as a Behavioral Science

One perspective on practical theology views it as a churchly oriented application of the behavioral sciences. Thus, pastoral counseling is understood as a form of psychotherapy informed by Christian values, ecclesiology as the sociology of religion, preaching as motivational oral communication, Christian nurture as a subset of education, and missiology as an application of anthropology or demographic analysis.

The appeal of this approach is understandable. Pastors are called to guide people toward personal growth and to exercise leadership in a group of diverse people, promoting both interpersonal harmony and the accomplishment of a common mission. It stands to reason that, in order to accomplish these goals, one would draw on those academic disciplines that research human personality and society and those methods that have proven effective in influencing people. One might expect that reconceiving practical theology as a derivative of the behavioral sciences would appeal to mainline (theologically liberal) circles, where confidence in the Bible's authority and sufficiency to guide the church is sometimes tenuous. Examples are not hard to find.[10] On the other hand, evangelicals, who are more interested in grounding their theology in the divinely authoritative revelation of Scripture, seem equally ready to allow the behavioral sciences to set the agenda for pastoral ministry. Pollster George Barna might not present himself as a "practical theologian" *per se*, but his research into the religious tastes of Americans and the conclusions that he draws from it have *de facto* normativity for the ministry priorities and practices of many evangelical pastors.[11] Like-

10. James N. Lapsley, "Practical Theology and Pastoral Care: An Essay in Pastoral Theology," in Browning, *Practical Theology*, 167–86.

11. E.g., George Barna, *User Friendly Churches: What Christians Need to Know about the Churches People Love to Go To* (Ventura: Regal, 1991); *Virtual America: What Every Church Leader Needs to Know about Ministering in an Age of Spiritual and Technological Revolution* (Ventura: Regal, 1994); *Grow Your Church from the Outside In: Understand-*

wise, the leadership principles that many evangelical pastors have imbibed from the works of John Maxwell are as applicable to the entrepreneurial sphere as to the ecclesiastical arena.[12] A third example would be the embrace of cultural anthropology by some evangelical missiologists.[13]

We should not dismiss as pure pragmatism the appeal of letting such sciences set the agenda for practical theology. A theological case can be made for the responsibility of practical theology to understand not only Scripture but also the complexities of the human beings to whom it is addressed and the life contexts in which they must respond to it. Biblical wisdom entails not only insight into the special revelation imparted in the Bible but also discernment of the general revelation embedded in the universe and in human nature and cultures.[14] God has given us not only the written Word but also, as the Belgic Confession says, the created universe "as a most elegant book, wherein all creatures, great and small, are as so many characters, leading us to contemplate the invisible things of God. . . ."[15] Even as Reformed theology focuses on special revelation, it also takes account of general revelation.[16] This is particularly true of practical theology, which con-

---

ing the Unchurched and How to Reach Them (Ventura: Regal, 2002); and the Web site of the Barna Research Group, www.barna.org.

12. John C. Maxwell, *Developing the Leader within You* (Nashville: Thomas Nelson, 1993).

13. E.g., Charles H. Kraft, *Christianity in Culture* (Maryknoll: Orbis, 1979). Note the balance of critique and appreciation in Harvie M. Conn, *Eternal Word and Changing Worlds: Theology, Anthropology, and Mission in Trialogue* (Grand Rapids: Baker, 1984), 129–205.

14. See Dennis E. Johnson, "Spiritual Antithesis, Common Grace, and Practical Theology," *Westminster Theological Journal* 63 (2002): 73–94, especially pp. 81–85, 92–93.

15. Belgic Confession, art. 2. Arthur C. Cochrane, ed., *Reformed Confessions of the 16th Century* (Philadelphia: Westminster, 1966), 189–90.

16. John Murray, "Systematic Theology," *Westminster Theological Journal* 25 (1963): 134: "The chief source of revelation for theology is the special revelation incorporated in Holy Scripture. But the latter comes to us in the life which we live in this world and therefore in a context which is filled with the manifestation of the glory of the same God who specially reveals himself to us in his Word. It would be an abstraction to suppose that we could deal with special revelation and ignore the revelatory data with which the context of our life is replete."

stantly confronts "wisdom" issues at the intersection of biblical principle and life experience.

Nevertheless, both mainline and conservative practical theologians have warned against the tendency to *subsume* practical theology under the disciplines of behavioral science. Edward Farley blamed "the alienation of theology and practice" on the narrowing of the concept of theology from a medieval frame of mind, which included wisdom and commitment, to the modern academic specialization.[17] Once this reductionism had isolated ministry practices from the "pure" academic disciplines, reducing the former from subjects of reflection to mere "techniques," the question arose:

> What is it that establishes these [areas of practical theology] as disciplines if there is no discipline of practical theology and if they are virtually severed from the structure of theological study? The answer is, their discrete subject matter (some area of ministerial work) as it is rendered objective and scholarly by some satellite science, by rhetoric, psychology, social science, business science, and so forth.[18]

When we define practical theology in terms of the behavioral sciences, practical theology ceases to be *theological*. The linkage is broken between the structure of biblical truth, on the one hand, and the strategies for conveying that truth, on the other. Consequently, a practical theology that looks to the behavioral sciences for its identity risks ceasing to be uniquely Christian at all. Along with valid insights or strategies that the sciences have to offer, an alien theoretical framework may be absorbed into practical theology, and thereby into pastoral practice. Don S. Browning observed:

> More and more, I fear, we have tried to intervene into these life-cycle issues with increasingly diffuse and confused theo-

17. Edward Farley, "Theology and Practice," 22–31.
18. Ibid., 33. Farley also critiques efforts to overcome the theory/practice division by means of "the therapeutic, which masquerades as a pseudo-theological *habitus*" (p. 29).

logical images. . . . We borrow from psychotherapeutic and developmental psychologies. But we are sometimes oblivious to the fact that we appropriate from them not only scientific information and therapeutic techniques but various normative visions of human fulfillment that are often neither philosophically sound nor theologically defensible.[19]

Jay E. Adams made the same point in critiquing evangelical counselors who invoke "common grace" to defend their dependence on the psychological views of Rogers, Freud, and Skinner, not recognizing that such thinkers have produced "rival systems [of interpreting reality] competitive to the Bible."[20] Browning and Adams make a valid point: scientific disciplines are never spiritually neutral. Both their methods and their outcomes reflect ultimate truth claims and value commitments, which are sometimes antithetical to Christian faith.

God's remedy for the guilt, alienation, and impotence of fallen humanity contradicts our expectations, not only as to its *message*—God's power to save through the weakness of Christ's cross—but also as to its *methods*—the folly of preaching in "weakness and fear and much trembling," and the paradox of leadership exercised in sacrificial servanthood (1 Cor. 1:18; 2:1–4; Mark 10:42–45). The counterintuitive "divine factor" in the ministries that practical theology seeks to understand could not have been anticipated through the behavioral sciences.

Practical Theology as Historical Theology

In Eastern Orthodox, conservative Roman Catholic, and confessional Protestant circles, it is more credible to define prac-

19. Don S. Browning, "Pastoral Theology in a Pluralistic Age," in Browning, *Practical Theology*, 188. Ogletree, "Dimensions," 83, likewise notes that when theological education isolates academic from practical studies, the "means" employed to achieve ministry "ends" are often "borrowed without criticism or adaptation from secular frames of reference: management, psychotherapy, communications, education. . . . Theological understandings are displaced by unexamined assumptions and premises."

20. Jay E. Adams, *More than Redemption: A Theology of Christian Counseling* (Phillipsburg, N.J.: Presbyterian and Reformed, 1979), 8.

tical theology in relation to historical theology than in terms of "Christianized" behavioral sciences. If the behavioral science view appeals to some mainline Protestants and evangelicals who desire maximum impact on the *present*, the historical theology approach attracts those who place higher value on continuity with the *past*.

This view gives weight to the reality that the church is catholic not only geographically and ethnically but also temporally.[21] Because the church extends through time from the patriarchs through the prophets, the apostles, the fathers, and the Reformers, common sense and humility dictate that contemporary pastors not turn a deaf ear to the insights and the missteps of those who have preceded us. Abraham Kuyper observed that it is an "unhistoric" illusion to think that, Bible in hand, one could "leap backward" across the centuries to study the Scriptures as though there had been no intervening history of interpretation, theological debate, and confessional formulation.[22] Even if such a move were possible, since the church has tested many viewpoints and found them wanting, it would be "the height of folly" to ignore this history: "In its rich and many-sided life, extending across so many ages, the Church tells you at once what fallible interpretations you need no longer try, and what interpretation on the other hand offers you the best chances of success."[23]

Our moment in church history has its own unique features. The church in the West can no longer assume a broader culture of "Christendom," as in the medieval and Reformation periods. The context of our ministry more closely resembles the pagan plu-

21. Thomas Aquinas, Opusculum VII, "In Symbolum Apostolorum, scil., Credo in Deum, Exposition": "The Church is Catholic . . . *with respect to time*. . . . This church began from the time of Abel and will last to the end of the world." Philip Melancthon, "De Appellatione Ecclesiae Catholicae": "Why is this epithet added . . . so that the Church is called Catholic? Because it is an assembly dispersed throughout the whole earth and because its members, wherever they are, . . . profess one and the same utterance of true doctrine *in all ages* from the beginning until the very end . . ." (emphasis added). Cited from Avery Dulles, *The Catholicity of the Church* (Oxford: Clarendon, 1985), 181–82.

22. Kuyper, *Encyclopedia*, 574.

23. Ibid., 576.

ralism that confronted the early church.[24] Yet even the parallel to the Patristic period is inexact: unlike the apostles and the church fathers, the Western church today confronts a culture that, thinking it has understood Christianity, has deliberately rejected it, returning to paganism. Nevertheless, despite the differences between previous epochs and ours, deep continuities link our context and calling in the twenty-first century with the challenges confronting earlier generations. Like our predecessors, we address God's good news to people created in God's image, yet deeply stained by sin, spiritually dead apart from the Spirit's power. We and our predecessors use humble tools common to human experience: spoken words, water, bread, and wine. Yet they and we minister in the confidence that God's sovereign Spirit is strong to save through means that seem ineffective by the prevailing criteria of anthropocentric culture, whether Greek rhetoric or modern communication theory. In view of such continuities in context and calling through the ages, it would be foolish arrogance to succumb to the Enlightenment's temporal parochialism and turn one's back on the accumulated wisdom of the church's teachers.

Nevertheless our Reformation tradition cautions against idolizing any tradition, including itself.[25] Because the accumulated wisdom of the church's past is not internally consistent, we need criteria to winnow wheat from chaff. Those alarmed by the theological and methodological homogenization in American evangelicalism seek such criteria by looking *ad fontes*, to

24. Robert L. Wilken, *Remembering the Christian Past* (Grand Rapids: Eerdmans, 1995), 25–62.

25. Westminster Confession of Faith, 1.10: "The supreme judge by which . . . all decrees of councils, opinions of ancient writers, doctrines of men, and private spirits, are to be examined, and in whose sentence we are to rest, can be no other but the Holy Spirit speaking in Scripture." 31.4: "All synods or councils, since the Apostles' times, whether general or particular, may err; and many have erred. Therefore they are not to be made the rule of faith, or practice; but to be used as a help in both." Note the salutary humility with which the First Confession of Basel (1534) concludes: "Finally, we desire to submit this our confession to the judgment of the divine Biblical Scriptures. And should we be informed from the same Holy Scriptures of a better one, we have thereby expressed our readiness to be willing at any time to obey God and his holy Word with great thanksgiving." Cited from Cochrane, *Reformed Confessions*, 96.

the sixteenth-century Reformers and, through them, to the early church fathers. Yet the practices of the Reformers were not always consistent with each other. Calvin and his followers, despite their solidarity with Luther with respect to biblical authority, law and gospel, and faith's unique role in justification, parted ways with their Lutheran colleagues over worship. Even the Calvinists, who affirmed together that no element may be introduced into corporate worship without convincing biblical warrant, diverged in implementing this principle.[26] Both Protestant theology and Protestant experience render implausible the Roman Catholic appeal to ecclesiastical tradition as *ultimately* normative, infallibly interpreting Scripture. In its place one sometimes hears a humbler, postmodern appeal to a particular ecclesiastical heritage as *functionally* normative for those who find themselves in that tradition. Yet even in this subdued expression, a particular stream of tradition is sometimes accorded a hegemony over the church's practice that rightly belongs only to the Word of God itself.

For example, D. G. Hart, a distinguished historian of American Christianity, wants to reform the theology and practice of worship among American Reformed churches, sounding the alarm against the infiltration of the revivalist and pietist influences.[27] In *Recovering Mother Kirk*, he advocates a return to a standardized liturgy, including written prayers and a fixed order of liturgical elements such as that which Calvin composed for the church of Geneva.[28] Hart cites Calvin's rationales for "highly approving" of a standardized liturgical form: "First, some ministers are unskilled in leading worship; second, forms and rites

26. These variations are surveyed in Hughes Oliphant Old, *Guides to the Reformed Tradition: Worship That Is Reformed According to the Scripture* (Philadelphia: Westminster John Knox, 1984); and Horton Davies, *The Worship of the English Puritans* (1948; reprint, Morgan, Pennsylvania: Soli Deo Gloria, 1997).

27. Reviewers cited on the back cover of *Recovering Mother Kirk: The Case for Liturgy in the Reformed Tradition* (Grand Rapids: Baker, 2003) commend it as "a lively polemic" (William Willimon) written to "rouse" Hart's fellow Presbyterians (Ken Myers).

28. The order is found in Hart, *Recovering*, 72.

ensure uniformity among the churches; and finally, they prevent 'capricious giddiness and levity' from surfacing in worship."[29]

These rationales constitute an interesting argument. The first and third assume that some pastors who can proclaim God's Word are incompetent to lead the people of God in prayer or so immature as to debase worship with "giddiness and levity." If Calvin viewed these defects as temporary results of inadequate pastoral preparation, his endorsement of a fixed liturgy of written prayers might be a pragmatic expedient to address transient problems. If, however, Calvin believed that God calls men to preach without also gifting them for liturgical leadership,[30] his assumption seems to contradict the link that Scripture draws between the ministries of Word and of prayer (Acts 6:4; 13:1–3; Phil. 1:3–5; etc.).

Although Calvin hoped that a fixed liturgy would "ensure" trans-congregational uniformity, he "hesitated to prescribe a specific liturgy for all churches."[31] If liturgical uniformity were the ideal, such was available in the Roman Mass (which claimed worldwide catholicity through the use of Latin) and, after Calvin, in the Anglican *Book of Common Prayer*. Yet Calvin's Puritan heirs rejected the latter as an unwarranted abuse of centralized authority by a state church. Thus the Westminster Assembly (1644–47) reformed English worship not by revising the *Book of Common Prayer*, but by issuing a *Directory for the Publick Worship of God*, which provided guidelines but not required formulae for the minister's conduct of worship. Hart attributes the Assembly's departure to ecclesiastical compromise, "a concession to Congregationalists and Independents who believed a set liturgy smacked of tyranny."[32] This explanation is historically plausible, but it does not vitiate the Congregationalists' and Independents' objection to tyranny, nor does it offer a *biblical* warrant for the standardized

29. Ibid., 199, quoting Charles W. Baird, *Presbyterian Liturgies: Historical Sketches* (1855; reprint, Grand Rapids: Baker, 1957), 23.

30. Old, *Guides*, 100.

31. Hart, *Recovering*, 73.

32. Ibid., 33.

liturgy that Hart advocates, even though such a warrant is required by the Reformed regulative principle that Calvin and his Puritan heirs shared.[33] Instead of refuting the Assembly's theological and exegetical rationales (summarized in Horton Davies's study of Puritan worship[34]), Hart laments the "liturgical chaos" that resulted from its decision, dismissing as "usually a smoke screen for an experiential piety that is at odds with the formality inherent in set liturgies" the concern that the imposition of a standardized liturgy may violate Christians' consciences.[35]

The point of this illustration is not to side either with Calvin and Hart or with the Westminster Puritans. I agree with Hart that well-crafted written prayers, especially those written by mature pastors, can enrich the substance and enhance the dignity with which we lead congregations in prayer. I also empathize with Puritans' objections to the imposition—without biblical warrant—of a universal liturgical form, whether by a state church or by a disestablished ecclesiastical body. My point, however, is that in calling Reformed churches back to their roots, Hart must pick and choose between different strands of past Reformed practice. Historical theology—even within the narrow and relatively homogeneous tradition of historic Calvinism—does not provide a unified, and therefore credibly normative, answer to many ministry questions.

Practical Theology as the Systematic Theology of Ministry

Reformed systematic theology tries to offer a faithful and coherent account of God's revelation of himself and his creatures,

33. In *With Reverence and Awe: Returning to the Basics of Reformed Worship* (Phillipsburg, N.J.: P&R, 2002), Hart and co-author John R. Muether offer more biblical and theological argumentation for their understanding of Reformed worship, but the idea of a standardized written liturgy does not appear even in their chapter on "Reformed Liturgy" (pp. 91–102). They later quote, without objection, the Orthodox Presbyterian Church's *Directory for Worship*, which stands in the Westminster tradition: "The Lord Jesus Christ has prescribed no fixed forms for public worship but, in the interest of life and power in worship, has given his church a large measure of liberty in this matter" (p. 151).

34. Davies, *Worship*, 81, 98–114.

35. Hart, *Recovering*, 33–34. Hart cites Charles Hodge as a Presbyterian whose defense of extemporaneous pastoral prayer was "afflicted" with the influence of revivalism (34–35).

as that revelation comes preeminently in his Son and the Scriptures and, secondarily, in the general revelation that surrounds us in the universe, including the cultures, pursuits, and problems of humanity. Theology needs to be faithful *conceptually*: congruent, to the best of our ability, with the truth unveiled in Scripture—a "faithful portrait" of the components of biblical truth and of their interconnectedness. It is not the compilation of biblical truths distilled from individual scriptural texts as freestanding "bullet points." It aims to reflect the organic interrelationships between the various facets of God's self-revelation.

Theology must also be faithful *covenantally*: The Lord speaks his Word not merely to convey information but to lay claim to our trust, devotion, and obedience. We do not mistake mere intellectual comprehension for the whole-personed response of covenantal trust and allegiance that are always entailed in knowing God. The covenantal character of divine revelation forbids the dissociation of theory from practice. Nothing that God reveals in Scripture is intended merely to satisfy our curiosity.[36] All revealed truth serves the Creator's covenantal relationship to his human creatures: establishing covenant, maintaining covenant, enforcing covenant, restoring covenant, or consummating covenant.[37] Revealed truth therefore evokes a response that is richer than (though not less than) cognitive, and a systematic theology that faithfully reflects it does likewise. Thus all systematic theology is "practical" theology, designed to transform the whole range of our being and practice: intellectual (perceiving, reasoning, dis-

36. Kuyper, *Encyclopedia*, 605: ". . . this ectypal knowledge of God is revealed, not in the abstract sense to satisfy our desire for knowledge, but very concretely, as one of the means by which this all-excelling work of re-creation is accomplished. . . ."

37. Geerhardus Vos, "The Idea of Biblical Theology as a Science and as a Theological Discipline" in *Redemptive History and Biblical Interpretation: The Shorter Writings of Geerhardus Vos*, Richard B. Gaffin Jr., ed. (Phillipsburg, N.J.: Presbyterian and Reformed, 1980), 10: "The knowledge of God communicated by [revelation] is nowhere for a purely intellectual purpose. From beginning to end it is a knowledge intended to enter into the actual life of man, to be worked out by him in all its practical bearings. . . . God has not revealed Himself in a school, but in the covenant; and the covenant as a communion of life is all-comprehensive, embracing all the conditions and interests of those contracting it."

cerning), affective (valuing, delighting in), relational (loving, reconciling, consoling), and even physical (working, giving, resting, serving).

How, then, should we relate the family of disciplines that belong to "practical theology" (homiletics, poimenics, missiology, etc.) to the traditional *loci* (theology proper, anthropology, Christology, soteriology, ecclesiology, eschatology) that we normally call "systematic theology"? One approach would be to demonstrate the relevance of each theological *locus* to a particular practice of ministry. Adams develops a "theology of Christian counseling" by tracing how counseling should be molded by the doctrines of Scripture (chap. 3), God (chaps. 4–7), man (chaps. 8–11), salvation (chaps. 12–13), sanctification (chaps. 14–18), the church (chaps. 19–22), and last things (chaps. 23–24).[38] This approach demonstrates how deeply any ministry practice—in this case, pastoral counseling—must be rooted in the whole range of revealed truth.

It seems more precise, however, to start with the observation that the practices with which practical theology is concerned are congregated under those systematic-theological *loci* that address the topics of *soteriology*—specifically, effectual calling, regeneration, justification, adoption, and sanctification—and *ecclesiology*. Practical theology inhabits the territory in which soteriology and ecclesiology overlap because it concentrates reflection on those means by which God applies his saving grace to individuals in the context of the church.

Two examples illustrate how practical theology blends motifs that are both soteriological and ecclesiological, inquiring how these motifs mold the ministry methods by which they are conveyed to and through the church. The ministry of the Word— whether preaching in public worship or pastoral counsel in a private home—is the means by which the Spirit evokes and deepens faith in God's elect (effectual calling, sanctification). The ministry of the Word is also the exercise of gifts bestowed by the Spirit on

38. Adams, *More Than Redemption*.

Christ's Body, and gratefully acknowledged by that Body in ecclesiastical office (ecclesiology, edification). The sacraments, likewise, are appropriately discussed as means of grace in connection with sanctification; and, no less appropriately, they belong to the doctrine of the church and its marks. Both their soteriological and their ecclesiological significance should inform their administration in worship, a topic addressed in the practical theology curriculum.

When practical theology is understood as reflection on the methodological implications of the biblical doctrines of salvation and church, an indivisible integration of theory and practice is built into its very identity. Practical theologians ask questions about ministry practices: speaking and listening, caring and confronting. Asking those questions within the framework of the Bible's teaching about salvation and the church invites methodological answers that are shaped by the gospel itself. God's message of judgment on sin and grace toward sinners in Jesus controls the media in which we deliver it, and this gospel-centered focus minimizes the danger of importing paradigms and values alien to Scripture.

Space does not permit a detailed description of what a gospel-driven, churchly theology of ministry practice would look like.[39] I can only suggest certain praxis-oriented implications of the two focal events of the gospel, Christ's death for our sins and his resurrection (1 Cor. 15:3–4). These implications gripped Paul's heart and molded his motive and conduct as a minister of the new covenant.[40]

39. Many details are found in Paul's "pastoral epistles" to his apprentices, Timothy and Titus: qualifications for church offices; the pastor's responsibilities to his Lord, duties in office, and relationships to various groups; the dangers of false teaching; and other matters promoting church order and health (1 Tim. 3:15).

40. Anderson, *Structure*, finds in Scripture a recurring principle, "There can be no resurrection without a pattern of death" (p. 70). God first confronts his covenant servants with the human impossibility of effective ministry, and only then intervenes with a sovereign promise that creates what it demands. This principle, so counterintuitive to our self-reliant inclinations, judges every ministry practice: "Every pragmatic principle of ministry must be subjected to the critical dogmatic test: has it gone through the death and resurrection process? Have we allowed the ministry as such to reveal to us its impossibility before we have assumed its possibility?" (p. 74).

Christ's death to atone for our sins entails a complex diagnosis of the human condition. Since Christ's death implies the *incarnation* of the second person of the Trinity, it affirms that the universe is not to be regarded as evil simply because it is physical. God is Spirit, yet as Creator and Redeemer he reveals his glories in the material world: his wisdom and power in the created universe, and his grace, preeminently, in the Word made flesh. Humanity was created in the image of God originally. Then, despite our sin, the eternal Son assumed our flesh and blood to rescue us from our rebellion and its consequences. God appoints material elements as means of grace. By the consecration of the Word and the Spirit's presence, water, bread, and wine nourish faith. Since the redemption inaugurated through the incarnate Son's suffering and glory is to embrace whole persons, body and soul, in the consummation, our semi-eschatological ministry today, though focusing on faith and heart allegiance, must not artificially subdivide those we serve by disregarding their corporeality.

The fact that nothing less than Christ's *death* could deal with our sins reveals the gravity of our guilt and spiritual impotence. Implied in this death is the whole complex of human fallenness: alienation, self-delusion, idolatry, despair, pride, corrupt desire, pain, suffering, want, decay, and misery. This dire divine diagnosis does not permit ministerial methods that ameliorate symptoms while failing to attack the infection itself. If humanity's problem were merely ignorance, education would be the remedy. If it were political oppression, armed revolution or peaceful reform could be pursued. If economic inequity were the root of our troubles, the solution could be sought in generosity or job training. If one's personal dysfunction is inflicted from without by others, counseling that bolsters self-esteem might suffice. But if these and other miseries, in which we may be sinned against as well as sinners, stem from our breach of covenant with the Creator, our ministry strategies—whether in the pulpit, the study, the hospital room, or the mortuary—must aim to unveil how Christ's death and resurrection remove guilt, break the tyranny of evil desire, heal relationships, and restore hope. Our calling is not merely to reprogram behavior from destructive to constructive patterns, nor to assuage emotional wounds. Rather, God's grace in the cross of Christ pierces deeper, to reorient the heart, the wellspring of our identity, from self-centeredness (both lawless self-indulgence and law-abiding self-righteousness) to Christ-centeredness.

The radical diagnosis of human need implied in Christ's death corresponds to an equally counterintuitive cure: "The word of the cross is foolishness to those who are perishing, but to us who are being saved it is God's power. . . . Christ crucified—to Jews a stumblingstone, to Gentiles foolishness . . ." (1 Cor. 1:18, 23). God's saving power slipped incognito into human history, unrecognized by those who wield influence and mold opinion (2:7–8). Yet to those who recognize Christ's cross as exposing their shameful self-reliance, the cross speaks an astonishing message of grace: "God showed his own love for us, because while we were still sinners Christ died for us. . . . We were reconciled to God through the death of his Son" (Rom. 5:8, 10).[41]

This counterintuitive message consequently entails *methods* that appear foolish, weak, and ineffective according to the standards of "normal" human culture: "My word and preaching were not in persuasive words of wisdom but in demonstration of the Spirit and power, in order that your faith might not be in men's wisdom but in God's power" (1 Cor. 2:3–5). Although Paul's written words resonate to believers, when delivered in person they fell short of expectations: " 'His epistles,' they say, 'are weighty and strong, but his personal presence is weak and his speech despicable" (2 Cor. 10:10). Such communication defects, however, were strengths in disguise, showing that the Spirit's power, not Paul's cleverness, changes people.

Paul's gospel announced not only Christ's death but also his resurrection, the inauguration of a new creation in the Last Adam who had become life-giving Spirit (1 Cor. 15:20–23, 45). Through a message (the cross) and a method (preaching) easily dismissed

41. Cf. Timothy J. Keller, "The Centrality of the Gospel." Available [Online]: <http://www.redeemer2.com/resources/papers/centrality.pdf> [1 May 2003]. Keller sketches the gospel's implications for such issues as motivation for ministry, worship, the poor, doctrinal distinctives, holiness, church health, and social change.

as ineffective by the standards of this present age, the Spirit breathes life into the dead, giving birth even now to citizens of the age to come.

Here, however, we face a problem for pastoral education: If the Spirit's power is most evident where the minister's weaknesses are most obvious, is it not an insult to the Spirit when teachers of practical theology drive students to develop skills for ministry, such as articulate speaking, insight into counselees' problems, pedagogical effectiveness, or leadership skills? Should we avoid excellence and cultivate incompetence to enhance God's glory in converting sinners and building Christ's church?[42]

This inference, however, sounds suspiciously familiar: "Let us remain in sin, that grace may abound" (Rom. 6:1). Paul rebuffs the antinomian excuse by drawing out the life-transforming implications of our union with Christ in his death and resurrection. This same apostolic answer, grounded in the gospel, refutes excuses of ministerial sloth and sloppiness. Certainly, if we *rely on* our proficiencies in preaching, counseling, or leadership, assuming that our skills secure outcomes or obligate God to bless our efforts, such self-reliance contradicts the sovereign grace that we proclaim. If, however, through Christ's cross "the world" (with its assumption that human resources can remedy the human predicament) has been crucified to us and we to the world (Gal. 6:14), we can offer our best efforts in preaching, worship, counseling, and leadership out of a new motive: not to obligate a Master but to delight a Father, acknowledging that his grace alone has made us willing and able to serve his purposes. Only in the mind of the slave, who can see no reason to obey beyond avoiding punishment or obligating compensation, does grace destroy motivation for holy living. Likewise, only in the mind of a slave, who serves not for love but for recognition or reward, will the fact that

---

42. We might also ask, Do Paul's own writings and the sermons attributed to him in Acts really display *indifference* to rhetorical skill and persuasive effectiveness? Although his speaking style may not have satisfied the reigning norms of Greek rhetoric, he was both intentional and strategic in analyzing audiences, identifying points of contact, and marshaling arguments and evidence.

the sovereign Spirit (not the preacher's eloquence) makes preaching productive destroy motivation for serving strenuously.

Jesus warned his disciples against the slave's mindset. Those who approach him in the last day boasting of their effective ministry in Jesus's name will be shocked to hear his word of disavowal and banishment (Matt. 7:23). Although their ministry allegedly was performed by Jesus's authority, those who trust in their achievements have not "done the will of my Father in heaven" (v. 21)—the will that requires, first of all, "that you believe in the one he has sent" (John 6:29). Jesus also indicts the slavish fear that excuses its unbelieving indolence: "Master, I knew you, that you are a harsh man . . . and because I was afraid I went and hid your talent in the ground" (Matt. 25:24–25). Such slaves, paralyzed by fear of a Master's harsh justice, will receive harsh justice (vv. 28–30), no less than those who imagine that their ministerial exploits have placed the Master in their debt.

The minister who serves out of confidence in sovereign grace, on the other hand, secure in his status as a son of the Father and knowing that God does not need our excellence to accomplish his aims, has the strongest motive to serve skillfully and strenuously: we offer our best out of grateful love. The minister's performance of his responsibilities is itself a dimension of his personal sanctification, which is the Spirit's sovereign work of grace, not our own self-renovation. When Galatian Christians, having been justified by faith in Christ, nevertheless listened sympathetically to a pseudo-gospel that made their spiritual security contingent on their Torah-keeping, Paul shamed their folly: "Was it by the works of the Law that you received the Spirit, or by faith in the heard message [of Christ crucified, v. 1]? Are you so senseless? Having begun by the Spirit are you now going to achieve perfection by the flesh?" (Gal. 3:2–3). The faith that looks away from oneself to Christ crucified and risen is as instrumental to our sanctification as it is to our justification.[43] So also ministry must draw its moti-

43. Thomas Chalmers, "The Expulsive Power of a New Affection," in *The Selected Works of Thomas Chalmers*, 4 vols. (New York: Robert Carter, 1848), 4:271–78. Available [Online]: <http://www.newble.co.uk/chalmers/comm9.html> [1 May 2003]. "The best way of cast-

vation and its methods from the faith that rests in Christ alone. In his cross God condemns our self-reliant efforts and commends his all-sufficient love, and in his resurrection the new creation power of the age to come is unleashed by the Spirit.

We should also consider the implications of the gospel for the spiritual *gifts of grace (charismata)* through which the members of Christ's Body minister to one another. In the Old Testament the skills of artisans who constructed God's tabernacle were recognized as gifts bestowed by God's Spirit (Exod. 31:1–11). How much more, now that the risen Lord has poured his Spirit on the church, must we recognize that abilities to build the Lord's new sanctuary flow from "the grace given us" (Rom. 12:6–8)! Paul rebuked Corinthian believers who forgot the gracious source of their capacities to serve: "What do you have that you did not receive?" (1 Cor. 4:7 NIV). Their forgetfulness lured "high profile" Christians to despise others (12:21–25), while those with modest ministries were tempted to belittle their own gifts, perhaps excusing lethargy (12:15–20). The grace revealed in the gospel, however, destroys both pride and passivity, as Paul implied to Timothy: "Rekindle the gracious gift [*charisma*] of God, which is in you through the laying on of my hands" (2 Tim. 1:6). Timothy must exercise his gift by reading and teaching Scripture (1 Tim.

---

ing out an impure affection is to admit a pure one; and by the love of what is good to expel the love of what is evil. Thus it is, that the freer the gospel, the more sanctifying is the gospel; and the more it is received as a doctrine of grace, the more will it be felt as a doctrine according to godliness. . . . It is only when, as in the gospel, acceptance is bestowed as a present, without money and without price, that the security which man feels in God is placed beyond the reach of disturbance, or that he can repose in Him as one friend reposes in another, . . . the one party rejoicing over the other to do him good, the other finding that the truest gladness of his heart lies in the impulse of a gratitude by which it is awakened to the charms of a new moral existence. Salvation by grace—salvation by free grace—salvation not of works, but according to the mercy of God, salvation on such a footing is not more indispensable to the deliverance of our persons from the hand of justice than it is to the deliverance of our hearts from the chill and the weight of ungodliness" (p. 277). Chalmers's insight into the sanctifying power of the gospel of grace was anticipated by Walter Marshall, *The Gospel Mystery of Sanctification* (1692; reprint, Welwyn, Hertfordshire, England: Evangelical Press, 1981). See also G. C. Berkouwer, *Faith and Sanctification* (Studies in Dogmatics. Grand Rapids: Eerdmans, 1952), 17–44.

4:13–14). These duties require strenuous effort, like that of the soldier, the athlete, the farmer, and the craftsman (2 Tim. 2:4–6, 15). Recalling that the gracious gift entrusted to his stewardship is the Spirit of power, love, and self-control would guard Timothy's heart from both self-reliance and timid indolence (1:7).

Christ's cross and resurrection must refashion our practice of leadership. When the Son of Man came not to receive service but to serve others, giving his life to ransom many, his cross turned society's expectations regarding leadership on their head (Mark 10:42–45). In contrast to the surrounding culture, in which rulers enjoy privilege, leaders in Jesus's community take the slave's role, subordinating their comfort and convenience to the welfare of those they lead. Those who lead "under the cross" have, and must exercise, genuine authority: they bear the keys of the kingdom (Matt. 16:19). Yet their leadership is qualified by the suffering servanthood of the Lord in whose name they lead.

Conclusion

Practical theology in the Reformed tradition has an extraordinary opportunity to demonstrate the unity of theory and practice, the harmony of faith-filled conviction and faithful action. The covenantal structure of Scripture keeps us from segregating intellectual and ethical responses to the divine Word. Sovereign grace and its corollary, utter human dependence, forbid trust in ministry techniques. Yet the fact that God extends grace through creaturely means forestalls passivity, and the love that such mercy evokes should move us to serve our Redeemer to the full extent of the gifts, insight, and strength that his Spirit supplies. The catholicity of the church encourages us to listen respectfully to the consensus (and the dissent) of those who preceded us as stewards of the mysteries of God, while the norm of *sola Scriptura* enables us to assess both the church's past and contemporary trends. Foundational to our practical theology is the gospel itself: Christ crucified, buried, and risen according to the Scriptures, the climax of redemptive history in a death that exposes the depths of human depravity and the height of divine grace, and the dawn of a new creation in a resurrection that vindicates the Last Adam and ushers his people into the life of God's Spirit.

Much remains to be done to develop in detail a systematic, gospel-driven, Christ-centered theology of ministry in all the activities by which God's Word is to be implemented in and through the church. Recently resources have multiplied to help preachers proclaim Christ as the fulfillment of all the Scriptures.[44] Progress is being made in pastoral counseling that addresses the complexity of personal and interpersonal problems by exposing their roots in the depths of the human heart, applying Christ's cross and resurrection to counselees' misdirected worship and misplaced trust.[45] The gospel's implications for conflict resolution are receiving more widespread attention and implementation in the Body of Christ.[46] Christian education materials are being developed that place Christ and his grace "center stage" rather than treating Scripture as a repository of moral examples.[47] In adult discipleship rediscovery of an older Reformed emphasis on filial assurance is enabling believers to pursue sanctification with fresh freedom.[48]

44. Edmund P. Clowney, *Preaching and Biblical Theology* (Grand Rapids: Eerdmans, 1961); Clowney, "Preaching Christ from All the Scriptures," pp. 163–91 in Samuel T. Logan Jr., ed., *The Preacher and Preaching: Reviving the Art in the Twentieth Century* (Phillipsburg, N.J.: Presbyterian and Reformed, 1986); Bryan Chapell, *Christ-Centered Preaching: Redeeming the Expository Sermon* (Grand Rapids: Baker, 1994) ; Sidney Greidanus, *Preaching Christ from the Old Testament: A Contemporary Hermeneutical Method* (Grand Rapids: Eerdmans, 1999); Graeme Goldsworthy, *Preaching the Whole Bible as Christian Scripture: The Application of Biblical Theology to Expository Preaching* (Grand Rapids: Eerdmans, 2000).

45. Recent articles in the *Journal of Biblical Counseling* evidence the nouthetic counseling movement's deepening analysis of heart-idolatries and of grace's role in sanctification.

46. E.g., Ken Sande, *The Peacemaker* (Grand Rapids: Baker, 1977), and the influence of Peacemaker Ministries (www.hispeace.org) through education and conciliation.

47. E.g., the *Show Me Jesus* curriculum of Great Commission Publications, the joint publisher of the Orthodox Presbyterian Church and the Presbyterian Church in America. See also S. G. De Graaf, *Promise and Deliverance*, 4 vols. (St. Catherines, Ontario: Paideia, 1977–81).

48. See, e.g., Jerry Bridges, *The Discipline of Grace* (Colorado Springs: NavPress, 1994); Bridges, *The Gospel for Real Life* (Colorado Springs: NavPress, 2002); *Gospel Transfor-*

Reflection must continue in these areas. Attention should also be given to the implications of the gospel for such topics as worship, leadership, church discipline, and diaconal ministry. God-glorifying ministry, which gathers God's elect as his new covenant people, nurtures them toward maturity in Christ, and mobilizes their witness in word and deed, involves thinking and acting from our new identity as those united to Christ "whom we proclaim, admonishing everyone and teaching everyone in all wisdom, in order that we might present everyone perfect in Christ" (Col. 1:28).

---

mation (Jenkintown: World Harvest Mission, 2001); Neil H. Williams, *The Theology of Sonship* (Jenkintown: World Harvest Mission, 2002).

Part Three

Particular Issues in Westminster Systematics

6

Westminster Seminary, the Doctrine of Justification, and the Reformed Confessions

W. Robert Godfrey

Why is it so difficult to get the doctrine of justification right? This study will seek to show that throughout the history of the church—even in the strict Reformed circles of Westminster theology—many churches and theologians have gotten the doctrine of justification seriously wrong. It will examine some of the reasons for that error and argue for the importance of the Reformed confessions as a key to upholding the biblical doctrine of justification.

The Difficulty of Justification

The gospel of justification in Christ alone by grace alone through faith alone is taught repeatedly throughout the Bible. The apostle Paul in particular taught the doctrine clearly, fully, and passionately. Yet, he faced misunderstanding and criticism even in the churches that he had gathered by his preaching. He had to write to the Galatians: "I am astonished that you are so quickly deserting the one who called you by the grace of Christ and are turning to a different gospel—which is really no gospel at all" (Gal. 1:6–7).

Because Paul has so often been misunderstood, it is important to keep some key biblical texts before us—especially in our day of deconstruction when they have so often been wrested from their clear meaning:

Ephesians 2:8–10

For it is by grace you have been saved, through faith—and this not from yourselves, it is the gift of God—not by works, so that no one can boast. For we are God's workmanship, created in Christ Jesus to do good works, which God prepared in advance for us to do.

Romans 3:20–25a, 28

Therefore no one will be declared righteous in his sight by observing the law; rather, through the law we become conscious of sin. But now a righteousness from God, apart from law, has been made known, to which the Law and the Prophets testify. This righteousness from God comes through faith in Jesus Christ to all who believe. There is no difference, for all have sinned and fall short of the glory of God, and are justified freely by his grace through the redemption that came by Christ Jesus. God presented him as a sacrifice of atonement, through faith in his blood. . . . For we maintain that a man is justified by faith apart from observing the law.

Romans 4:4–5

Now when a man works, his wages are not credited to him as a gift, but as an obligation. However, to the man who does not work but trusts God who justifies the wicked, his faith is credited to him as righteousness.

Galatians 2:16

So we, too, have put our faith in Christ Jesus that we may be justified by faith in Christ and not by observing the law, because by observing the law no one will be justified.

Galatians 3:21–22

For if a law had been given that could impart life, then righteousness would certainly have come by the law. But the Scripture declares that the whole world is a prisoner of sin, so that what was promised, being given through faith in Jesus Christ, might be given to those who believe.

These passages show Paul's concern to highlight the work of Christ and the necessity of faith as key components of the doctrine of justification and show his determination to contrast faith with works. These passages must be central to understanding the biblical doctrine of justification because they represent the most comprehensive and detailed discussion of that doctrine in Scripture. It is a critical Reformed principle of biblical interpretation that the fuller and clearer passages of Scripture should guide the understanding of briefer passages.

If Paul in his own day was not always understood by his own churches on the doctrine of justification, we should perhaps not be surprised that the churches since that time have so often failed to get it. The true doctrine of justification always strikes some as antinomian, even though it is not. Paul must often have faced the question: "Shall we go on sinning so that grace may increase?" (Rom. 6:1). A doctrine of justification that does not from time to time evoke that question is not the biblical doctrine of justification.

After the time of Paul churches continued to fail to get the gospel straight. At their best they taught that the sinner is saved by Christ alone through grace alone, but until the Reformation they seldom taught justification by faith alone. Even those Christian teachers who emphasized grace (like Augustine or Aquinas) did not have a truly stable, balanced theology. Until one understands the biblical teaching on faith, one cannot have a reliable theology of grace. As Paul taught in Romans 4:16, "Therefore, the promise comes by faith, so that it may be by grace and may be guaranteed to all Abraham's offspring. . . ."

The great Reformers—out of the superb education they received in Renaissance learning—studied the Scriptures carefully. Seldom in the history of the church have so many leaders been so well-educated. They had exceptional knowledge of the original languages in which the Scriptures were written and had learned how to read and interpret a text with profound insight. As they applied their talents and skill to the text of the Bible, they recaptured the Pauline doctrine of justification.

The Reformation churches accepting *sola Scriptura* faced not only criticism and misrepresentation for their faith but also persecution. Both to present their faith clearly to the world and to answer their critics the churches produced confessions. A confession (derived from the Latin word for what we believe together) was a new sort of church document in the sixteenth century. Confessions were longer and more detailed than creeds. Since the Reformation led to several different churches with different teachings, more detailed statements of faith became necessary so that what a given church taught would be clear. In addition to the confessions the Reformers wrote theological studies to elaborate and explain their theology. John Calvin wrote the most influential systematic theology of the sixteenth century, his *Institutes of the Christian Religion*. There he presented a full statement of his understanding of justification. He showed both in his *Institutes* and in his commentaries the biblical foundation and character of his doctrine.

Calvin confronted a long theological tradition that insisted that God could only justify those who had been morally changed. For this tradition Paul's contrast between faith and works was really a contrast between real faithfulness and some legalistic or ceremonial works. Calvin rightly rejected this approach, arguing that "the works of the law" are the best possible works because they are the works in accordance with God's holy will as revealed in his law. Consequently he stressed that even the best works of the Christian cannot meet God's standard for justification. Only a perfect conformity to the law—which Christ alone accomplished—can stand in the judgment.

After the Reformation Protestantism developed and changed. Most changes claimed to advance and refine the cause of the

Reformation. Many changes arose from a concern to protect the church from formalism. Formalism meant outward conformity to true doctrine and practice, but no true faith in the heart. Movements like Puritanism, Pietism, Methodism, Evangelicalism, and Pentecostalism sought in different ways to ensure that Christians did not just have correct doctrine, but also had a true experience of living faith. The danger in all of these movements was that a religious experience would undermine the importance of doctrinal integrity. Real Christianity would become more a matter of experience than truth. That danger became a reality in quite diverse circles from the eighteenth century on. One expression of the triumph of experience can be seen in the rise of liberal Protestantism and especially in its attack on the Reformation doctrine of Scripture. The Reformation had taught that the Bible was the completely true revelation of God, the only trustworthy source of religious truth. Liberalism began to undermine this Protestant conviction, in time turning the Bible from the revelation of God to a human record of religious experiences. Liberals insisted that they were not rejecting Christianity, but placing it on the more modern and vital foundation of experience. To insist on the old teaching that the Bible was divine truth, the liberals said, would destroy Christianity.

If the great Reformation teaching on the Bible could be attacked, we should not be surprised that the great Reformation doctrine of justification would also be attacked. In the nineteenth century that attack came from liberals like Albrecht Ritschl in *The Christian Doctrine of Justification and Reconciliation*, but also from evangelicals like Charles G. Finney in his *Lectures on Systematic Theology*.

The Deconstruction of Justification in the Twentieth Century

In the last century the attacks on justification not only came from a number of different sources, but also had a remarkably similar character. Those attacking the Reformation doctrine may have had quite different views on the work of Christ and on grace, but they agreed that the idea of justification by faith alone was false. At least in a formal way they all agreed that justification was not by faith alone, but was by faithfulness.

One source of these attacks has been systematic theological reflection, often in an ecumenical context. We can see several examples of this in the twentieth century from very different theological backgrounds. First, in 1935 Karl Barth published a little book entitled *Gospel and Law*. In reversing the usual Protestant order of law and gospel Barth was indicating by the title itself his dissent from ordinary Protestant ways of thinking and speaking. Hans Küng helps us to see Barth's conflict with the Reformation clearly in his book on Barth and justification. Küng wrote, "It is to be presupposed that the justified man is truly just—inwardly in his heart. At this point Barth does side with Trent against the Reformation. . . . Justification is not merely an externally pasted-on 'as if.' Man is not only *called* just but *is* just."[1] In the preface to Küng's book Barth acknowledges that Küng has presented Barth's position accurately and states that if Küng accurately has presented the Roman Catholic view, then they are agreed.

Second, Daniel Fuller of Fuller Theological Seminary adopted fundamentally the same position as that of Barth in a book the title of which he borrowed from Barth. In 1980 Fuller published *Gospel and Law: Contrast or Continuum?*[2] In that book he claimed to go beyond the limitations of both dispensationalism and covenant theology to a more genuinely biblical approach to justification. Some of his critique of dispensationalism seems just, especially in the context of the clear antinomianism of Charles Ryrie and Zane Hodges.[3]

1. Hans Küng, *Justification: The Doctrine of Karl Barth and a Catholic Reflection* (New York: Westminster, 1964), 236.

2. Daniel Fuller, *Gospel and Law: Contrast or Continuum? The Hermeneutics of Dispensationalism and Covenant Theology* (Grand Rapids: Eerdmans, 1980).

3. This antinomianism was criticized by John F. MacArthur Jr. in *The Gospel According to Jesus: What Does Jesus Mean When He Says "Follow Me"?* (Grand Rapids: Zondervan, 1988).

But his understanding of the Reformation and covenant theology is weak, and his critique and suggested alternative are wrong.[4]

Third, in 1983 a group of Lutherans and Roman Catholics in the United States issued a statement showing their agreement entitled "Justification by Faith."[5] Here again a redefinition of the role of faith in justification has taken place. The witness of the Reformation on justification does not seem to be understood or appreciated.

Fourth, we can see compromises of the Reformation doctrine of justification in two statements, "Evangelicals and Catholics Together" (1994), and "The Gift of Salvation" (1997). These two statements claim to bring evangelicals and Roman Catholics to basic agreement on justification and were endorsed on the Protestant side by some very prominent North American evangelical leaders. Yet the Roman Catholic signatories insisted nothing in these documents contradicted the canons of the Council of Trent, which in the sixteenth century anathematized the Reformation doctrine of justification.[6]

Fifth, on October 31, 1999, Lutherans and Roman Catholics gathered in Augsburg, Germany to issue a "Joint Declaration on the Doctrine of Justification." This Declaration was released on Reformation Day in the city where the basic Lutheran confession, the Augsburg Confession, had been presented to the Holy Roman Emperor as a statement of Protestant faith. Many hailed this action as a major ecumenical accomplishment. But the Lutheran Church, Missouri Synod, released an official reaction from the Office of the President on October 15, 1999, calling the future Joint Declaration "a clear, stunning departure from the Reformation" and "a betrayal of the Gospel of Jesus Christ."

4. For several articles discussing Fuller's position, see *Presbyterion* 9 (Spring–Fall 1983).

5. The text is printed in *Origins* 13 (October 6, 1983): 277–304. For a brief analysis of this statement, see W. Robert Godfrey, "Reversing the Reformation," *Eternity* 35 (September 1984): 26–28.

6. For a brief response to "The Gift of Salvation," see W. Robert Godfrey, "A Discussion of Justification," *The Outlook* 49 (February 1999): 5–7. For other critical materials see the publications of the Alliance of Confessing Evangelicals.

Another source of attacks on the Reformation doctrine of justification has been from historical studies. The most remarkable of these has come from the so-called Finnish school of interpretation of Luther. Here the argument has been that Protestant churches have misunderstood Luther, who did not teach justification and imputation as the Reformation confessions and later orthodox theologians do.[7]

Still another source has been biblical studies. In the course of the twentieth century several new approaches to the theology of Paul have been suggested that to one extent or another have challenged the Reformation understanding of Paul. We can see that in the work of Krister Stendahl and later the so-called New Perspective on Paul (promoted by James D. G. Dunn and N. T. Wright).[8] The new perspective does not, in fact, seem very new, but rather is another reiteration of the view that justification is by faithfulness. Another example can be found in a recent article by the evangelical biblical scholar Robert Gundry. He wrote against aspects of the Reformation doctrine of justification in an article entitled "Why I Didn't Endorse 'The Gospel of Jesus Christ: An Evangelical Celebration.' "[9] A key focus of this article was an exegetical argument against the Reformation doctrine of the active obedience of Christ for our justification.

The reasons for these assaults on the Reformation doctrine of justification are varied. Still we can see some common threads that run through many or all of them. First, the claim is usually made that the new doctrine is more biblical. No doubt these claims are sincere and must be seriously examined. But often they show a surprising level of ignorance of the careful exegetical work of the orthodox Protestants for centuries. This historical igno-

7. For a critical evaluation of this Finnish interpretation, see Carl R. Trueman, "Is the Finnish Line a New Beginning? A Critical Assessment of the Reading of Luther Offered by the Helsinki Circle," *Westminster Theological Journal* 65 (Fall 2003): 231–44.

8. For an excellent critique of the New Perspective on Paul, see Richard B. Gaffin Jr., "Paul the Theologian," *Westminster Theological Journal* 62 (Spring 2000): 121–41.

9. Robert Gundry, "Why I Didn't Endorse 'The Gospel of Jesus Christ: An Evangelical Celebration,' " *Books and Culture* (January-February 2001): 6–9.

rance often reflects considerable modern arrogance. Often the "new" analysis of the Bible presents arguments long known and well answered by orthodox scholars.

Second, these attacks often rest on a rejection of the whole idea of a system of theology. The Bible is treated as not possessing a system or internal consistency. This rejection is often linked more specifically to a disdain for scholastic theology as too concerned with reason, distinctions, and harmonization. In fact, Reformed scholastics have discussed the doctrine of justification with extraordinary clarity and fidelity to Scripture and have anticipated most contemporary concerns. The work of the Reformed scholastics of the seventeenth century is a treasury of theological insight, and we neglect it only to our peril. Third, these attacks often reflect a conviction that new formulas of justification will better express and reinforce religious experience. Faithfulness is offered as the antidote to formalism and the great foundation of vital, active Christianity. Fourth, these assaults serve the cause of unity in the churches. The hope is that new definitions will at last overcome the divisions of the sixteenth century. While the goal is noble, the new formulations to this point have offered statements that are at best ambiguous and are not faithful to the Scriptures.

Westminster Theology and Justification

What role does the Westminster theology play in the twentieth-century controversies about justification? The origins of Westminster theology lie in the Calvinistic Reformation, Old School Presbyterianism in America, and the work of Dr. J. Gresham Machen of Princeton Seminary. Machen became the leading intellectual voice in America in the 1920s defending orthodox Protestantism or "fundamentalism" against the rising tide of theological liberalism or "modernism." He established Westminster Theological Seminary in Philadelphia in 1929 to educate future ministers in true, Reformed theology. Today the Westminster theology is taught particularly at the Westminster seminaries.

The major focus of this Westminster theology at the beginning was defending the authority of the Bible as the foundation of the basic truths of orthodox Protestantism. In his most famous book, *Christianity and Liberalism*, Machen enthusiastically identified with the Reformation doctrine of justification: "At the beginning of the sixteenth century, God raised up a man who began to read the Epistle to the Galatians with his own eyes. The result was the recovery of the doctrine of justification by faith. As expounded by Luther and Calvin the Epistle to the Galatians became the 'Magna Charta of Christian liberty.' "[10] Even more eloquently Machen gave testimony to his commitment to the Reformation doctrine of justification when, as he lay dying, he declared, "I'm so thankful for active obedience of Christ. No hope without it."[11]

John Murray, the first systematic theologian at Westminster Seminary (1930–66), followed in the footsteps of Machen, giving a clear and faithful exposition of the Reformed doctrine of justification in his writings. His *Redemption Accomplished and Applied* (1955) and his *Commentary on the Epistle to the Romans* (1959 and 1965) bear eloquent testimony to that orthodox teaching. Murray's clear teaching on this point was continued first in Philadelphia and then at Westminster in California by Robert B. Strimple.

That controversy should arise within the context of this Westminster theology on justification is therefore most surprising. Yet controversy did arise in relation to the teaching of Professor Norman Shepherd, who also taught systematic theology at Westminster Theological Seminary in Philadelphia. Shepherd, in the fall of 1974, reported to the faculty on the fruit of his sabbatical study on the doctrine of justification.[12] Certain key themes came to the fore in the early faculty discussions of Shepherd's ideas.

10. J. Gresham Machen, *Christianity and Liberalism* (1923; reprint, Grand Rapids: Eerdmans, 2002), 143–44.

11. Ned B. Stonehouse, *J. Gresham Machen* (Edinburgh: Banner of Truth, 1987), 508.

12. The author of this essay was a member of the Westminster Theological Seminary, Philadelphia, faculty from 1974 to 1981 and participated as a critic of Shepherd's theology in the various discussions held during that time. For a recent account by another participant in those discussions that is also critical of Shepherd's views, see O. Palmer Robertson, *The Justification Controversy* (Unicoi, Tenn.: Trinity Foundation, 2003).

Shepherd called for a more distinctively and consistently Reformed doctrine of justification. He believed that Reformed theology needed to distance itself from a Lutheran understanding of justification. A truly Reformed doctrine would incorporate more fully both the teaching of James and the biblical revelation of a final judgment according to works. The keys to formulating a more Reformed doctrine were to recognize first that justification was both definitive and progressive, and second that there were two instruments of justification: faith and works. He claimed that this revised understanding of justification could not lead to self-righteousness or boasting because both faith and works were the gift of grace alone.

Continuing discussions within the faculty led to a prolonged controversy. The faculty under the leadership of President Edmund Clowney spent many hours and discussed many papers in an effort to find truth and unity on this important doctrine. Shepherd soon changed his language to say that the instrument of justification was obedient faith. His critics believed that this formula was functionally indistinguishable from saying that faith and works were the instrument. His defenders believed that he was simply saying that the faith which justifies also obeys. The long and painful controversy came to an end in 1982. A majority of the faculty still supported Shepherd as orthodox. The Board of Trustees finally dismissed him from the faculty. About one-third of the Board believed that he was not within the bounds of the confession. About one-third believed that he was too unclear in his teaching to teach systematic theology. About one-third believed that he was orthodox.

How could Westminster theology, ostensibly committed unreservedly to Reformed orthodoxy, have had so much trouble getting justification right? The attractiveness of Shepherd's doctrine of justification rested on its apparent resolution of some problems in the Reformed tradition. Shepherd argued that his emphasis on works would answer the tendency of some of the Reformed to be too introspective and to lack assurance. It would also prevent any movement in an antinomian direction, but would rather encourage the pursuit of holiness. It would clarify the centrality of the doctrine of the covenant in Reformed theology and would eliminate any notions of merit, since all works would clearly be the gift of grace. Also his view would be more biblical by incorporating more fully the biblical material in the Epistle of James and on judgment.

Shepherd had a significant tension in his thought, however. On the one hand he insisted that his theology was Reformed and in accord with the Reformed confessions. On the other hand he claimed that his position was significantly new and gave to the Reformed a distinctively Reformed doctrine of justification. He made clear that we ought not to embrace a Lutheran doctrine of justification. Those who supported Shepherd tended to agree with him on both sides of this tension. They argued that he was confessional and that he was making a helpful addition or clarification in Reformed theology.

Four interconnected factors contributed to the difficulty some adherents of the Westminster theology had in seeing the problems in Shepherd's theology. First, the Westminster theology had become somewhat ingrown and isolated both from its Reformation roots and from the developments within the broader theological world. Second, Shepherd and his associates shared a long friendship and a common education and very similar church connections. For many he seemed almost indistinguishable from John Murray. They seemed to feel that it was impossible for a serious error to arise within Westminster's theology. Third, the pioneering work of Geerhardus Vos, Cornelius Van Til, and Jay Adams seemed to inspire a number of those within the Westminster theology to seek a distinctively Reformed approach to various theological subjects. Shepherd similarly desired to have a uniquely Reformed view of justification. Fourth, many of Shepherd's supporters seemed less acquainted with the issues that had produced Reformation theology and seemed not always to be fully familiar with the Reformed confessions. Westminster's focus on the Bible and on the developments in Reformed theology, especially in the Netherlands in the twentieth century, left some ill-prepared in a knowledge of the confessions. John Murray in his teaching had urged a knowledge of the confessions, but he stressed particularly the biblical evidence for Reformed doctrine. Some of his students seem to have come away, contrary to his intention, focusing on the Bible, but not knowing their confessional heritage as they ought.

Shepherd left the Orthodox Presbyterian Church for the Christian Reformed Church in 1982 just before charges were to be brought against him. After being dismissed from Westminster Seminary, he served as a pastor in the Christian Reformed Church. He has continued to promote his views in various conferences at which he lectured and in a recent book, *The Call of Grace*.[13] His deviations from Reformed orthodoxy have recently become more clear and more radical. On August 9, 2003, at a conference entitled "Contemporary Perspectives on Covenant Theology" sponsored by the Southern California Center for Christian Studies, Shepherd clearly rejected the classic Reformed doctrine of the active obedience of Christ. He argued that while that doctrine is taught in seventeenth-century Reformed theology, it is not taught in the sixteenth-century Reformed theology of Calvin and the Heidelberg Catechism.[14] His denial of the active obedience of Christ

13. Norman Shepherd, *The Call of Grace: How the Covenant Illuminates Salvation and Evangelism* (Phillipsburg, N.J.: P&R, 2000).

14. Shepherd's claim that the doctrine of active obedience was not widely taught among the Reformed in the sixteenth century is wrong. While the emphasis in the theology of the sixteenth century was on the passive obedience of Christ (as indeed it is in the Bible), the substance of the doctrine of active obedience is clearly taught. It is taught in the confessions of the Reformed churches (see quotations from the Belgic Confession, art. 22, and Heidelberg Catechism, Qq. 60 and 61, cited later in the body of this study). The great Reformed theologians of the sixteenth century also taught active obedience. For example, John Calvin wrote, "When, however, we come to Christ, we first find in Him the exact righteousness of the law, and this also becomes ours by imputation." See *The Epistles of Paul the Apostle to the Romans and to the Thessalonians*, trans. Ross Mackenzie (Grand Rapids: Eerdmans, 1960), on Rom. 3:31. He also wrote, "We are not accounted righteous because we have righteousness within us, but we possess Christ Himself with all His blessings, given to us by the Father's bounty" (ibid., on Rom 5:17). In his *Institutes of the Christian Religion* he wrote, "Therefore, we explain justification simply as the acceptance with which God receives us into his favor as righteous men. And we say that it consists in the remission of sins and the imputation of Christ's righteousness." *Institutes of the Christian*

for sinners seems linked to his insistence on the necessity of personal obedience of the believer for justification in the judgment on the last day.

Confessing the Gospel

The controversy surrounding Shepherd's theology of justification helps to focus for us the relationship of Westminster theology to the Reformed confessions. It shows us that for some who belong to the Westminster school of theology, there is a weakness in understanding both the role and the content of the confessions in the life of the Reformed churches.

The Reformed churches adopted confessions to summarize what they as churches believed was essential in the teaching of the Bible. A confession is a statement of what a church believes that the Bible teaches. In orthodox Reformed churches the confessions are subscribed because they agree with the Word of God, not in so far as they agree with the Word of God. A confession does not seek to summarize everything that the Bible teaches and

---

Religion, ed. John T. McNeill, trans. Ford Lewis Battles (Philadelphia: Westminster, 1960), 3.11.2. Zacharias Ursinus wrote similarly in his *Commentary on the Heidelberg Catechism* (Grand Rapids: Eerdmans, 1954), "*Evangelical righteousness* is the fulfilling of the law, performed not by us, but by another in our stead, and imputed unto us of God by faith" (p. 325). "Christ fulfilled the law by the holiness of his human nature, and by his obedience, even unto the death of the cross. The holiness of his human nature was necessary to his obedience; for it became our mediator to be holy and righteous in himself, that he might be able to perform obedience, and make satisfaction for us" (p. 328). John Murray saw rightly how active obedience and passive obedience are simply useful distinctions for expressing aspects of the unity of Jesus's life and death in obedience to God: "It is our Lord's whole work of obedience in every phase and period that is described as active and passive, and we must avoid the mistake of thinking that the active obedience applies to the obedience of his life and the passive to the obedience of his final sufferings and death. The real use and purpose of the formula is to emphasize the two distinct aspects of our Lord's vicarious obedience. The truth expressed rests upon the recognition that the law of God has both penal sanctions and positive demands. . . . Christ's obedience was vicarious in the bearing of the full judgment of God upon sin, and it was vicarious in the full discharge of the demands of righteousness. His obedience becomes the ground of the remission of sin and of actual justification." See *Redemption Accomplished and Applied* (Grand Rapids: Eerdmans, 1955), 21–22.

does not speak to all the issues that would be addressed in a full systematic theology. It is a statement of the corporate faith of the church. It is also a statement of the central or foundational truths that the church believes. Many theological issues are peripheral to the center and are not part of the confession of the church. Many theological issues are the superstructure built on the foundation of the church's confession. The church's confession is not an exercise in writing a brief systematic theology. To be sure, a confession is to some extent the product of systematic reflection, but even more it is the result of Bible study.

The attitude that the confession is basically a brief form of systematic theology can perhaps be seen in a phrase attributed to Professor Klaas Schilder of the Netherlands. Schilder stated that a theologian ought to have a "sympathetic-critical" relationship with the confessions and theology of his tradition. This phrase has been used recently by two Westminster theologians, Dr. Richard Gaffin and Dr. Tim Trumper.[15] A similar attitude can be seen in the comments of Professor John Frame. He wrote that in his education at Westminster Seminary he perceived a "relative absence . . . of a confessional or traditional focus." In contrast he wrote of his own practice: "I always assign relevant portions of the confessions, and I try to make sure that every student understands the traditional formulations, even when I seek to improve upon them."[16]

Reformed systematic theologians should indeed have a "sympathetic-critical" relation to our Reformed theological tradition.

15. Richard B. Gaffin Jr. used this phrase in a discussion of the function of systematic theology. He wrote, "The basic stance of dogmatics to adopt toward the doctrines and confessions of the church is, as Schilder has neatly captured it, 'sympathetic-critical.'" See Richard B. Gaffin Jr., "The Vitality of Reformed Dogmatics," in *The Vitality of Reformed Dogmatics*, ed. J. M. Batteau et al. (Kampen: Kok, 1994), 21. Tim Trumper picked up the phrase "sympathetic-critical" and used it with reference to "the history and theology of the [Reformed] tradition." See Tim J. R. Trumper, "Covenant Theology and Constructive Theology," *Westminster Theological Journal* 64 (Fall 2002): 388.

16. John Frame, "In Defense of Something Close to Biblicism: Reflections on *Sola Scriptura* and History in Theological Method," *Westminster Theological Journal* 59 (Fall 1997): 279.

But that should not be their attitude toward our confessions. We need to distinguish clearly between our confessions and our tradition. While fully recognizing that our confessions are human writings and may need to be changed in light of clearer understanding of the Word of God, our attitude to them in the first place is not critical, not even "sympathetic-critical." Our attitude in the first place is one of confidence because we have subscribed them as our confession of faith.

This point becomes crucial when we come to controversy over a central doctrine like justification. Too many Protestants—whether Lutherans, evangelicals, or Reformed—have acted as if the confessions of their churches were out-dated historical documents or pious advice that could be rejected as easily as followed or as brief systematic theologies that they were free to improve upon. Such a procedure misses the communal, ecclesiastical character of confessions. Confessions are not just a declaration of the faith of an individual, but the faith of a church. Only the church can change its confession, and then only through orderly procedure. Until that happens, those who have confessed their faith by subscribing a confession are under a moral obligation to uphold that confession.

Among American Presbyterians confusion on the relation of confession and systematic theology is exacerbated by distinctive features of their history. We can see that problem in two particular practices of most American Presbyterian churches. The first is the practice of not requiring the lay members of the church to embrace the teachings of the confession. One must be a Christian to join their churches, but one need not necessarily be a Reformed Christian. In such situations the confession of the church does not communicate to the world the faith of the church—at least when we define the church as the body of the faithful. It means that the church may be Reformed only in the hierarchical sense that the officebearers of the church are Reformed. Second, however, American Presbyterian churches allow even the officebearers to take significant exceptions to the confessional standards as part of their subscription. The practice of allowing exceptions to the confessions arose understandably in American Presbyterianism because the Westminster Standards are long and detailed. While the practice of allowing exceptions may make sense for a variety of reasons, it weakens the proper function of the confession as a clear testimony to what the church believes. It also tends to relativize and undermine the authority of the confession in the life of the church.

In light of the proper role that confessions ought to play in the life of Reformed churches, we must turn again to the content of those confessions to find the true Reformed doctrine of justification. The Reformed churches have produced a significant number of confessions in different countries and at different times. While they have some differences, their basic teaching is quite unified. Certainly on the doctrine of justification they speak the same truth as with one voice. The reader of this study will want to consult all that the Reformed standards confess about justification. The following quotations offer representative key selections.

In reading the following quotations, notice how they contain the essential elements of the Reformation doctrine of justification. The work of Christ is clearly presented in terms of his active and passive obedience. Justification is clearly an undeserved gift of grace that does not depend on anything in the one justified. The work of Christ is imputed to the sinner. The justified person is in the judgment of God as perfect as Christ himself. Faith is not itself meritorious, but is the only instrument by which justifying grace is received. The good works of Christians always accompany justifying faith, but are not part of justification.

The Belgic Confession (1561)

Article 22: Our Justification Through Faith in Jesus Christ

We believe that, to attain the true knowledge of this great mystery, the Holy Spirit kindles in our hearts an upright faith, which embraces Jesus Christ with all His merits, appropriates Him, and seeks nothing more besides Him. . . . However, to speak more clearly, we do not mean that faith itself justifies us, for it is only an instrument with which we embrace Christ our righteousness. But Jesus Christ, imputing to us all His merits, and so many holy works which he has done for us and in our stead, is our righteousness. And faith is an instrument that keeps us in communion with Him in all His benefits, which, when they become ours, are more than sufficient to acquit us of our sins.

Article 24: *Man's Sanctification and Good Works*

These works, as they proceed from the good root of faith, are good and acceptable in the sight of God, forasmuch as they are all sanctified by His grace. Nevertheless they are of no account towards our justification, for it is by faith in Christ that we are justified, even before we do good works; otherwise they could not be good works, any more than the fruit of a tree can be good before the tree itself is good.

Heidelberg Catechism (1563)[17]

Question 60

How are you righteous before God? Only by a true faith in Jesus Christ; that is, though my conscience accuse me that I have grievously sinned against all the commandments of God and kept none of them, and am still inclined to all evil, yet God, without any merit of mine, of mere grace, grants and imputes to me the perfect satisfaction, righteousness, and holiness of Christ, as if I had never had nor committed any sin, and myself had accomplished all obedience which Christ has rendered for me; if only I accept such benefit with a believing heart.

Question 61

Why do you say that you are righteous only by faith? Not that I am acceptable to God on account of the worthiness of my

17. Justification in the Reformation catechisms is more fully discussed in W. Robert Godfrey, "Teaching Justification: The Approach of the Reformation Catechisms," *The Banner of Truth Magazine* (August-September 2003): 29–40.

faith, but because only the satisfaction, righteousness, and holiness of Christ is my righteousness before God, and I can receive the same and make it my own in no other way than by faith only.

Question 64

But does not this doctrine make men careless and profane? By no means; for it is impossible that those who are implanted into Christ by a true faith should not bring forth fruits of thankfulness.

The Westminster Confession on Justification

Chapter 11: Of Justification

1. Those whom God effectually calleth, He also freely justifieth: not by infusing righteousness into them, but by pardoning their sins, and by accounting and accepting their persons as righteous; not for any thing wrought in them, or done by them, but for Christ's sake alone; nor by imputing faith itself, the act of believing, or any other evangelical obedience to them, as their righteousness; but by imputing the obedience and satisfaction of Christ unto them, they receiving and resting on Him and His righteousness by faith; which faith they have not of themselves, it is the gift of God.

2. Faith, thus receiving and resting on Christ and His righteousness, is the alone instrument of justification: yet is it not alone in the person justified, but is ever accompanied with all other saving graces, and is no dead faith, but worketh by love.

The Westminster Catechisms on Justification

Shorter Catechism, Q. 33

Justification is an act of God's free grace, wherein he pardoneth all our sins, and accepteth us as righteous in his sight, only for the righteousness of Christ imputed to us, and received by faith alone.

Larger Catechism, Q. 72

Justifying faith is a saving grace, wrought in the heart of a
sinner by the Spirit and word of God, whereby he, being convinced of his sin and misery, and of the disability in himself
and all other creatures to recover him out of his lost condition, not only assenteth to the truth of the promise of the
gospel, but receiveth and resteth upon Christ and his righteousness, therein held forth, for pardon of sin, and for the
accepting and accounting of his person righteous in the sight
of God for salvation.

Larger Catechism, Q. 73

Faith justifies a sinner in the sight of God, not because of
those other graces which do always accompany it, or of good
works that are the fruits of it, nor as if the grace of faith, or
any act thereof, were imputed to him for his justification; but
only as it is an instrument by which he receiveth and appli-
eth Christ and his righteousness.

Larger Catechism, Q. 77

Wherein do justification and sanctification differ? Although
sanctification be inseparably joined with justification, yet
they differ, in that God in justification imputeth the righteousness of Christ; in sanctification his Spirit infuseth grace,
and enableth to the exercise thereof; in the former, sin is par-
doned; in the other, it is subdued: the one doth equally free
all believers from the revenging wrath of God, and that perfectly in this life, that they never fall into condemnation; the
other is neither equal in all, nor in this life perfect in any, but
growing up to perfection.

These confessions and catechisms cited above speak with great
clarity and precision of the content of the doctrine of justification
as confessed by the Reformed churches. Especially the last citation
from question 77 of the Westminster Larger Catechism highlights
the spiritual importance of the doctrine for the people of God: all

believers in this life are perfectly freed from the wrath of God by the work of Christ and will never fall into condemnation.

What we find in the Reformed confessions is the biblical and Pauline doctrine of justification. This is why I am a member of a Reformed church. Against all of the attacks on that doctrine—whether outside or inside the Westminster school of theology—the church must continue to confess that biblical truth. The defense of the Reformed doctrine of justification is not a nit-picking exercise in irrelevant theology. Justification is central to the lives as well as the confession of the churches and of Christians individually. Without a clear understanding of justification we soon lose a sense of God's holiness and his uncompromising demand for perfection—a demand only met in the perfection of Christ.[18] We soon lose a sense of the continuing sinfulness of the regenerate and begin to think that we are pretty good.[19] We soon lose a proper understanding of justifying faith as the instrument that looks away from ourselves and rests in Christ and his work for us alone for justification. We soon lose assurance because we can have no assurance of peace with God on any other foundation than the perfect, finished work of Christ for us, received forever when we first truly believe. We soon lose the comfort of gospel preaching in our churches and hear instead the deadening false gospel: "Try harder." As Calvin wrote, "No one will stand without fear before God, unless he relies on free reconciliation, for as long as God is judge, all men must be filled with fear and confusion. . . . wretched souls are always uneasy, unless they rest in the grace of Christ."[20]

---

18. Calvin is especially eloquent on this point at many places in his writings. For example, he wrote, "In the shady cloisters of the schools anyone can easily and readily prattle about the value of works in justifying men. But when we come before the presence of God we must put away such amusements! For there we deal with a serious matter, and do not engage in frivolous word battles." (*Institutes*, 3.12.1)

19. The real state of the regenerate Christian is best summed up in Heidelberg Catechism, Q. 114, ". . . even the holiest of men, while in this life, have only small beginnings of this obedience, yet so, that with a sincere resolution, they begin to live, not only according to some, but all the commands of God."

20. Calvin, *Commentary on Romans*, Rom. 5:1.

Why then is it so difficult to get the doctrine of justification right? Paul and the Reformation knew. Human nature in its pride wants to contribute and help in its own justification. But any confidence in one's own spiritual progress for justification denigrates Christ and imperils the soul. As Calvin wrote,

> Therefore, those who prate that we are justified by faith because, being reborn, we are righteous by living spiritually have never tasted the sweetness of grace, so as to consider that God will be favorable to them. . . . Therefore, we must come to this remedy: that believers should be convinced that their only ground of hope for the inheritance of a Heavenly Kingdom lies in the fact that, being engrafted in the body of Christ, they are freely accounted righteous. For, as regards justification, faith is something merely passive, bringing nothing of ours to the recovering of God's favor but receiving from Christ that which we lack.[21]

Every generation must take up the responsibility of teaching and defending the biblical doctrine of justification. Although the attacks on the doctrine from one generation to another are fundamentally the same, yet they come with just enough difference to intrigue and attract some followers. As Paul in his epistles and the Reformers in their confessions taught the doctrine faithfully, so must we in our churches and our theological writings. The glory of Christ, the well-being of the churches, and the peace of Christian consciences demand it.

21. Calvin, *Institutes*, 3.14.5.

7

Janus, the Well-Meant Offer of the Gospel, and Westminster Theology

R. Scott Clark

I t is a pleasure to contribute to a *festschrift* for my teacher, colleague, and friend, Bob Strimple. One of the most important moments in my theological education was hearing him present the exegetical and biblical-theological case for the well-meant offer of the gospel. His explanation of the 1948 majority report to the Fifteenth General Assembly of the Orthodox Presbyterian Church (OPC) by John Murray (1898–1975) was a turning point in my hermeneutic, doctrine of God, and theology of evangelism.[1] He helped me to appreciate Scripture as an accommodated revelation, the distinction between God "in himself" *(in se)* and "toward us" *(erga nos)*, and that the proper motivations for the free, serious, well-meant offer of the gospel are God's glory and the salvation of the lost. The Murray-Strimple approach provided a clear biblical, exegetical, and theological rationale for the proclamation of the gospel.

1. *Minutes of the Fifteenth General Assembly of the Orthodox Presbyterian Church* (1948), Appendix, 01–63. See also *The Collected Writings of John Murray*, 4 vols. (Edinburgh: Banner of Truth, 1976–82), 4:113–32; idem, *Redemption Accomplished and Applied* (Grand Rapids: Eerdmans, 1955), 75, 134–37; idem, "The Atonement and the Free Offer of the Gospel" in *Collected Writings*, 1:59–85; idem, "Common Grace," in *Collected Writings*, 2:93–119. On this question generally see Cornelius Venema, "Reformed Evangelism: Elec-

It seemed impossible to me, a naïve student, that confessional Reformed folk should not embrace the doctrine of the well-meant offer, but as influential as it has been among some of us, it has not found universal acceptance in either contemporary Reformed theory or our practice. In the Three Points of Synod Kalamazoo (1924) the Christian Reformed Churches in North America (CRC) came out solidly for the well-meant offer of the gospel.[2] In reaction, the well-meant offer came under sustained criticism from Herman Hoeksema (1886–1965) and his followers, who contended that the well-meant offer is a form of Arminianism.[3] One of their theolo-

---

tion and the Free Offer of the Gospel," *The Outlook* 52 (2002), no. 5–7; Joseph H. Hall, "The Marrow Controversy: A Defense of Grace and the Free Offer of the Gospel," *Mid-America Theological Journal* 10 (1999): 239–57; Craig A. Sheppard, "The Compatibility of the Doctrine of Election with the Free Offer of the Gospel in James Henley Thornwell," Th.M. thesis, (Jackson, Miss.: Reformed Theological Seminary, 1997); Evangelical Presbyterian Church of Eastern Australia, *Universalism and the Reformed Churches: A Defence of Calvin's Calvinism* (reprint, Launceston, Tasmania, 1997); Iain H. Murray, *Spurgeon and Hyper-Calvinism: The Battle for Gospel Preaching* (Edinburgh: Banner of Truth, 1996); J. I. Packer, "The Love of God," in *The Grace of God/The Bondage of the Will*, 2 vols. (Grand Rapids: Baker, 1995), 1:413–27; John Piper, "Are There Two Wills in God? Divine Election and God's Desire for All to Be Saved," in *The Grace of God/Bondage of the Will*, 1:107–31; E. Hulse, *The Free Offer of the Gospel* (Hertfordshire: Evangelical, 1986); H. Bavinck, "Calvin and Common Grace," in *Calvin and the Reformation* (reprint, Grand Rapids: Baker, 1980); Cornelius Van Til, *Common Grace and the Gospel* (Nutley, N.J.: Presbyterian and Reformed, 1977); Peter Toon, *The Emergence of Hyper-Calvinism in English Non-conformity, 1689–1765* (London: The Olive Tree, 1967); James Daane, "The Free Offer of the Gospel," *The Reformed Journal* 6, no. 8 (1956): 6–9. See also the debate between Daane and Van Til in *The Reformed Journal* 6, no. 11 (1956): 20–23; Daane, *A Theology of Grace: An Inquiry into and Evaluation of Dr. C. Van Til's Doctrine of Common Grace* (Grand Rapids: Eerdmans, 1954); A. C. DeJong, *The Well-Meant Offer: The Views of H. Hoeksema and K. Schilder* (Franeker: Weaver, 1954); H. Kuiper, *Calvin on Common Grace* (Goes: Oosterbaan & Le Cointre; Grand Rapids: Smiter, 1928).

2. The original text of the "Three Points" is found in the *Acta der Synode 1924* van de Christelijke Gereformeerde Kerk (18 June–8 July 1924, Kalamazoo, Mich.): 145–47. A full English translation was published in *The Banner* in 1939 and was reproduced in C. Van Til, *Common Grace* (Philadelphia: Presbyterian and Reformed, 1947), 19–22.

The first point says in part, "Synod declares that it is certain, according to Scripture and the Confessions that there is, besides the saving grace of God shown only to those chosen to eternal life, also a certain favor or grace of God which He shows to His creatures in general. This is evident from the quoted Scripture passages and from the Canons of Dort II, 5 and III and IV:8 and 9, where the general offer of the Gospel is discussed. . . ."

3. Herman Hoeksema, *Reformed Dogmatics* (Grand Rapids: Reformed Free, 1966), 471; idem, *A Triple Breach in the Foundation of the Reformed Truth: A Critical Treatise on*

gians recently identified this issue as "the chief point of controversy" between themselves and proponents of common grace.[4] The doctrine of the well-meant offer has also been rejected by the followers of Gordon Clark (1902–85), and his opposition to the well-meant offer played a major part of the Clark-Van Til Controversy in the Orthodox Presbyterian Church in the 1940s.[5] More recently, even John Gerstner (1914–96) revealed his opposition to the well-meant offer in a book against dispensationalism.[6]

---

the "Three Points" Adopted by the Synod of the Christian Reformed Churches in 1924 (reprint, Grand Rapids: Reformed Free, 1942), 28–45; Herman Hanko, For Thy Truth's Sake: A Doctrinal History of the Protestant Reformed Churches (Grandville, Mich.: Reformed Free, 2000), 53, 71 n. 6, 87–91; Herman Hoeksema, The Clark-Van Til Controversy (Hobbs, N.Mex.: The Trinity Foundation, 1995), 39–44, 64–67; David Engelsma, Hyper-Calvinism and the Call of the Gospel (Grand Rapids: Reformed Free, 1980), 3, 27, 36.

4. Hanko, For Thy Truth's Sake, 53 n. 9.

5. The critique by Westminster Seminary professor Cornelius Van Til and others was published privately as "The Text of a Complaint Against Actions of the Presbytery of Philadelphia on the Matter of the Licensure and Ordination of Dr. Gordon H. Clark," (1944), hereafter denominated as The Complaint. The response by a committee composed of Gordon Clark and others was published as The Answer to a Complaint Against Several Actions and Decisions of the Presbytery of Philadelphia taken in a Special Meeting Held on July 7, 1944, hereafter denominated, The Answer. See also The Minutes of the Twelfth General Assembly of the Orthodox Presbyterian Church (1945), 5–30; Minutes of the Thirteenth General Assembly of the Orthodox Presbyterian Church (1946), 38–82, 88–89; The Minutes of the Fifteenth General Assembly of the Orthodox Presbyterian Church (1948), appendix, 1–96. On the controversy generally see Fred H. Klooster, The Incomprehensibility of God in the Orthodox Presbyterian Conflict (Franeker: Weaver, 1951). In his Doctrine of the Knowledge of God (Phillipsburg, N.J.: Presbyterian and Reformed, 1987), 21–40 (hereafter DKG) and his Cornelius Van Til: An Analysis of His Thought (Phillipsburg, N.J.: P&R, 1995), 97–113, John M. Frame proposed a resolution of the Clark-Van Til controversy. He discusses and approves of Van Til's doctrine of analogy and indicates support for Van Til's distinction between the Creator and the creature, but then substantially subverts them both by affirming and denying that humans can know God's "essence" (DKG, 30–32) and God "in se" (DKG, 32–35). Such claims are incompatible with the classical Protestant understanding of Scripture and should be rejected as incoherent. Frame seeks a reconciliation of Clark and Van Til via tri-perspectivalism and ethical criticisms of the parties in the debate. If one does not accept his method (and there are good reasons to reject this method, since it tends to erase the archetypal/ectypal distinction), his redefinition of several key terms in the debate, his ethical analysis, or his hypotheses about what parties in the debate might have said under different circumstances, then his resolution is unsatisfactory.

6. John Gerstner, Wrongly Dividing the Word of Truth: A Critique of Dispensationalism, ed. Don Kistler, 2nd ed. (Morgan, Pa.: Soli Deo Gloria, 2000), 142–47. Gerstner misstates the date of the CRC Synod Kalamazoo as 1920.

In his exposition and defense of the well-meant offer, Murray offered a highly detailed exegetical case. In its brief explanation, Synod Kalamazoo appealed to Scripture and some standard Reformed theologians. In analyzing the criticisms of the well-meant offer by Hoeksema and Clark, however, it is apparent that it was neither biblical exegesis nor historical theology which animated the discussion, but rather matters of theological method, specifically hermeneutics and assumptions about the nature of divine-human relations. This essay contends that the reason the well-meant offer has not been more persuasive is that its critics have not understood or sympathized with the fundamental assumption on which the doctrine of the well-meant offer was premised: the distinction between theology as God knows it (*theologia archetypa*) and theology as it is revealed to and done by us (*theologia ectypa*). In making the biblical case for the claim that God reveals himself as desiring what he has not secretly willed to do, Murray and Strimple assumed this distinction which they did not articulate explicitly.[7]

The critics have been sometimes more direct in their rejection of the archetypal/ectypal distinction than the proponents of the well-meant offer have been in their exposition of it. Gordon Clark and his supporters rejected as a "strange doctrine" the notion that "there are mysterious areas of knowledge which God has, incapable of being revealed by God to man or of being understood by man even if God revealed them."[8] According to Clark, divine-human relations are such that God could reveal to us anything he wills. According to Clark, there is no evidence in Scripture that a proposition is qualitatively different for us from what it is for God.[9] Whereas Deuteronomy 29:29 has traditionally been used in Reformed dogmatics as a proof of the archetypal/ectypal

7. A possible exception to this claim would be Murray's "Minority Report to the Committee Elected by the Twelfth General Assembly to Consider the Doctrinal Portion of the Complaint of Certain Members of the Presbytery of Philadelphia," in *Minutes of the Thirteenth General Assembly*, 68–81.

8. Clark, *The Answer*, 14. See also Klooster, *Incomprehensibility*, 20–26.

9. Clark, *The Answer*, 14.

distinction, of the necessity of analogical knowledge of and speech about God, Clark understood it to teach only that certain things are hidden solely because they are unrevealed, not because *finitum non capax infiniti*.[10] From this, it appears that for Clark, our theology is partly ectypal and partly archetypal. When we correctly formulate a theological proposition, we have come into contact with the divine mind immediately.[11]

For his part, Hoeksema rejected categorically the well-meant offer as making God into a sort of "Janus," that is, a two-faced god. The best interpretation of Hoeksema's language is that it was an implicit rejection of the archetypal/ectypal distinction. This is why he alleged that Louis Berkhof (1873–1957) was a sort of crypto-Arminian:

> For, fact is, that the first point [of Synod Kalamazoo on common grace] reminds one of the two-faced Janus. Janus was a Roman idol, distinguished by the remarkable feature of having two faces and looking in two opposite directions. And in this respect there is a marked similarity between Janus and the first point. The latter is also two-faced and casts wistful looks in opposite directions. . . . One of his faces reminds you of Augustine, Calvin, Gomarus; but the other shows the unmistakable features of Pelagius, Arminius, Episcopius. And your troubles begin when you would inquire of this two-faced oracle, what may be the exact meaning of the first point. For, then this modern Janus begins to revolve, alternatively showing you one face and the other, till you hardly know whether you are dealing with Calvin or Arminius.[12]

10. Ibid., 11. See also Richard A. Muller, *Dictionary of Latin and Greek Theological Terms* (Grand Rapids: Baker, 1985), s.v., "finitum."

11. Klooster, *Incomprehensibility*, 133. As further evidence of Clark's intellectualism, one could point to his commentary on the Gospel of John in which he argued that the correct translation of *logos* in the prologue is not "word" but "Reason, Wisdom or Logic. . . ." See Gordon H. Clark, *The Johannine Logos* (Nutley, N.J.: Presbyterian and Reformed, 1972), 23, 38–46. The theological function of such an interpretation of Scripture is to put us into immediate contact with the divine intellect.

12. Hoeksema, *A Triple Breach*, 30.

Since the nature of divine-human relations is fundamental to the recovery and re-expression of the well-meant offer, a consideration of the rise and function of the basic assumption on which the well-meant offer is based also offers avenues for discussion between the proponents and opponents of the well-meant offer.

The Background of the Modern Debate

The proponents of the free or well-meant offer of the gospel (e.g., Van Til and Synod Kalamazoo) have argued that they were merely continuing an approach long-established in the Reformed tradition.[13] Certainly the terms of debate in the two periods were different and therefore they must be compared with caution. The orthodox Reformed theologians in the early seventeenth century were defending the gospel of free grace against what they perceived to be a semi-Pelagian corruption. The controversy over the "Three Points" of 1924 and the Clark case (1944–48) were concerned with the problem of hyper-Calvinism. The Arminian and modern problems are connected, however, by a suspicion common to both the opponents of the well-meant offer and the Remonstrants that the well-meant offer was built on a false foundation, the archetypal/ectypal distinction.

The basic premise of the well-meant offer has it roots in the earliest days of the Protestant Reformation. At the 1518 *Heidelberg Disputation*, Martin Luther (1483–1546) unveiled what he called the theology of the cross (*theologia crucis*), against Aristotle and Rome's theology of glory (*theologia gloriae*). By the latter he meant to define a complex of ideas, including the notion that one is ultimately justified before God on the basis of graciously infused sanctity, and the notion that, at some point, the human intellect intersects with God's. The theologian of the cross "says what a thing is," because he relies on divine revelation in Scripture rather than on a neo-Platonic continuum of being.[14]

13. *Acta*, 146; Clark, *The Complaint*, 14–15.
14. "Theologus gloriae dicit malum bonum et bonum malum, Theologus [22] crucis dicit id quod res est." *Disputatio Heidelbergae habita. 1518* in M. Luther, *Luthers*

Behind his distinction between the *theologia crucis et gloriae* was another: the distinction between God revealed (*Deus revelatus*) and God hidden (*Deus absconditus*).[15] Luther's entire argument with Erasmus in his *Bondage of the Will* (1525) was grounded in this distinction. God as he is *in se*, is hidden to us. We only know God as he has revealed himself to us (*erga nos*). For Luther, we do not know God's absolute power (*potentia absoluta*); though it exists, we only know what he has ordained (*potentia ordinata*). Against Erasmus's rationalism and in the midst of explaining the distinction between law and gospel in Ezekiel 18:23, 32, Luther developed the Scotist distinction between God *in se* and *erga nos* in dramatic and definite way for Protestant theology. He wrote,

> For he is here speaking of the preached and offered mercy of God, not that hidden and awful will of God whereby he ordains by his own counsel which and what sort of persons he wills to be recipients and partakers of his preached and offered mercy . . . we have to argue in one way about God or the will of God as preached, revealed, offered and worshipped, and in another way about God as he is not preached, not revealed not offered, not worshipped. To the extent, therefore, that God hides himself and wills to be unknown to us, it is no business of ours. . . .

Luther clearly demarcated between God as he is *in se* and God as he reveals himself to us. The former is the theology of glory, and the latter is the theology of the cross. The medieval theologians believed they had a sort of access to the mind and will of God which we cannot have. To such rationalism, Luther responded:

> God must therefore be left alone to himself in his own majesty, for in this regard, we should have nothing to do with

---

Werke Kritische Gesamtausgabe, ed. by J. K. F. Knaake et al (Weimar, 1883), 1:354. Hereafter, *WA*.

15. Fred Klooster's otherwise excellent study unfortunately links Luther's distinction between God hidden and revealed with Barth's doctrine of God (idem, *Incomprehensibility*, 111).

him, nor has he willed that we should have anything to do
with him. But we have something to do with him insofar as
he is clothed and set forth in his Word, through which he
offers himself to us. . . .[16]

For Luther (and for Calvin after him), for sinners to know God as
he is in himself is to know him only as judge. To know him in the
incarnation is to know his grace, mercy, and forgiveness. The theology of glory leads sinners to believe that they can present themselves to God, either with condign merit wrought graciously in them
by the Spirit (*meritum de condigno*) or with those acts God is graciously pleased to accept and to which he imputes perfection (*meritum de congruo*). In distinction, the theologian of the cross clings
to the foolishness of the gospel of imputed righteousness received
through faith alone.[17] The theologian of the cross submits to divine
revelation and does not seek to look behind it, as it were. The distinctions became the basis for Protestant theological method. They
were applied differently by the Lutheran orthodox and the
Reformed in Christology, but both traditions have agreed that there
are fundamentally two distinct sorts of knowledge, that possessed
by God and that which he reveals to humans.[18]

The Development of the Archetypal/Ectypal Distinction

John Calvin (1509–64) accepted Luther's fundamental distinction between God hidden (*Deus absconditus*) and God
revealed (*Deus revelatus*). In *Institutes* 1.17.2 he argued from
Deuteronomy 29:29, 30:11–14, and Romans 11:33–34 (among
other places) that there is a distinction to be made between God's

16. *Luther's Works*, trans. and ed. J. Pelikan et al. (Philadelphia and St. Louis: Con-
cordia, 1955), 33:139. *WA* 17:684–85.
17. Paul Althaus, *The Theology of Martin Luther*, trans. Robert C. Schultz (Philadelphia: Fortress, 1966), 25–34. See also Walther von Loewenich, *Luther's Theology of the
Cross*, trans. Herbert J. A. Bouman (Minneapolis: Augsburg, 1972), 27–49; A. E. McGrath,
Luther's Theology of the Cross (Oxford: Blackwell, 1985), 148–81.
18. Louis Berkhof, *Systematic Theology*, 4th ed. (Grand Rapids: Eerdmans, 1941), 43.

will as it is revealed and his will as it is hidden (*voluntatem abscon-ditam*) from us. Whereas the hidden, secret, providential, decre-tive, mysterious will of God is like an abyss (*abyssus*), such is not the case with God's revealed will, which becomes to us a "school of truth" (*veritatis schola*).[19] The Sophists (i.e., the Roman Catholic theologians of the Sorbonne) argue about God's "absolute will" (*absoluta voluntas*), in which they "separate his justice from his power," but we respect the boundary between the secret and the revealed.[20] Thus, Calvin required the Christian theologian to adhere to the "rule of modesty and sobriety" (*modestiae et sobri-etatis regulam*), that is, those things revealed in Scripture.[21] According to Calvin, religion is either true or false.[22] That which is according to the Bible is true; that which is not according to the Bible is false. We only know what God has willed to reveal to us, and all revelation is accommodated to our weakness: it is "baby talk."[23] Despite the fact that all revelation is necessarily accom-modated and analogical, it is nevertheless true and that theology that conforms to Holy Scripture is also true.

In *De vera theologia* (1594), Franciscus Junius (1545–1602) followed Calvin's pattern by distinguishing between "true theol-ogy" and "false theology."[24] The latter is that which does not come from God and does not conform to his accommodated self-revelation. The former is "twofold" (*duplex*). Because of the nature

19. Joannis Calvini, *Opera selecta*, 5 vols., ed. P. Barth and W. Niesel, 3rd ed. (Munich: Christian Kaiser, 1963–74), 3.204.15, 23, 25. Hereafter, *OS*.

20. "separantes eius iustitiam a potentia . . .". Calvin, *OS* 3.205.16, 17.

21. Calvin, *Institutes* 1.14.4; *OS*, 3.156.19.

22. Calvin, *Institutes* 1.14.4.

23. Ibid., 1.13.1, "Quis enim vel parum ingeniosus non intelligit Deum ita nobiscum, ceu nutrices solent cum infantibus, quodammodo balbutire?" (*OS*, 3.109.13–15). See Ford Lewis Battles, "God Was Accommodating Himself to Human Capacity," *Interpretation* 31 (1977): 19–38.

24. Franciscus Junius, *De theologia vera* in *Opera theologica Fransci Iunii*, 2 vols. (Geneva, 1613). On this topic see the excellent introduction by Willem J. van Asselt, "The Fundamental Meaning of Theology: Archetypal and Ectypal Theology in Seventeenth-Century Reformed Thought," *Westminster Theological Journal* 64 (2003): 319–35. See also Richard A. Muller, *Post-Reformation Reformed Dogmatics*, 4 vols., 2nd ed. (Grand Rapids: Baker, 2003), 1:225–69.

of divine-human relations, we must speak analogically about God's theology and understand that theology that he reveals to us is an analogue of what is proper to God.[25] He distinguished theology into two types, archetypal theology, that is, theology as God knows it in himself, and ectypal theology or theology as he reveals it to creatures.[26] *Theologia archetypa* is the "divine understanding (*sapientia*) of divine matters, such things we adore but do not investigate."[27] Indeed, Junius was careful to stress that this is not even a definition, since it is impossible for humans to define divine knowledge. Rather it is an analogical account of it.[28]

In 1609 Amandus Polanus (1561–1610) expanded Junius's explanation of the archetypal/ectypal distinction. True theology is either archetypal or ectypal, but only God knows the former and creatures only know the latter.[29] With Junius, he argued that the division itself is analogical (*analogica*), which is to say, it does not exist in God himself, but he accommodates himself to us to make this division.[30] Archetypal theology is "first and principally" (*primo et principaliter*) theology, as the (medieval) scholastics were accustomed to saying, it is "God's theology" (*theologia Dei*), it is the original example (*exemplum primigenium*) and "immutable" (*immutabile*).[31] Whatever qualities may be found in rational creatures (e.g., wisdom, goodness, justice, power) their archetype is in God the Creator. In these things we are but the image of God.[32] Because archetypal theology is the understanding residing in God, it is essential (as opposed to accidental or acquired) and uncreated (*increata*).[33]

25. Junius, *Opera*, 1.1767.
26. Ibid., 1.1759–61, 1767–68.
27. "Theologia archetypa est divinarum rerum divina Sapientiaem, hanc vero nos adoramus, ac non investigamus." Junius, *Opera* 1.1768.58–59. Polanus quotes this aphorism in *Syntagma theologiae christianae*, 13 vols. (Geneva, 1612) 1.3.3. Citations from the *Syntagma* give the volume, chapter, and page numbers.
28. Junius, *Opera*, 1.1768.62–67.
29. Polanus, *Syntagma*, 1.3.3.
30. Ibid.
31. Ibid.
32. Ibid.
33. Ibid.

Nevertheless, ectypal theology is a true and "complete" (*tota*) theology, capable of being communicated to rational creatures in "this life and the next."[34] It is the "understanding (*sapientia*) of divine matters communicated according to the mode or capacity of rational creatures, so that knowing him rightly and loving him *ex animo*, we might live with him in eternal blessedness. . . ."[35] Even though it is accommodated to the intellectual capacity of rational creatures, and even though it is only analogical of the archetype, nevertheless, according to Polanus, ectypal theology, as a "*vera theologia*," is sufficient to guide believers to two ends, the first and highest of which is God's glory and the second of which is human blessedness.[36]

Johannes Wollebius (1586–1629) in his *Compendium theologiae Christianae* (1626) adopted the same fundamental distinction:[37]

> True theology is called archetypal or ectypal. Archetypal theology is the knowledge by which God knows himself, which in reality is no different from the essence of God. Ectypal theology is a kind of copy (*effigies*) of archetypal theology which is first of all in Christ the God-Man and secondarily, to be sure, in the members of Christ.[38]

It is important to notice that for Wollebius, as for Junius and Polanus and most other orthodox Reformed theologians in the clas-

---

34. "Theologia ectypa in se, est tota sapietntia rerum divinarum cum creaturibis rationalibus communicabilis, in hac et in furtura vita, pro modo Dei illam coummicantis" (Polanus, *Syntagma*, 1.4.4).

35. "Theologia ectypa considerata ut est in creaturis rationalibus, est sapientia rerum divnarum cum creaturis rationalibus communicata pro modo seu captu ipsarum, ut illae Deum recte agnoscentes et ex animo diligentes, cum eo beate in aeternum vivant . . ." (Polanus, *Syntagma*, 1.4.4).

36. Polanus, *Syntagma*, 1.4.5.

37. Johannes Wollebius, *Christianae theologiae compendium*, ed. E. Bizer (Neukirchen, 1935), 1. (Citations of the *Compendium* give the page numbers.) For an English translation see J. W. Beardslee III, trans. and ed., *Reformed Dogmatics* (New York: Oxford University Press, 1965).

38. "Vere autem dicta theologia archetypa est aut ectypa. Archetypa est cognitio, qua Deus cognoscit se ipsum, quae reipsa non differt a Dei esssentia, Ectypa est archetypae qaedam effigies, primario quidem in Christo *theanthropo* secondario vero in mebris Christi" (Wollebius, *Compendium*, 1).

sical period, there was a clear distinction made between archetypal
and ectypal theology, because they affirmed a clear distinction
between God and man. Wollebius, with all the Reformed orthodox
theologians, over against the Lutherans, assigned to Jesus's humanity only ectypal knowledge, lest the Creator-creature distinction be
destroyed by divinizing Jesus's humanity. Even though ectypal theology is a "copy" of the archetypal, it is nevertheless true. Intersection between our intellect and God's was not considered a pre-
requisite for true knowledge. This distinction continued as a basic
assumption of function in Reformed theology throughout the seventeenth century, although it received less prominence in the late
orthodox period than it did in the earlier periods.[39]

In the 1920s controversy over the "Three Points," there was
a clear demarcation between those who accepted the traditional
distinction and those who did not. While those who accepted the
archetypal/ectypal distinction tended to favor the well-meant offer,
those who rejected the analogical model of theology also rejected
the well-meant offer. For example, Louis Berkhof's *Systematic Theology* (first published in 1932 as a *Reformed Dogmatics*) restated
the traditional position distinguishing between archetypal and
ectypal theology.[40] Even more clearly, another proponent of the
well-meant offer and a Westminster theologian, Cornelius Van Til
(1895–1987), upheld the archetypal/ectypal distinction, even if he
did not use the traditional terminology consistently.[41]

In Herman Hoeksema's *Reformed Dogmatics* (1966), however, there was no explicit discussion of the archetypal/ectypal
distinction. At times he seemed to acknowledge a distinction
between God as he is in himself and as he reveals himself to us,
saying that we know God "in part," but not a "part of God." We
have only a reflection in finite form of the "infinite Essence."[42]

39. I discuss the history of the archetype/ectype distinction in the forthcoming book,
Recovering the Reformed Tradition.

40. Louis Berkhof, *Introductory Volume to Systematic Theology*, 2nd ed. (Grand Rapids:
1932), 93–95.

41. See for example, C. Van Til, *An Introduction to Systematic Theology* (Nutley, N.J.:
Presbyterian and Reformed, 1974), 203.

42. Hoeksema, *Reformed Dogmatics*, 41.

Most of the time, however, he argued against the substance of the archetypal/ectypal distinction. He said, "If we want to make separation between revelation and Himself, there is no knowledge of God."[43] This approach influenced how he structured his theology. For Hoeksema, God himself is the *principium cognoscendi*, whereas, in contrast, for Berkhof, Scripture performs that role.[44] This is a significant difference. Berkhof's doctrine of the knowledge of God began with revelation. Hoeksema, however, began not with revelation, but with God himself as the beginning of knowledge. This move suggests a sort of intellectualism, that is, an intersection between our mind and God's, in Hoeksema's theology. There was tension in his *Dogmatics*. At one point he nodded politely to the Creator-creature distinction, but elsewhere he argued against the substance of the archetypal/ectypal distinction, and the historical record is that his rhetoric against the well-meant offer tended to militate against the distinction.[45]

The Arminian and Remonstrant Rejection of Analogical Theology

Luther and Calvin established and maintained assiduously a strict analogy between theology as God knows it and as he reveals it to us. Jacob Arminius (1559/60–1609) was trained in this theological milieu. At the outset it was not clear that Arminius would be anything but an orthodox Reformed pastor. His student disputation in Geneva was orthodox, and he left Geneva with a letter of commendation from Theodore Beza (1509–1605).[46] Even

43. Ibid., 6.

44. Ibid., 15–16; Berkhof, *Introductory Volume*, 96–97.

45. E.g., Herman Hoeksema, *Predestination: Revealed Not Hidden nor Confused* (Grand Rapids: The Radio Committee of the First Protestant Reformed Church, 1948).

46. *Theses theologicae in schola Genevensi ab aliquot sacrarum literarum studiosis sub DD. theol. Beza & Antonio Fayo S.S. theologiae professoribus propositae & disputatae. In quibus methodica locorum communium S.S. theologiae epitome continetur* (Geneva, 1586). Translated and published in English as *Propositions and Principles of Divinitie propounded and disputed in the universitie of Geneua, by certaine students of Diuinitie there, vnder M. Theod. Beza, and M. Anthonie Faius, professors of Divinitie* (Edinburgh, 1591). Among the

after he entered into controversy with Junius on predestination and later Franciscus Gomarus (1563–1641), as Richard Muller has shown, he had far more in common with the orthodox Reformed theologians of his day than has been sometimes recognized.[47] Specifically, late in his career, after he had engaged in his most famous public disputations, Arminius was still using the categories he inherited from Junius.[48]

Despite certain similarities between Arminius and Junius, however, there were indications in Arminius's theology that what Luther called *theologia gloriae* was not entirely vanquished. "Arminius' argument for the priority of intellect in the final vision of God perfectly reproduces the classic intellectualist thesis of Thomas Aquinas."[49] Arminius's intellectualism was "quite unparalleled" among the early orthodox Reformed and signaled "the profound soteriological disagreement between Arminius and the Reformed and, consequently, toward the greater receptivity of the Arminian system to philosophical rationalism." More than that, as Muller writes, Arminius's method proposed an "interrelationship of the Being of God with the being of the world that is both rational and regularized, and interrelationship of the two levels of being, the eternal and temporal that is ordained by God and cannot be undone, not by sin and surely not by the work of redemption."[50] This is all to say that, in Arminius, the analogy between God and man, established by the Reformers and systematized by the early orthodox Reformed theologians, was fundamentally

disputants were Jacobus Arminius (*Theses Theologiae*, 147) and the Remonstrant Johannes Uitenbogaert (ibid., 64, 117).

47. Richard A. Muller, *God, Creation and Providence in the Thought of Jacob Arminius: Sources and Directions of Scholastic Protestantism in the Era of Early Orthodoxy* (Grand Rapids: Baker, 1991), 40–70.

48. Muller, *God, Creation and Providence*, 50–51. See Arminius's "Private Disputations," which gives an indication of his dogmatic lectures in Leiden. James Arminius, *The Works of James Arminius: The London Edition*, 3 vols., trans. and ed. James Nichols and William Nichols (reprint, Grand Rapids: Baker, 1996), 1:318–21.

49. Muller, *God, Creation and Providence*, 78.

50. Ibid., 79, 228–29.

undone in favor of an intersection of divine and human intellects of the sort discarded at the outset of the Reformation.

In order to understand the Reformed orthodox insistence on analogical theology, that is, the archetypal/ectypal distinction and its corollary, the well-meant offer, it is useful to consider how the Remonstrants applied evangelical intellectualism to their soteriology. After Arminius's death in 1609, the rationalism implicit in Arminius became explicit in the Remonstrants.[51] In the Five Arminian Articles of 1610, the Remonstrants argued that God has an immutable decree "to save, in Christ, for Christ's sake and through Christ, those who, through the grace of the Holy Spirit will believe in this same Son, and in this same faith and obedience of faith through this grace, who will persevere to the end."[52] That is, unlike Luther and the Reformed, election is not grounded solely in God's free grace and good pleasure, but rather God's foresight of our faith and works. The Remonstrant version of prevenient or "common" grace is substantially identical to what William of Ockham (c. 1285–1347) called the "antecedent will" of God to save whoever is willing to be saved.[53] In this definition of common grace, the emphasis is not on restraint of sin or a general favor of the Creator toward his creatures as such, but rather on the human will.[54]

Having rejected the analogical model, the Remonstrants were unwilling to embrace the paradoxes of the orthodox Reformed

51. On the rise of rationalism among the Remonstrants see John Platt, *Reformed Thought and Scholasticism: The Arguments for the Existence of God in Dutch Theology, 1575–1650* (Leiden: Brill, 1982).

52. My translation from the Latin text. See Philip Schaff, ed., *The Creeds of Christendom*, 3 vols., 6th ed. (reprint, Grand Rapids: Baker, 1983), 3:545.

53. E.g., William Ockham, *Predestination, God's Foreknowledge, and Future Contingents*, 2nd ed., trans. Marilyn McCord Adams and Norman Kretzmann (Indianapolis and Cambridge: Hackett, 1983), 7–11, 34–53. Arminius was quite conversant with these distinctions. See Arminius, *Works*, 2:343–47; William Ames, *The Marrow of Theology*, trans. John Dykstra Eusden (Durham, N.C.: Labyrinth, 1983), 98–99; Muller, *God, Creation and Providence*, 187–88.

54. CD RE 3/4.5; RE 1.2; 3/4.14. Which view was rejected explicitly in CD 3/4.10 among other places. Turretin imputed this view also to the orthodox Lutherans. See F. Turretin, *Institutes of Elenctic Theology*, 3 vols., trans. G. M. Giger, ed. J. T. Dennison Jr. (Phillipsburg, N.J.: P&R, 1992–97), 1:395.

soteriology. Where the Synod of Dort would have preachers make
a well-meant offer of the gospel indiscriminately, despite the fact
that not all hearers are elect, the Remonstrants resolved the paradox by saying that Christ died not only for the elect, but rather
"for all men and for every man" (*pro omnibus et singulis
hominibus*).[55] Now the gospel is not that Christ has accomplished
redemption, but that he has made it possible. They also revised
the doctrine of grace. The Remonstrants described the grace by
which men are able to actualize for themselves the salvation that
Christ has made possible as "prevenient," and "exciting," "assist-
ing," "awakening," that is, "cooperating."[56] This was not the mys-
teriously free and sovereign grace of Calvin or the orthodox; rather
this language was substantially Thomas's doctrine *de gratia co-
operans*.[57] In the Remonstrant scheme, the ground of justification,
as the ground of election, has moved to include our sanctity, that
is, our cooperation with grace. The sole instrument of justification was no longer a passive, receptive trust in Christ's active and
passive obedience, but rather our trusting and obeying. In the intellectualist Remonstrant construction, the gospel message changed
fundamentally, and with it the nature of the gospel offer. It was a
turn away from the Protestant theology of the cross (purely ectypal
theology) toward a rationalist and moralist message of human
cooperation with divine grace toward justification.

The Recovery of the Gospel and the Offer at Dort and After

Junius had taught in Heidelberg before the *"Relutheranisierung"*
of the Palatinate in 1576, and then in exile in the Casimirianum at
Neustadt am der Haardt until his restoration, with several other
Reformed theologians, to Heidelberg in 1584. For the last ten years
of his life he taught theology at the University of Leiden, where he
exercised considerable influence over the development of Dutch

55. Schaff, *Creeds*, 3:546.
56. Ibid., 3.547.
57. Thomas Aquinas, *Summa Theologiae*, 1a2ae 111.2

Reformed orthodoxy. By the time the Synod of Dort convened, Junius's distinction between archetypal and ectypal theology was twenty-eight years old. Polanus's well-known and highly regarded *Syntagma* was published nine years before the Synod. Thus, the delegates to the Synod were quite familiar with these distinctions and applied them in their response to the Remonstrant challenge. In its defense of the gospel and teaching on the well-meant offer, the Synod of Dort appealed not to the decree, God's hidden will, or *theologia archetypa*, but to *theologia ectypa*, that is, to God's revealed will and the outworking of the decree in history.

Against the Remonstrant intellectualism and denial of analogical theology, the Synod of Dort reasserted the doctrines of total depravity, divine sovereignty, and the well-meant offer of justification by grace alone, through faith alone, in Christ alone.[58] They taught that God, sovereignly and efficaciously, has decreed not only sovereignly and efficaciously to save the elect, not on the basis of "foreseen faith and the obedience of faith" (CD 1.9; RE 1.5), and to reprobate others, but also to use certain means to save those whom he has chosen in Christ from all eternity. In other words, they taught the foolishness of the well-meant offer of the gospel. Under the first head of doctrine the synod declared:

> And that men may be brought to believe, God mercifully sends the messengers of these most joyful (*laetissimi nunti*) tiding to whom He will and at what time He pleases; by whose ministry men are called to repentance and faith in Christ crucified. "How, then, can they call on the one they have not believed in? And how can they believe in the one of whom they have not heard? And how can they hear without someone preaching to them? And how can they preach unless they are sent?"[59]

It is significant that under the Second Head of Doctrine, when they addressed the question of definite atonement, the Synod did

58. CD 1.1; 3/4.3. Schaff, *Creeds*, 3.
59. CD 1.3; Schaff, *Creeds*, 3:552, 581.

not reason that since Christ died only for his elect we ought to preach only to the elect. Rather they said,

> Moreover, the promise of the gospel is that whoever believes (*credit*) in Christ crucified shall not perish, but have eternal life. This promise, together with the command to repent and believe, ought to be announced and propounded to all nations, and to all persons promiscuously (*promiscue*) and indiscriminately (*indiscriminatim*), to whom God by his good pleasure sends the gospel.[60]

We are to "announce and propound" (*annunciari et proponi*) to all nations the promise that "whoever believes in Christ shall not perish." The Synod defined the gospel very carefully. The gospel is not that one is elect, though the truth of the decree of election and reprobation was fundamental to their understanding of the accomplishment and application of redemption. Neither is the gospel that God will justify and save those who cooperate sufficiently with his grace. This is the very error the Synod was called to repudiate. Rather, the gospel is that whoever (*quisquis*) trusts in Christ's finished work shall be justified and saved.

The Synod began with the well-meant offer, and though it included properly the "command to repent and believe," it also established an attitude toward the lost. In view of the fact that the number and identity of the elect is a matter of archetypal theology, the divines used the notable adverbs "*promiscuously* and *indiscriminately.*" For the Synod, ectypal theology demanded that the gospel be preached as a full and free promise of salvation to all who trust the finished work of Christ for their justification and salvation.

The next article under the Second Head of Doctrine is less famous but equally important to this discussion:

> And, whereas many who are called through the gospel neither repent (*resipiscunt*) nor believe (*credunt*) in Christ, but

---

60. CD 2.5; Schaff, *Creeds*, 3:51, 586. I have slightly modified Schaff's translation.

perish in unbelief (*infidelitate*), this is not owing to any defect or insufficiency (*defectu vel insufficientia*) in the sacrifice offered by Christ upon the cross, but is to be blamed to themselves. (CD 2.6)

The Synod recognized that, in the providential outworking of the divine decree, not all would believe the promise because not all are elect. This did not stop them, however, from requiring the preaching of the promise. Notice too that the Synod did not turn to the decree to explain the rejection of the promise by the reprobate, even though the decree is the *sine qua non* of the entire argument. The Synod was pointed: the moral culpability of unbelievers is their own (*sed propria ipsorum culpa*).[61]

They were also quite clear about the relations between the promise and faith. "But as many as truly believe, and are delivered and saved from sin and destruction through the death of Christ, are indebted for this benefit solely to the grace of God given them in Christ from everlasting, and not to any merit of their own."[62] The promise is not that the gospel will be preached, but that as many as believe will be saved. At the same time, the Canons would have us always regard saving faith as nothing else than the free gift of God. It is God's will that the benefits of Christ's work should "extend to all the elect" for whom he has "an everlasting love."[63] The work, however, of regenerating the elect from the mixed visible congregation is God's, not ours. This was also their approach in 3/4.8:

> As many as are called by the gospel are called earnestly (*serio*). For God has most earnestly (*serio*) and truly declared in His Word what is acceptable to Him, namely, that those who are called should come unto Him. He also seriously promises rest of soul and eternal life to all who come to Him and believe.[64]

61. See also CD 3/4.9; Schaff, *Creeds*, 3:566, 589. I have slightly modified Schaff's translation.

62. CD 2.7; Schaff, *Creeds*, 3:564, 586–87.

63. CD 2.8; Schaff, *Creeds*, 3:565, 587.

64. Schaff, *Creeds*, 3.565–66, 589. I have slightly modified Schaff's translation.

Those who are called are called *"serio."* Those who are promised rest and eternal life are promised them *"serio,"* which is sometimes translated "seriously" or better, "earnestly" or "urgently." According to Dort, this is the sort of gospel offer required of us by God's Word because this is precisely how God himself speaks to us.[65]

Again, the Synod turned not to the decree, but to the revealed will of God, wherein we learn what is "acceptable" (*gratum*) to him. Following Heidelberg Catechism Q. 65, which taught that it is through the "preaching of the Holy Gospel" that God works saving faith in the hearts of sinners, the Synod also taught that Christ

> not only causes the gospel to be externally preached (*externe praedicari*) to them, and powerfully illuminates their minds by His Holy Spirit, that they may rightly understand and discern the things of the Spirit of God; but by the efficacy of the same regenerating Spirit He pervades the inmost recesses of man; He opens the closed and softens the hardened heart. . . .[66]

How God the Spirit so works "cannot be fully comprehended by believers in this life" (3/4.13), but it is nevertheless the case.

According to the Synod, nature and grace are not opposed. Grace does not destroy nature, but renews it. Though totally depraved and unable to save themselves or to will the good, sinful humans, even the reprobate, are to be regarded as God's image-bearers, since the sinner "did not cease to be a creature endowed with understanding and will" and because "this grace of regeneration does not treat men as senseless stocks and blocks" (*truncis et stipitibus*), nor does it "take away their will and its properties, or do violence thereto." Rather, God the Spirit, through the gospel, "spiritually quickens, heals, corrects, and at the same time sweetly and powerfully bends" the fallen human will of the elect.[67]

---

65. For the Protestant Reformed understanding of "serio," see H. Hanko, *For Thy Truth's Sake*, 88–89.

66. CD 3/4.11; Schaff, *Creeds*, 3:566, 590.

67. CD 3/4.16. See also 3/4.17; Schaff, *Creeds*, 3:568, 591–92.

Both Klaas Schilder (1890–1952) and Herman Hoeksema and more recently David Engelsma and Randy Blacketer have argued that when Dort and our theologians said *"offero"* they only meant "to present" or "to demand."[68] There is weighty evidence to the contrary, however. For example, Caspar Olevian (1536–87) used this term and its cognates frequently to mean "to offer with intention that the offer should be fulfilled if the recipients meet the condition of trust in Christ." In his massive 1579 commentary on Romans and in his final commentary on the Apostles' Creed, *De substantia foederis gratuiti inter Deum et electos* (1585), he used it frequently this way (e.g., *"oblatum beneficium"*), just as Dort later used it.[69] When our theologians wished to say "present" or "exhibit" or "demand," they had other verbs (e.g., *"exhibeo"* or *"mando"*) with which to do it. They did not need *"offero"* to perform the same function. Rather, when our theologians spoke of the *"evangelium oblatum,"* that is, "gospel offered" in preaching, they believed that it entailed a well and sincerely meant revealed divine intention that whoever believes should be saved. As we shall see below, the semantic range of *"offero,"* as it was used by the orthodox, is closer to "invitation" than "demand."

There are good reasons arising from the Canons of Dort themselves, however, to reject the proposed reinterpretation of *"offero."* In 2.6 the Canons describe Christ's sacrifice (*hostia*) as *"oblatae,"* "offered" on the cross. While "presented" is not utterly remote from the sense of the text, "demand" and "exhibit" make little sense here. The divines meant to say that Jesus gave himself

---

68. Herman Hoeksema, *The Clark-Van Til Controversy*, 33–38. See also R. Blacketer, "The Three Points in Most Parts Reformed: A Reexamination of the So-Called Well-Meant Offer of Salvation," *Calvin Theological Journal* 35 (2000), 37–65. Olevian's usage was not unique. Blacketer errs, in part, by using a modern dictionary of classical Latin to determine the meaning of the word. The meaning of *offero* must be determined by its immediate context and its actual use in Reformed theology. Blacketer's essay fails to account for the distinction between archetypal and ectypal theology, which is fundamental to this entire discussion. Schilder also defined "offer" to mean "to present" or "to demand." See also A. C. DeJong, *The Well-Meant Offer*, 56–58.

69. See *In epistolam . . . ad Romanos* notae (Geneva: 1579), 6, 475; De *substantia foederis gratuiti inter Deum et electos* (Geneva, 1585), 2:29; 2:30–31; 2.48.

and his obedience as a sacrifice for us to the justice of God, in
such a way that it was righteously received by God as payment
for the sins of all believers, that is, the elect. This is how the Vul-
gate and Theodore Beza's Latin translations of Hebrews 10:18
used the cognate *oblatio* (for the Greek *prosphora*).[70]

In the Rejection of Errors under the Second Head of Doctrine (RE 2.6), the Canons attacked vigorously the Remonstrant
abuse of the distinction between "meriting" and "appropriating"
Christ's benefits (*beneficia*), that is, justification and sanctification, such that God is said to have made them available to all on
condition that sinners exercise their free will (*libero arbitrio*). In
this construal, Christ's benefits depend not on the "singular gift
of mercy" (*singulari misericordiae dono*) but on our cooperation
with divine grace. The orthodox divines rejected the Remonstrant
view as a contradiction of the gospel.[71] Thus, by connecting the
Remonstrant doctrine of "free will" to the "grace freely offered"
(*gratiam indifferenter oblatam applicante*), the divines were endors-
ing the notion that in the preaching of the gospel grace is offered
freely, while simultaneously repudiating the notion that the well-
meant offer implies or should become an occasion for "the per-
nicious poison of Pelagianism" (*"perniciosum Pelagianismi
venenum"*).[72] The well-meant offer of grace was not to be interpreted by the Remonstrants to imply that justification is contingent (*pendere*) upon a Remonstrant form of congruent merit (*faci-
entibus quod in se est, Deus non denegat gratiam*).

In the Third and Fourth Heads of Doctrine (3/4.9), the divines
took virtually the same approach as in 2.6. When, in the providence of God, many are outwardly called (*vocati*) through the
(well-meant offer of the) gospel, and they do not come or are not
converted, the blame rests not *"in Christo,"* in the *"Evangelium
oblato"* (the offered gospel), nor in "God calling through the

70. *Biblia Sacra Iuxta Vulgatam Versionem*, ed. R. Weber et al. (Beuron and Tübingen:
Deutsche Bibelgesellschaft, 1983); *Novum testamentum domini nostri Jesu Christi*, ed.
Theodore Beza (reprint, London: 1834).
    71. Schaff, *Creeds*, 3.563–64.
    72. Ibid.

Gospel." Having ordained the means of grace, God is free to confer faith or not through the external gospel call. The moral culpability for unbelief lies in those who "carelessly do not receive the Word of life" (*verbum vitae non admittunt securi*).[73] "Therefore," Dort says, justifying faith is the "*Dei donum*," not because "it is offered by God to man's free will," (*a Deo hominis arbitrio offeratur*), but because faith is "conferred" (*conferatur*), "inspired" (*inspiretur*), and "infused" (*infundatur*).[74]

The divines were not saying that the gospel is not freely and sincerely offered in the preaching of the Word. Rather, the divines were complaining about Remonstrant rationalism, that is, the illegitimate inference that, since the gospel is offered freely, sinners therefore have a free will and the ability to will contrary to God. In fact, the next point presupposes the existence of the well-meant offer, since the article distinguishes between the external administration and call of the gospel offered seriously and freely and the internal application of Christ's benefits by the Holy Spirit wrought through and in conjunction with the external gospel preaching. This is why the divines used a series of passive verbs. Justifying faith is not the product of the human will, but of sovereign divine operation upon and within humans.

This was the typical Reformed way of distinguishing between the external, well-meant offer of the gospel and the internal, efficacious work of the Spirit through it. Because the success of the external or common call is contingent upon the divine decree and application of redemption, and not on the preacher's rhetorical skill or the hearer's free will, the preacher is free to offer grace to all who will receive it, knowing that it is, as the Canons remind us, God who "produces both the will to believe" (*velle credere*) and "the act of believing" (*actum credendi*).[75]

In the interests of space, we can only compare the language and approach of Dort to the teaching of a few post-Dort documents. First, in the *Synopsis purioris theologiae* (Leiden, 1625), a

73. Ibid., 3.566.
74. CD 3/4.14; Schaff, *Creeds*, 3:567.
75. Schaff, *Creeds*, 3:567.

compilation of school disputations by Johannes Polyander (1568–1646), Andreas Rivet (1572–1651), Antonius Walaeus (1573–1639), and Antonius Thysius (1603–65), of whom only Rivet was not delegated to the Synod, we find the archetypal/ectypal distinction taught (in *Disputatio I, De sacrosancta theologia*) and from it a corollary, the internal/exernal distinction in the *ordo salutis*.[76] Under *Disputatio XXX, De hominum vocatione ad salutem*, in Article 21, the *Synopsis* taught that through the "preaching of the Gospel" (an external operation performed according to ectypal theology) the "good" (*bonum*) of salvation (Art. 20) is "offered" (*offertur*), and the Holy Spirit "kindles" (*accendit*) "genuine knowledge" (*serias cogitationes*) and "pious desire" (*pium desiderium*) in our hearts.[77] Not surprisingly, the language of the *Leiden Synopsis* was virtually identical to that of Dort.

Johannes Wollebius (1586–1629), in his *Compendium theologiae Christianae* (1626), under the heading *De foedere gratiae*, distinguished between the covenant of grace, which is *"post lapsum,"* and the covenant of works that was initiated with our "first parents" (*primis nostris parentiubus*). He distinguished between the covenant of grace considered externally and internally. By analogy, there is both an "offering" (*oblatio*) and "sealing" (*obsignatio*) of the covenant of grace. The offer comes to all externally, but the sealing comes only to the elect who actually receive the benefits of the covenant.[78] The external or "common call" (*communis vocatio*) is that by which all are "invited" (*invitantur*) to "a state of grace or participation of Christ the Mediator."[79] His proof that the external call was an invitation was Matthew 22:2–3. According to Wollebius, the well-meant offer is addressed neither to all nor only to the elect, but to people of every sort.[80] The form of the call is an "offer of the benefits of redemption" (*beneficii redemptionis*).[81] The substance

76. *Synopsis purioris theologiae*, ed. H. Bavinck (Leiden: D. Donner, 1881), 2–3, 294–300.
77. Ibid., 296.
78. Wollebius, *Compendium*, 92.
79. ". . . qua ad statum gratiae seu participationem Christi Mediatoris . . ." (Wollebius, *Compendium*, 90).
80. Ibid., 91.
81. Ibid.

of the offer is that "God promises by himself to be a Father, in Christ, if we will fulfill filial obedience."[82] The "end" (*finis*) of this "offered covenant," that is, "the common call, is the glory of God and the salvation of the elect."[83] The covenant is "offered" (*offertur*) to all, but only the elect "profit" from the promises of the covenant.[84] Therefore, the external call comes "earnestly" (*serio*) to both the elect and the reprobate.[85] That one is called by the preaching of the gospel does not make one elect, because this call is common to elect and reprobates, on the condition of faith (*sub conditione fidei*).[86]

In the high orthodox period, Herman Witsius (1636–1708) and Peter van Mastricht (1630–1706) used the same categories and language about the relations between the external "common call," and the efficacious call by the Holy Spirit of the elect through it.[87] In the latter's *Theoretico-practica theologia* (1699), in his chapter on "The Love, Grace, Mercy, Longsuffering and Clemency of God," van Mastricht wrote at length about God's "universal benevolence and beneficence" toward creatures.[88] In his chapter on calling, he defended the sincerity and genuineness of the well-meant offer of the gospel. He made the invitation to trust in Christ of the essence of the call.[89] From this brief survey of the Canons and just

82. "Oblatio foederis gratiae est, qua Deus vocatis promittit se ipsis in Christo Patrem fore, si filialem praestiterint oboedientiam" (Wollebius, *Compendium*, 92).

83. "Finis oblatio foederis idem est, qui vocationis communis, Dei gloria et electorum salus" (Wollebius, *Compendium*, 93).

84. Ibid., 93.

85. Wollebius, *Compendium*, 91.

86. Ibid., 92.

87. See H. Witsius, *Economy of the Covenants Between God and Man: Comprehending a Complete Body of Divinity*, 2 vols., trans. W. Crookshank (Phillipsburg, N.J.: Presbyterian and Reformed, 1990), 1:350–56.

88. P. van Mastricht, *Theoretico-Practica Theologia*, editio nova (Utrecht, 1699). Synod Kalamazoo, under the first point, appealed to Van Mastricht to support the doctrine of the free offer of the gospel. See Van Til, *Common Grace*, 20. The quotation is cited as "First Part, page 439." Presumably "First Part" refers to the doctrinal section of the work. If so, the citation is not correct, for Van Mastricht was discussing the two natures of Christ on p. 439. The citations that follow give the book, chapter, and section. See also the related discussion in Kuiper, *Calvin on Common Grace*, "Appendix," i–xv. See also *Theoretico-Practica Theologia*, 2.17.3, 22.

89. P. van Mastricht, *Theoretico-Practica Theologia*, 2.6.5–6.649.

a few classic Reformed theologians, it appears that Synod Kalamazoo was right to say that, in substance, if not in absolute verbal identity, well-meant offer was the teaching of the "writers of
the flowering period of Reformed theology" (*schrijvers uit de
bloeitijd der Gereformeerde Theologie*).[90]

According to Dort and both early orthodox theologians such
as Olevianus and early Reformed dogmatic theologies such as the
Synopsis purioris and the high orthodox theologian Peter van Mastricht, the *praxis* of the free and sincere offer of the gospel is not
controlled by our knowledge of archetypal theology (e.g., the
decree), but by *theologia ectypa*. In this regard, the approach of
the Synod of Dort is in contrast to that of both the Remonstrants
and the modern critics of the well-meant offer. Rather than making deductions from the revealed fact of God's sovereign eternal
decree, the Synod was committed to learning and obeying God's
revealed will, even if it seems paradoxical to us.

Conclusions: The Free Offer and Westminster Theology

In 1948 John Murray offered a highly detailed exegesis of a
number of biblical passages. Since that time, however, the critics
of the well-meant offer have not often engaged that exegesis because
they reject the hermeneutical assumptions that shaped Murray's
reading of the key texts in the debate. It would appear that, like the
Remonstrants, the critics of the well-meant offer have misunderstood, rejected, or ignored this distinction and its implications for
the nature of divine-human relations, biblical revelation, and theological method. This much would seem to be clear from the fact
that, during the controversy, the archetypal/ectypal distinction was
never formally discussed as a Reformed theological category or
proposed as a way to resolve the issue and from Hoeksema's char-
acterization of the well-meant offer as schizophrenic.

Given the archetypal/ectypal distinction, however, the free
or well-meant offer does not contradict absolute predestination,

90. *Acta*, 146.

but rather necessarily presupposes its truth. Here the adjective *free* is of paramount importance. If the promiscuous and indiscriminate offer of the gospel really were a sort of crypto-Arminianism, of course the gospel offer would no longer be free. As Reformed theology understands the nature of grace, however, if the offer of the gospel were ultimately conditioned upon the *ability* of sinners to respond, then, to quote Paul, "grace would no longer be grace" (Rom. 11:6). The well-meant offer is part of the divinely ordained administration of his decree(s) of predestination and reprobation. The fact of the decree is presupposed in and animates the well-meant offer, but since its contents are archetypal, we are shut up to ectypal theology of which the well-meant offer is correlative.

It is also apparent that, in rejecting this implicit correlation, the modern critics of the well-meant offer find themselves using the same theological method as the Remonstrants, which they repudiate so strongly: in place of the Reformed analogical scheme, they posit an intellectualism that is hard to distinguish from that of Arminius. The irony of this situation is acute. For its entire history, Reformed orthodoxy has been accused of beginning with a rationalist *a priori*, (i.e., a theory of absolute double predestination), which either ignored Christ or made him merely the means to an end. The Reformed orthodox have been accused repeatedly of more or less inventing Christ-less doctrines out of whole cloth. This charge has been shown by modern historical theology to be patently false when applied to the mainstream of historic Reformed theology.[91] In their rejection of the archetypal/ectypal distinction, however, Herman Hoeksema and Gordon Clark came close to fulfilling at least some of the caricature.

Against Herman Hoeksema and Gordon Clark, however, if the archetypal/ectypal distinction represents the mainstream of

---

91. See Richard Muller, *Christ and the Decree: Christology and Predestination in Reformed Theology from Calvin to Perkins* (Grand Rapids: Baker, 1986). See also C. R. Trueman and R. S. Clark, ed., *Protestant Scholasticism: Essays in Reassessment* (Carlisle, U.K.: Paternoster, 1999); W. van Asselt and E. Dekker, eds., *Reformation and Scholasticism: An Ecumenical Enterprise* (Grand Rapids: Baker, 2001).

Reformed theological method, and if its corollary is the doctrine of the well-meant offer as articulated by Dort, Reformed orthodoxy, and later by Synod Kalamazoo, John Murray, and Bob Strimple, then it is not the well-meant offer of the gospel that is a concession to Arminianism, but rather the opposite is true. Those who have rejected the basic premise that our theology is categorically different from and only analogical to God's and that any revealed theology is what Johannes Markius (1656–1713) called *"analogica communicata"* of the archetype have, like Arminius, posited a direct point of contact between divine intellect and ours.[92]

The classical Reformed view has been that, because of the natural disparity between God and humans, all revelation is necessarily accommodated. It is not as if we sometimes have direct, unmediated access to God and at other times we do not. This is precisely Jesus's argument when he said, "Not that any man has seen the Father, except the One who is from God; he has seen the Father" (John 6:46). Jesus Christ is nothing less than the incarnate self-disclosure of God (John 1:1–3). According to Scripture, because of the nature of divine-human relations, God's Word must necessarily "come down" to us (Eph. 4:9; John 6:51). Accommodation is constitutive of divine-human relations for the simple fact that unaccommodated revelation (*Deus in se*) would necessarily be fatal to its human objects, since no human may see the unmediated face of God and live (Exod. 34:20).

The classical Reformed theologians described reading Scripture in this way is as *pilgrim* theology (*theologia viatorum*), which is a sub-species of ectypal theology. Following the tradition, Murray, Van Til, and Strimple understood that God is also free to reveal himself as desiring certain things that he also reveals that he has not willed decretively. Murray's essay begins by saying, "The real point in dispute in connection with the well-meant offer of the gospel is whether it can properly be said

92. Johannes Marckius, *Compendium theologiae Christianae didactico-elencticum* (Amsterdam, 1690), 4.9, cited in H. Heppe, *Die Dogmatik der Evangelisch-Reformirten Kirche* (Elberfeld, 1861), 43.

that God desires the salvation of all men."[93] As he explained, in speaking this way, he was working within the confines of the distinction between God's revealed or preceptive will and his hidden or decretive will (Deut. 29:29).[94] So the proponents of the well-meant offer have spoken analogically, equivocally, and even metaphorically about God's attitude toward and will for sinners.[95] They were not saying that God decretively wills to save and reprobate the same people. God does not have two wills, *per se*, but given the archetypal/ectypal distinction, there is a distinction to be made in our understanding of and speech about his will.[96] This is the same approach followed in the Reformed discussion of the divine attributes. Considering God *in se*, there is no distinction between his attributes. Because of our finitude, however, we must make some logical distinctions among them in order to discuss them.

Recognizing divine accommodation is not skepticism, but rather it is submission to divine revelation as it comes to us. To affirm the reality behind accommodated language we need only know that such a reality exists.[97] We do not need and cannot have immediate contact with God *in se* to validate the biblical revelation. Therefore, the distance between God's theology and ours, the analogical nature of our theology relative to God's, necessarily creates tension in all our speech about God. This is evident in Murray's discussion of the difficulty of describing

93. *Minutes of the Fifteenth General Assembly*, Appendix, 51.

94. See Engelsma, *Hyper-Calvinism*, 118, where, after attacking the well-meant offer as Arminianism, he comes close to conceding this point. See also Turretin, *Institutes*, 1:415–16; Herman Bavinck, *Our Reasonable Faith*, trans. H. Zylstra (Grand Rapids: 1956), 415–16.

95. C. Van Til, *Common Grace and the Gospel* (Nutley, N.J.: Presbyterian and Reformed, 1977), 37.

96. Cf. Engelsma, *Hyper-Calvinism*, 31. See Turretin, *Institutes*, 1:412; J. H. Thornwell, *The Collected Writings of John Henley Thornwell*, 4 vols. (Edinburgh: Banner of Truth, 1979), 2:164; Berkhof, *Systematic Theology*, 397.

97. This was J. H. Thornwell's argument. See Sheppard, "Compatibility," 121–23. See also Robert L. Dabney, *Lectures in Systematic Theology* (reprint, Grand Rapids: Zondervan, 1975), 554–59; idem, "God's Indiscriminate Proposals of Mercy," *Princeton Review* 54 (July-December 1878): 33–66.

accurately God's attitude toward human beings in the well-meant offer:

> There is expressed not simply the bare preceptive will of God but the disposition of lovingkindness on the part of God pointing to the salvation to be gained through compliance with the overtures of gospel grace. In other words, the gospel is not simply an offer or invitation but also implies that God delights that those to whom the offer comes would enjoy what is offered in all its fullness.[98]

Even more pointedly, Murray explained that we are not to think of a mere " 'seeming' disposition of God," but a "real attitude, a real disposition of lovingkindness inherent in the well-meant offer to all."[99] In view of the archetypal/ectypal distinction, this way of speaking is not only permissible, but also necessary. As Van Til said in 1947, "We are entitled and compelled to use anthropomorphism not apologetically but fearlessly. We need not fear to say that God's attitude has changed with respect to mankind. We know well enough that God in himself is changeless. But we know that we are able to affirm that our words have meaning for no other reason than that we use them analogically."[100] In short, the warrant of our speech to sinners is God's speech to us.

With his commitment to careful exegesis of the biblical text, as seen in his 1979 essay, "Philippians 2:5–11 in Recent Studies: Some Exegetical Conclusions," Bob Strimple demonstrated a theological method that applied the archetypal/ectypal distinction.[101] Abandoning himself to the biblical text, he is able

98. *Minutes of the Fifteenth General Assembly*, Appendix, 52.

99. Ibid.

100. Van Til, *Common Grace*, 73. See also B. B. Warfield, *The Person and Work of Christ* (Philadelphia: Presbyterian and Reformed, 1950), 569–71.

100. Van Til, *Common Grace*, 73. See also B. B. Warfield, *The Person and Work of Christ* (Philadelphia: Presbyterian and Reformed, 1950), 569–71.

101. Robert B. Strimple, "Philippians 2:5–11 in Recent Studies: Some Exegetical Conclusions," *Westminster Theological Journal* 41 (1979): 247–68.

to say that Christ has "poured himself out" (*ekenōsen*), taking the way of the cross, humiliation, and shame, that is, the highest example of the *theologia crucis* as God's accommodation to us. It is this Suffering Servant whom we freely, sincerely, and indiscriminately offer, knowing that our proclamation of the gospel is in obedience to God's revealed will, and part of the administration of Christ's hidden eternal decree.

8

Speech and the Image of God: Biblical Reflections on Language and Its Uses

Richard B. Gaffin Jr.

Reformed theology, specifically systematic theology at Westminster Seminary with the distinctive cast given to it by John Murray and ably maintained by the honoree of this volume, Robert B. Strimple, is radically nonspeculative. This is so in the sense that, as the presentation under appropriate topics (*loci*) of the unified teaching of the Bible as a whole, its very existence depends upon sound biblical interpretation. Since systematic theology is a statement overall of what "is either expressly set down in Scripture, or by good and necessary consequence may be deduced from Scripture" (Westminster Confession of Faith, 1.6), exegesis is its lifeblood.

Plainly, then, systematic theology has a hermeneutical concern. No less than Old and New Testament studies, though perhaps not so explicitly, it ought to be alert to issues of exegetical method as well as the wide range of principles and procedures that inform sound interpretation. Put most elementally, systematic theology, along with the other theological disciplines, has a vital interest in *language*, in the language of the Bible and how it functions as well as in our own language and its usage. Something of theology's fundamental stake in language will occupy us in this chapter.

Language, linguistic reality, is exceedingly diverse and complicated and thus is capable of being explored and reflected upon in a multiplicity of ways. In what follows here, however, I will not undertake to scrutinize this or that specific aspect of language in appropriate scholarly depth. Instead, I intend something less ambitious, what may be viewed as a theological meditation on Scripture pertinent to language and its use. I offer these reflections not because they are particularly new or insightful, but rather as reminders, reminders that are perhaps needed all the more in the heightened hermeneutical times that have overtaken theology over the past half century or so, including, increasingly, evangelical and Reformed theology. I see them as biblical baselines, first principles worth highlighting because while for the most part they are obvious, just for that reason they may be looked past or even brushed aside in wrestling with admittedly difficult and complex issues of interpretation.

Language and the Divine Image

I begin by highlighting two passages. Juxtaposing them, along with several other related passages, will bring into view a state of affairs, in fact, a basic dilemma, about which we need to remain aware in assessing the functioning of language, broadly considered to include all media of communication. With that dilemma confronting us, we will then consider some basic dimensions of its resolution.

Psalm 94:9–10 poses several questions. Among them, the psalmist asks: "Does he who implanted the ear not hear? / Does he who formed the eye not see?" (v. 9). These questions are plainly rhetorical and, within the broader framework of biblical teaching, highlight that capacities in human beings, like hearing and seeing,[1] do not merely derive from God but are reflective of his own divine capacities.

Surely, then, by extension and in the same vein, we are to ask: "Does he who shaped the tongue not speak?" Here we are pointed to recognize this overall state of affairs: As our being itself is derived from God (we exist because he exists), and as our knowledge is an analogue of his knowledge (we know because he knows), so, too, our capacity for language and other forms of communication is derivative of his. We speak because God speaks, because he is a speaking God; that is his nature and so, derivatively, it is ours. In other words, man[2] in his linguistic functions, as in all he is and does, is to be understood as the creature who is the image and likeness of God (Gen. 1:26). In fact, should we not say that especially in his language man reflects the divine image he is?

I must resist attempting here to explicate in any depth the meaning of the *imago Dei* in Scripture, what it is that constitutes man, male and female, as the divine image. As the reader may be aware, that would involve us in a theological debate with a long and sometimes complicated history. Suffice it here to indicate briefly my own view, already intimated, and as it will come out along the way. Locating the image in a part or aspect of man, for example, the soul or one or more distinctively human functions, is problematic. Rather, the whole person, in full, body-and-soul integrity, is the image of God.

So, again, God in the person of his Son is originally and from all eternity *the* Word (John 1:1). He is ever Word, and so we, created as we are as his image-bearers, are, specifically, *Word*-bearers, and we are that essentially, inveterately, irremediably. We cannot help ourselves. We are born communicators, not just some of us,

1. Understanding and the power to judge are in view in the other parallel questions asked here ("Does he who disciplines nations not punish? Does he who teaches man lack knowledge?").

2. I use this generic singular advisedly, because it is particularly important here to be able to speak clearly and pointedly and not to lose sight of or otherwise obscure humanity, in all of its individuations, in its unique and specific unity.

but, apart from grievous, deeply abnormal exceptions, all human beings are communicators. Admittedly, some of us are that more gracefully and effectively than others, but that is not our concern just now. We are created for speech, for communication—in all of its attendant verbal, iconic, and graphic forms, whatever the medium.

As image-bearers we are, as such and in turn, image-fashioners and image-molders. In a broadened sense, that is really what we are all about as human beings. Or, as we may put it, as God's image-bearers, in our specific and absolute dependence on him as our Creator, we are made to be addressed and, in turn, to address, to see and to respond, to hear and to reply. This is so above all in our relationship to him, who is our pattern and original, and, out of that relationship, in our relationships with others, other likeness-bearers and image-shapers.

In terms of the fundamental biblical category of the covenant, which structures our image-bearing existence with God-given promises and commands, blessings and tasks—in covenant with God, we are created for communication, both with him as well as with others. That is at the heart both of our identity and our destiny. This radical "addressability," our covenantal identity as God's image-bearers, is utterly decisive for who we are and what is to become of us, for the protology as well as the eschatology that qualifies our ontology.

But now there is James 3:9–10 to consider, which also tells us of the tongue: "With the tongue we praise our Lord and Father, and with it we curse men, who have been made in God's likeness. Out of the same mouth come praise and cursing." Here we are confronted with a deeply troubling state of affairs, something gone terribly wrong: image-bearers cursing other image-bearers, and coupled, we are surely to infer, with praise of God that is anything but, praise so lacking in integrity that it in fact dishonors him. Here we are made to face up to an inescapable, undeniable reality: sin, human sin, our sin, and, specifically, sin's destructive impact on our speech, its subversion of language, its deep disruption of all our imaging-capacities, of our ability to communicate.

Further, we must not miss how in the immediate context, James, in part, pictures this situation. Though in itself small, "the tongue," he says, "is a fire" (v. 6); "consider what a great forest is set on fire by a small spark" (v. 5); within human beings, the tongue is "a world of evil" that "corrupts the whole person" (v. 6); as a "restless evil, full of deadly poison" (v. 8) it "sets the whole course of life on fire, and is itself set on fire by hell" (v. 6, my trans.).

This is strong language . . . about human language. The conflagration of communication that James sketches so severely is one of communication processes gone awry, perverted and in confusion, become harmful and destructive, because they are more than just tinged with hell-fire. We dare not shy away from such a depiction, for it does not take great imaging ability or much power of imagination to recognize here the malevolent potential of our own time, with its undeniably marvelous technologies, the potential for nothing less than media mayhem, a mayhem of mega proportions.

To the same effect are Paul's searching words in Romans 1. There, beginning at verse 18, he is intent on documenting the totality and universality of human sin, that all, without exception, are sinners, and that they are that pervasively. In clinching that indictment he writes (v. 21), "For although they knew God, they neither glorified him as God nor gave thanks to him." Here we have it; this is at the root of the sinful confusion, linguistic and otherwise, that permeates the entire creation. Where our language no longer functions for praising God, where the human tongue, with all the potential it evokes, has ceased to be an instrument for thanks, for thanking *him*—God—the results are calamitous.

The verses immediately following detail just some of the disastrous consequences of this creaturely, image-bearing and image-forming, ingratitude. Among them are "foolish, darkened hearts," "futile imaginings," which give rise to "exchang[ing] the glory of the immortal God" (v. 23) for images fashioned in the likeness of mortal man and other created beings, an exchange that unleashes in the human community the degradation that Paul goes on to document so unsparingly. All told, he says (v. 25), with their image-bearing capacities, human beings have "exchanged the truth of God for a lie," and that is the lie, preeminently, about who God is and who they are. With that fatal exchange, left to ourselves, we worship and serve, not our Creator, but one or another object or capacity in his creation, no longer properly acknowledged as his creation.

Because we are, each of us, the image of God, we will worship, in fact we must worship, someone or something, either our original, as we should, or, with the illusion that we are that original or our own ultimate point of reference, ourselves. If the latter, we will give ourselves over, with the full, still efficient resources of our imaging capacities, to some figment, some distorted image, focused on ourselves or on some aspect of the world, ultimately seen as an extension of ourselves. What Calvin observed long ago is no less true today: the human heart, our image-bearing and image-fashioning nature, is an idol factory.[3]

A couple of persisting misconceptions need challenging in this regard. The Fall, human sin, does not result in the complete loss of the divine image, but rather its radical distortion, its thorough defacement. Nor, alternatively, should we think that our continuing to bear or to be the image of God ameliorates or somehow offsets our sinfulness, as if here, in and of ourselves, is some remnant, a small spark that provides hope for us.

The divine image in us is not our "better self" (if only that were the case). Rather, we must recognize that being God's image reveals the true magnitude of our sinfulness. That image, however exactly it is to be defined, makes human sin, *human* sin. Quoting John Murray: "The higher is our conception of man in his intrinsic essence, the greater must be the gravity of his offense in rebellion and enmity against God. . . . Man conceived of as in the image of God, so far from toning down the doctrine of total depravity, points rather to its gravity, intensity, and irreversibility." "It may seem paradoxical, but the higher our view of man's

---

3. J. Calvin, *Institutes of the Christian Religion*, trans. F. L. Battles, ed. J. T. McNeill (The Library of Christian Classics, 20; Philadelphia: Westminster, 1960), 1:108 [1:11:8]: ". . . a perpetual factory of idols."

nature, the more aggravated becomes the depravity that characterizes man as fallen."[4]

Christ and the Consummation of Language

Juxtaposing Scripture as we have serves to highlight something of the full dimensions of our dilemma: our capacities as
God's image-bearers, granted to us for the high privilege of his
worship and service and for the good of the human community,
have been turned against him and others. The human tongue—
with all the media possibilities it symbolizes, with the varied
means of communication it embodies—has become an instrument of distortion, of perversion and degradation, of destruction.
The gift of the tongue, this God-given gift, is a gift that has been
prostituted—massively, thoroughly.

Should I have not yet made myself clear, I am not here simply pointing an accusing finger at others, at the glaring instances
all too readily and pervasively available currently in movies and
television, music and print media—something it is probably safe
enough to do with most readers of this chapter. Rather, this is *our*
prostitution, too, a prostitution in which, in and of ourselves,
every one us is implicated, to a greater or lesser degree, in one
way or another. Here, too, all of us "fall short of the glory of God"
(Rom. 3:23). The tongue, what ought to be our glory, is our shame,
and that is our desperate dilemma.

If all this were the final word about it, our situation, including prospects for communication, would in fact be hopeless. But
it is not the last word. There is still one word to consider, and that,
of course, is *the* Word, the Word who was in the beginning with
God and who was God, and who as such became flesh and lived
among us (John 1:1, 14). The eternal Word has become the *gospel*
Word and that is good news, perennial, for all times. He is the full
flesh-and-blood embodiment of good news. In his death and res-

---

4. *The Collected Writings of John Murray*, 4 vols. (Edinburgh: Banner of Truth, 1977):
2:38–39, 45–46.

urrection he has been glorified, to remove our culpability and restore our forfeited glory. He, Jesus Christ, is of the truth; he is the truth incarnate because he is God-incarnate. He embodies the truth; he images truth, uniquely and without peer, because he, at last, eschatologically, is the true image of God (Col. 1:15).

Here, finally, is a tongue, the Gospel writers tell us, that speaks "words of grace" (Luke 4:22, my trans.), "words of eternal life" (John 6:68), and, in that declaration that is so compelling, he claims for his disciples, "You are already clean because of the *word* I have spoken to you" (John 15:3). Finally, there is a word that meets our deepest and most desperate need, our need to be clean from our sin and all of its debilitating consequences, a word with power to cleanse, with a detergency strong enough to restore the image we bear to its full luster, and so, to strip away the impurities that pollute our communication at every level and in every form.

"God has in these last days spoken . . . in his Son" (Heb. 1:1–2, my trans.). Just as he, the Son, is this final, climactic speech, the nothing-less-than-eschatological speaking of God, he is, the writer goes on to say, "the radiance of God's glory and the exact representation of his being" (v. 3), the perfect imprint, the precise replica of God's very own being. He is, as Paul says, "the image of the invisible God" (Col. 1:15). Word and image together have their ultimate point of reference in Christ, however we are to expand on what that means.

And he is this, Word and image incarnate, it bears repeating, not merely for his own sake or for aspirations he has in isolation. Rather, God's purpose is that there be others who might be "conformed to the likeness of his Son, that he might be the firstborn among many brothers" (Rom. 8:29). In view here is a brotherhood, a family, where, with all the differences among them, each bears a common likeness, a quite striking resemblance; as bearers of the true image they are now imagers of the truth. Even now, what could otherwise never have been expected or even hoped for is in fact underway: reclamation of the divine image disfigured and debased in humanity, the removal of our shame and the restoration of our lost glory. Even now, believers "beholding as in a mirror the *glory* of the Lord [Christ] are being transformed into the *same* image from glory to glory" (2 Cor. 3:18, my trans.). Our shame, our image-bearing shame, is being replaced with his glory, our being conformed to his glory-image.

Among the components indicative of this renovated and reconstituted divine image, Paul singles out three in Ephesians 4:24 and Colossian 3:10: knowledge (understood as truth), righteousness, and holiness. What is striking, particularly in the context of our concerns, is how Paul goes on in the Ephesians 4 passage to expand on these qualities of the restored image. Moreover, it is surely not just coincidental that in the verses immediately following concerns about speech and communication are quite prominent. "Therefore [that is, because he is addressing those who have put on the new man in Christ and so bear the renewed image, v. 24] each of you must put off falsehood and speak the truth to his neighbor" (v. 25).

Of a number of angles that could be considered, it bears emphasizing, in the face of tendencies to the contrary, that we must not limit this exhortation to its merely private and personal dimensions. If it be pointed out that the corporate, communal context that Paul has in view is the church, will anyone want seriously to question that for him and the other New Testament writers what is true, in this respect, for the life of the church sets a standard for what ought also to be true in the world as well, individually and communally, publicly as well as privately? "Put off falsehood and speak the truth to [your] neighbor." It would be difficult to find a better wall plaque for a newsroom or motto for a magazine staff office, as well as for our homes and studies.

Then there is verse 29: "Do not let any unwholesome talk come out of your mouths, but only what is helpful for building others up according to their needs, that it may benefit those who listen"; and verse 31: "Get rid of all bitterness, rage and anger, brawling and slander, along with every form of malice." This may not say everything, but is there a more constructive guideline than this, say, for a television anchorperson as well as the members of a family with one another?

Here new prospects open up for communication, for imaging the truth, for truthful imaging and representation by image-bearers renewed according to the truth "as [it] is in Jesus" (v. 21, my trans.). These new, even unprecedented possibilities, we should also note, include controls, controls that will prove effective because, by the renewing power of the Spirit (see 5:18), they are ultimately uncoerced. Such possibilities culminate, at least in the framework of this passage, in the challenge of verse 32: "Be kind and compassionate to one another."

Some will dismiss all this out of hand as hopelessly simplistic, as impossible idealism, if not sentimentality, as inept and inadequate for the hardcore realism that is appropriate, even mandatory for communication in our times, certainly for the news media but for other communication as well. To them the response must suffice here that only those who look at life with the attitude of "forgiving each other, just as in Christ God forgave you"—for that is the grounding Paul provides here—only they, forgiven sinners, who themselves forgive, will grasp that this call to "be kind and compassionate to one another" breathes an air of realism, of resolute and, in fact, searching, unrelenting realism, realism that will spare nothing in uncovering and addressing sin and its myriad consequences. In prospect here is a truly kinder, gentler media far removed from a half-hearted, plaintive "Can't we all just get along?"

It is striking and sobering to contemplate that in a time of unprecedented advance and breakthroughs in communication technologies, we are likewise witnessing unprecedented breakdowns in communication itself. There is a growing lack of consensus not simply about how these technologies are to be used, but about what communication itself is for. Pessimism about the possibility of genuine communication, that our words have any meaning at all, continues to mount, a pessimism that in some has yielded to cynicism. I think, for example, of the already, in many respects, passe postmodern posturing of some that openly revels in the ultimate relativity of words and frankly celebrates language as a manipulative, self-serving tool, as an instrument of power for securing "my" interests and those of "our group," interests with no more ultimate justification than that they are self-asserted and self-satisfying. And, too often, justified protest against this exploitative use of language can rise no higher than some form of counterexploitation, producing a vicious cycle, without any real prospect of it being broken.

Ours, it is fair to say, is a "hyperhermeneutical" age. Most readers do not need to be reminded how in recent decades issues of interpretation have burgeoned in an overwhelming, almost unbelievable fashion and taken on unprecedented dimensions. Projects for construing texts have become paradigms for constructing, or deconstructing, reality as a whole. But the net result of this intensive expenditure of hermeneutical energy is a crisis in hermeneutics, an increasing hermeneutical despair.

I do not for a moment want to deny or even ignore the genuine problems, the real difficulties that come into view here, like the kinds of issues that sometimes confront even the biblical interpretation on which the vitality of systematic theology depends. But it is crucial to recognize what, as much as anything, is at the root of our contemporary hermeneutical malaise. That is the illusion that human language and all our other imaging capacities are self-generated and self-evolving.

Thus, we must be insistent that human language is not ultimately a human invention, but God's gift, a gift reflective of his own capacities as the Giver. That recognition engenders confidence, a confidence that needs to be focused negatively as well as positively. Our language is not innately ambiguous. Human language does not inherently veil and confuse as it seeks to communicate and disclose meaning. It does not inevitably create a distortion of the subject matter about which it speaks. Human language is not an intrinsically inadequate medium for communicating, for conveying meaning. Certainly our language, as we have seen, can confuse, veil, and distort. But this, we must remember, is directly attributable to our sin, to our varied misuse and deliberate abuse of language, not to any functional defect in our language itself.

Renewing conformity to the image of Christ brings healing and hope for the hermeneutical process and for release from the vicious cycles of postmodernity briefly noted above. The promise of Jesus that the Holy Spirit, as "the Spirit of truth," "will guide you into all truth" (John 16:13) carries a guarantee that "the problem of hermeneutics" will not so engulf the church as to produce a crisis of uncertainty. This promise made to the apostles (15:26–27) and so, through them as its foundation (Eph. 2:20), to the church in all ages, is fulfilled in the Spirit's own, properly authorial "speaking in the Scripture" (Westminster Confession of Faith, 1.10; see 1:4: "the author thereof") and his subsequent ever-attendant and efficacious witness in the church and within believers to the truth of Scripture. Or as Luther has so memorably put it, "the Holy Spirit is not a sceptic"!

The fact that for "now we see things imperfectly as in a poor mirror" (1 Cor. 13:12, my trans.), as the Reformers well understood, in no way obscures the central gospel clarity of the Bible as God's own words. Nor does this limitation deprive of their meaning and wholesome power our own words and images conformed to the standards of that gospel-Word. In fact, the reality of God's inscripturated Word, the phenomenon itself of human language that by virtue of its unique origin has a consequent character and authority that is "God-breathed" (2 Tim. 3:16), so that, like God himself and as his Word, it is "living and active" and all-discerning (Heb. 4:12)—that phenomenon stands as the promise that our own use of language, as part of our "labor in the Lord," is "not in vain" (1 Cor. 15:58).

Finally, there is one other aspect to consider. We must remain aware that our restoration in the divine image, even with all of the potential already unleashed, is, for now, only a beginning. We can only wonder at just what that means. Scripture challenges us with a transformation that will be complete, with its full glory evident, only at our future resurrection, when at last we will bear the image of Christ, consummately, bodily (1 Cor. 15:49). Then, when "we shall see him," the true image of God, "as he is," "we shall be like him" (1 John 3:2).

Then, and not until, as Romans 8:18ff. intimates, in the context of the renewed creation every vestige of groaning will finally be stripped from what so often, for now, proves to be our inarticulate and artless and frustrated imaging-efforts. And with this open revelation of "the glorious freedom of the children of God" (v. 21), undreamed-of media possibilities will open up, or, if that seems too speculative, we will communicate as never before. In store, we may anticipate, is a potential for our words and images that will be part of a creation order, which, especially because Jesus Christ, the true image, will be manifested there in his full glory, will have dimensions that, for now, are simply "beyond words" (2 Cor. 9:15), "too great for words" (1 Peter 1:8, my trans). The glorious magnitude of that new creation order so strains the limits of our language that for the meantime its realities are perhaps best intimated in evocative images like those resplendent in portions of the Old Testament prophets and the Book of Revelation.

I began these reflections with biblical questions about the eye and the ear and the tongue. So it seems particularly fitting to conclude by referring to that apostolic word which for those who have been blessed to glimpse something of its fulfillment already realized in Christ, the true image and veritable Word of God, remains such a thrilling word: "No eye has seen, no ear has heard, no mind can conceive"—and we may now surely gloss, "no tongue can tell"—"what God has prepared for those," those image-bearers, "who love him" (1 Cor. 2:9).

9

A *System* of Theology?
The Centrality of Covenant
for Westminster Systematics

David VanDrunen

The present volume, in which theologians associated with the Westminster Seminaries are evaluating the discipline of systematic theology, seems to be an excellent forum for raising a question of terminology. Why do we name a particular theological discipline "systematic"? The name implies that a system of theology exists, actually or at least potentially. And it implies that the discovery or construction of such a system is of crucial importance for a sound theological education. However, in the present day at least, there is perhaps no theological discipline whose name is less obvious. Surely no one would doubt the propriety of the names of disciplines such as New Testament, Old Testament, or church history—the fact that there is a New Testament and an Old Testament and that the church has a history is hardly in question. But that a system of doctrine exists or that theological truth is the sort of thing that can and ought to be systematized does not appear to be an immediately obvious claim. Also not immediately obvious is what the Westmin-

ster systematics tradition itself thinks about such claims and
whether consensus even exists among its systematicians on the
subject. A look at the historical record indicates that the question of the existence and nature of a system of theology may well
be answered differently by the great Old Princeton systematicians, Charles Hodge and B. B. Warfield, when compared to
Westminster's John Murray and the men who took up his responsibilities in the second generation, Norman Shepherd, John
Frame, Richard Gaffin, and Robert Strimple. This in turn raises
the question of how the third generation of Westminster systematicians will address this issue as the second generation
reaches the age of retirement.

As one who, at the moment, has been entrusted with the
task of teaching systematic theology at Westminster in California in lieu of one of the second generation figures (Strimple), I approach this matter with great interest and much at
stake. In this essay, therefore, I reflect upon the name that we
have accorded to this particular theological discipline and the
idea that lies behind it. Though the existence of a system of theology has been affirmed at Westminster in the past only with
some ambiguity, I argue that its defense must be taken up with
renewed vigor in the next generation. In response to doubts
that the development of a system of theology is even possible,
I point to the Reformed doctrine of the covenants as the place
where a system of theology can be centered and from which it
can emerge in orderly coherence and biblical fidelity. The
covenantal approach that I develop in this chapter seeks to capture the strengths of the Westminster theological tradition—
especially its exegetical rigor and biblical-theological insight—
as well as to put it in closer touch with a central theme of the
broader Reformed tradition. In this way, I hope to offer an
approach to *systematic* theology that meets the admirable goals
of being thoroughly biblical while remaining in the closest
organic connection with the theological heritage entrusted
to us.

Westminster *Systematic* Theology?

I begin with the provocative question of whether the Westminster Seminaries have ever actually done *systematic* theology.
The easy answer to this question is, of course, affirmative. Systematic theology courses have always been a prominent part of
the curriculum. The traditional *loci* of Reformed systematics have
been taught to every ministerial student from the beginning to
the present. The early history of Westminster Seminary certainly
demonstrated the central importance of systematics for the institution's key figure, J. Gresham Machen. When Westminster was
founded over a few hurried weeks in the summer of 1929, one of
Machen's key challenges was to find a qualified systematics
instructor. Machen believed that systematic theology was the most
important discipline in the curriculum, and he was relieved finally
to secure the services of R. B. Kuiper for the first year and of John
Murray thereafter.[1]

Nevertheless, certain aspects of Westminster history do legitimate the question concerning the degree to which *systematic*
theology has been done. One might consider first the self-
understanding of the nature of systematic theology among Westminster Seminary theologians. Cornelius Van Til speaks of systematic theology as offering "an ordered presentation of what the
Bible teaches about God." For Van Til, this means the construction
of a "system," a construction of theological truth that is unified and
harmonious: "Systematics alone seeks to offer the truth about God
as revealed in Scriptures as a *whole*, as a unified system." "Systematic theology . . . uses the fruits of the labors of exegetical and
biblical theology and brings them together into a concatenated system."[2] In making comments like these, Van Til seems to have echoed
the sentiments of Old Princeton theologians B. B. Warfield and

---

1. See Iain H. Murray, "The Life of John Murray," in *Collected Writings of John Murray*, 4 vols. (Edinburgh: Banner of Truth, 1982), 3:41–45; Ned B. Stonehouse, *J. Gresham
Machen: A Biographical Memoir* (Grand Rapids: Eerdmans, 1954), 449–52.

2. Cornelius Van Til, *An Introduction to Systematic Theology* (Nutley, N.J.: Presbyterian and Reformed, 1974), 1–2.

Charles Hodge. According to Warfield, systematic theology is unique among the theological disciplines in presenting "its material in the form of a system," or in dealing with its material "as an organizable system of knowledge" or "as a concatenated whole."[3] Warfield viewed this systematizing task as not only possible, but also necessary and inevitable.[4] Hodge wrote that while biblical theology was to state the facts of Scripture, systematic theology was "to take those facts, determine their relation to each other and to cognate truths, as well as to vindicate them and show their harmony and consistency." This meant the need "for the construction of systems of theology" and for bringing "all the facts of revelation into systematic order and mutual relation."[5]

In comparison, Murray's conception of systematic theology seems rather less broad. He writes, "The task of systematic theology is to set forth in orderly and coherent manner the truth respecting God and his relations to men and the world."[6] Later, Murray speaks of exegesis as "basic" to systematic theology. However, while exegesis is largely concerned with the exposition of particular passages, systematics "must coordinate the teaching of particular passages and systematize this teaching under the appropriate topics. There is thus a synthesis that belongs to systematics that does not belong to exegesis as such."[7] Hodge, Warfield, and even Van Til would probably not have disagreed with Murray's words as far as they go. However, these three seem to conceive of systematics as concerned with an architectonic system, whereas Murray speaks in terms of coordinating exegetical findings under particular topics. Murray does not, to my knowledge, speak in terms of the importance or structure of a system *per se*. Whereas Hodge's interest in the opening pages of his *Sys-*

---

3. Benjamin Breckinridge Warfield, "The Idea of Systematic Theology," in *Studies in Theology* (New York: Oxford University Press, 1932), 49, 51; and "The Task and Method of Systematic Theology," in *Studies in Theology*, 91.

4. See "The Idea," 83; and "The Task and Method," 95.

5. Charles Hodge, *Systematic Theology*, 3 vols. (reprint, Grand Rapids: Eerdmans, 1995), 1:1–3.

6. John Murray, "Systematic Theology," in *Collected Writings of John Murray*, 4:1.

7. Ibid., 17.

tematic Theology concerns the necessity of system-construction, Murray's interest in "Systematic Theology" lies centrally in promoting the exegetical and biblical-theological basis of his discipline. Some of Richard Gaffin's judgments have carried Murray yet another step away from Hodge. He claims, for example, that systematic theology, or dogmatics, is "essentially exegesis of Scripture."[8] Gaffin does not here deny some coordinating function to systematics, nor does he advocate the abandonment of "the so-called loci method of traditional dogmatics."[9] Nevertheless, his practical equating of systematics/dogmatics and exegesis is quite removed from the discussions of Hodge, Warfield, and Van Til, in which exegesis is no less important, but appears as a precursor discipline that must be distinguished from systematics itself.

The thoughts of twentieth-century German Reformed theologian Otto Weber offer some perspective on these intra-Westminster discussions. Weber, it ought to be noted, actually believed that theology should not be done as *systematic* theology, yet his comments on the nature of systematic theology are intriguing:

> We understand by "system" the totality of an intellectual structure which is based upon a fundamental concept (a "principle") and which develops it logically and methodically. The presupposition is, accordingly, that the "principle" contains potentially the one and total content which is then explained in greater detail in the systematic exposition. This means in turn that in its exposition the system cannot contain elements which are not already given in the "principle." The "principle" is, therefore, the intellectual condensation of an all-embracing totality.[10]

This is a great distance from the Murray-Gaffin talk about the nature of systematics, and goes further even than Hodge, Warfield,

8. Richard B. Gaffin Jr., "The Vitality of Reformed Dogmatics," in *The Vitality of Reformed Theology*, ed. J. M. Batteau, J. W. Maris, and K. Veling (Kampen: Kok, 1994), 20.

9. See ibid., 28–29.

10. Otto Weber, *Foundations of Dogmatics*, 2 vols., trans. Darrell L. Guder (Grand Rapids: Eerdmans, 1981), 1:51.

and Van Til. Systematics along these lines not only is concerned about the unity, coherence, and harmony of the whole of theological truth, but even posits a unifying principle that in some way encompasses the whole. Whether or not one agrees entirely with Weber's definition, it further presses the question whether what the Westminster theologians have been doing is "systematic" theology.

Perhaps a look at the written publications of Westminster systematics professors provides a degree of insight. The first two generations never produced a comprehensive systematic theology textbook, as, for example, Charles Hodge did for Old Princeton Seminary or Louis Berkhof did for Calvin Seminary. In fact, the first two generations produced relatively few shorter, occasional works of what would be considered systematic theology even by their own definition. Murray did write a few brief books that would qualify: *Redemption Accomplished and Applied*, *Christian Baptism*, and *The Imputation of Adam's Sin*. *The Covenant of Grace* is more a study in biblical theology than systematic theology, and it is really only a pamphlet, a transcription of a lecture. Much of the content of Murray's four volume *Collected Writings*, especially the second volume, covers topics in "systematic theology" seriatim, though, not insignificantly, someone other than Murray gathered and arranged these essays, many of which are transcriptions of class lectures.[11] The output of specifically systematics literature is no more extensive with Gaffin and Strimple, the longest-lasting among the second generation theologians. Strimple offered a robust defense of an amillennial eschatology as one of three contributors to *Three Views on the Millennium and Beyond*, but his one full-length book is a survey of modern New Testament criticism.[12] Though Gaffin's several books touch upon systematics themes, probably none can be considered sys-

---

11. See the comments of Iain H. Murray in *Collected Writings of John Murray*, 2:vii-ix.

12. Robert B. Strimple, "Amillennialism," in *Three Views on the Millennium and Beyond*, ed. Darrell L. Bock (Grand Rapids: Zondervan, 1999); Robert B. Strimple, *The Modern Search for the Real Jesus: An Introductory Survey of the Historical Roots of Gospels Criticism* (Phillipsburg, N.J.: P&R, 1995).

tematics volumes at heart. For example, *Resurrection and Redemption* is not a systematic study of the resurrection, nor is *Perspectives on Pentecost* a systematic study of the work of the Holy Spirit.[13]

Perhaps more illuminating than what these men did not write is what they did write, which as much as anything else was biblical exegesis. Murray's *opus magnum* was almost certainly his two-volume commentary on Romans. Even his (arguably) best systematics work, *The Imputation of Adam's Sin*, is to a great extent a rigorous exegetical study of one passage, Romans 5:12–19. Gaffin's first, and probably best-known, monograph, *Resurrection and Redemption*, originally written as a systematics dissertation under Murray at Westminster, is essentially a study in Pauline soteriology. Its application to the systematics themes of union with Christ and the *ordo salutis* are brief and rather tentative. Even what is perhaps Strimple's most rigorous written contribution to systematic theology besides his defense of amillennialism addresses the issue of Kenotic Christology through a detailed unfolding of Paul's thought in Philippians 2:5–11.[14]

Counting published volumes and tracking interest in other theological disciplines among Westminster systematicians is admittedly of limited conclusive value. What is perhaps of most value is analyzing *how* these theologians did systematics when they were consciously setting their minds to it. An analysis of how they did systematics in the classroom would theoretically be of great worth here, though realistically quite difficult, since the evidence would be mostly anecdotal and never comprehensive (few people have been students of Gaffin, Strimple, *and* Murray). The next generation must ultimately judge on the basis of written work, and let firsthand classroom experience with one or more

13. Richard B. Gaffin Jr., *Resurrection and Redemption: A Study in Paul's Soteriology* (Grand Rapids: Baker, 1978; reprint, Phillipsburg, N.J.: Presbyterian and Reformed, 1987); Richard B. Gaffin Jr., *Perspectives on Pentecost: New Testament Teaching on the Gifts of the Holy Spirit* (Phillipsburg, N.J.: Presbyterian and Reformed, 1979).

14. Robert B. Strimple, "Philippians 2:5–11 in Recent Studies: Some Exegetical Conclusions," *Westminster Theological Journal* 41 (Spring 1979): 247–68.

of these theologians confirm or question. On the basis of the standard of their written work, the conclusion most strongly commending itself to me is that these men all have felt most comfortable arguing a systematics position by exegeting one or a handful of discreet biblical passages. This is true of Murray's *Imputation*, Gaffin's *Resurrection*, and Strimple's "Philippians 2:5–11," which are among the most significant accomplishments of each. Undoubtedly, one's view of the imputation of Adam's sin must center on an understanding of Romans 5, and one's view of a kenotic interpretation of the incarnation must center on Philippians 2. Nevertheless, the very fact that Murray and Strimple chose these projects rather than others surely illustrates their distinctively exegetical bents. My conclusion, therefore, is that the practice of Murray and his successors has fairly well matched their self-understanding of it.[15] They have performed their "systematics" task by exegeting passages related to various topics under consideration, but have been relatively uninterested in developing a system as such, either in the weaker Hodge-Van Tillian sense of a unified, coherent, harmonious structure of the whole of theological truth or in the stronger Weberian sense of a single principle uniting and encompassing the whole.

Toward a More Systematic Systematic Theology

This leaves an evaluative question for the next generation to ponder: What should we make of this sort of systematics? I now turn to argue that the Westminster systematics tradition might helpfully develop in a more self-consciously systematic direction.

15. As a side note, it is worth recognizing that Murray and his successors, insofar as they draw a line directly from exegesis and biblical theology to systematics, are certainly working within the schema developed by Warfield; see Warfield, "The Idea of Systematic Theology," 68–74. In this sense, the Princeton-Westminster tradition together stands somewhat opposed to an alternative Reformed vision offered by Warfield's great contemporary, Abraham Kuyper, who argued that theologians should not move directly from exegesis to systematics, but only through the "middle-link" of church history; see Abraham Kuyper, *Encyclopedia of Sacred Theology: Its Principles*, trans. J. Hendrik de Vries (New York: Scribner, 1898), 635.

Before I do so, however, I wish to address a few concerns about what might or might not be lost in whatever development occurs. First, and perhaps most obviously, the rigorous exegesis that has marked the tradition must be sacrosanct. All theology—leaving aside the question of natural theology[16]—rightly emerges out of Scripture, and the first two generations of Westminster systematics have left an invaluable contribution in their detailed explorations of biblical texts in the quest to answer theological questions. Though observers have rightly pointed to exegesis as a distinguishing feature of Westminster systematics, they also do well to note that keen interest in exegesis is not *unique* to the Westminster tradition of Reformed systematics. The immediate historical predecessors to the Westminster theologians, those of Old Princeton, were undeniably engaged in exegetical study. The two most eminent figures of the Old Princeton systematics tradition, Charles Hodge and B. B. Warfield, both served for extended periods of time as professors of biblical studies before their appointments to systematics—this is a boast that Murray himself cannot make. Hodge wrote not only a commentary on Romans, as did Murray, but also on 1 and 2 Corinthians and Ephesians. The voluminous collections of Warfield's writings contain numerous studies of exegetical nature. This overt reciprocity between exegetical and systematic labor draws from the very font of the Reformed tradition, John Calvin himself. This greatest of systematic theologians wrote biblical commentaries and sermons from Scripture that far outnumber his *Institutes* in pages. In cherishing the exegetical labors of the Westminster systematicians, then, we are cherishing something that can rightly be judged a noble characteristic of Reformed systematics more broadly.

Another characteristic of Westminster systematics, and one that perhaps is more distinguishing, is its close relationship with biblical theology, or a redemptive-historical hermeneutic. The ori-

16. Murray, perhaps surprisingly, given contemporary Reformed discomfort with natural theology, defended the importance of natural revelation in the task of systematic theology. See "Systematic Theology," 1–2. In this, he followed the lead of Warfield in "The Idea of Systematic Theology," 59.

gin of this interest in biblical theology traces back to Geerhardus Vos's biblical-theological work at Old Princeton. Vos, a favorite teacher of both Murray and Van Til, called for biblical and systematic theology to exist in a reciprocal relationship, with biblical theology functioning, among other things, as a servant of systematics.[17] Vos's work focused on the progress of God's revelation through biblical history and emphasized the centrality of the eschatological in its intrusions into temporal reality. Murray and Gaffin both reflected explicitly on the importance of these perspectives for the systematics task,[18] and Gaffin edited *Redemptive History and Biblical Interpretation*, a published collection of Vos's shorter writings. The insights of Vosian biblical theology are clearly evident, in various degrees, in the writings of Murray as well as the second generation systematicians—and Ferguson's work half a generation later.[19] The originality of much of Vos's work cannot be doubted, though even here there is no uniqueness. The Reformed tradition—primarily by way of the theme of the covenant, as Vos himself recognized[20]—has had an interest in the historical progress of redemptive history and its significance

17. See "The Idea of Biblical Theology as a Science and as a Theological Discipline," in *Redemptive History and Biblical Interpretation: The Shorter Writings of Geerhardus Vos*, ed. Richard B. Gaffin (Phillipsburg, N.J.: Presbyterian and Reformed, 1980), 23–24. In the midst of his broader discussion here, Vos states: "Dogmatics [used by Vos interchangeably with "systematic theology"] is the crown which grows out of all the work that Biblical Theology can accomplish." See also Vos, *Biblical Theology: Old and New Testaments* (Grand Rapids: Eerdmans, 1948), 24–25. Warfield charted the relationship between biblical theology and systematic theology in almost identical fashion; see "The Idea of Systematic Theology," 65–67.

18. John Murray, "Systematic Theology," 4:9–19; Gaffin, "The Vitality of Reformed Dogmatics"; Richard B. Gaffin, "Systematic Theololgy and Biblical Theology, *Westminster Theological Journal* 38 (Spring 1976): 281–99.

19. Evident perhaps most eminently in his scholarly monograph on the Holy Spirit: Sinclair B. Ferguson, *The Holy Spirit* (Downers Grove, Ill.: InterVarsity, 1996).

20. Vos recognized and described the centrality of the doctrine of the covenant in Reformed theology in his extended article, "The Doctrine of the Covenant in Reformed Theology," in *Redemptive History*, 234–67; he hailed the importance of the covenant idea for his own biblical-theological task in, for example, "The Idea of Biblical Theology," in *Redemptive History*, 10. See also the comments in Murray, "Systematic Theology," 15; and Gaffin, "The Vitality," 24.

for making crucial theological claims that surpasses that of other Christian theological traditions. The *magnum opus* of the great seventeenth-century Dutch theologian Herman Witsius perhaps exemplifies as well as anything this classic Reformed intertwining of what today is called biblical and systematic theology.[21] Again, then, honoring this aspect of the Westminster systematics tradition puts us in close contact with the Reformed tradition more broadly.

In light of these admirable traits of Westminster systematics—especially seen as developments (rather than innovations) of historic Reformed theology—why the call for a more self-consciously *systematic* approach for the next generation? One reason commending itself derives from the so-called "postmodern" context in which systematic theology is done in the contemporary world. Perhaps as never before, systematic theologians must face a challenge to their work that precedes any particular substantive theological claim, that of the very possibility of a coherent and intelligible body of truth. The challenge, of course, emanates not simply from unbelieving postmodern philosophy, but also from within the church and its theologians. The claim that a coherent body of theological truth actually exists is closely related to another crucial claim, that the Scriptures are a harmonious, symphonic whole, whose message, though told from a wondrous variety of perspectives in a myriad number of ways, is ultimately one. Systematic theology, more than any other theological discipline, exists to promote, expound, and defend that conviction. To speak boldly of a *system* is to speak boldly of the reality and intelligibility of the truth, which itself springs from the unity and veracity of God himself. Moreover, the belief in a system undergirds the fundamental Reformed hermeneutical principle that one

---

21. *The Economy of the Covenants between God and Man: Comprehending a Complete Body of Divinity*, 2 vols., trans. William Crookshank (1822; reprint, The den Dulk Christian Foundation, 1990). One might note especially how Witsius weaves lengthy discussions of Christology into his treatment of the covenant of redemption and discussion of soteriology and the sacraments into his exposition of the nature and historical progress of the covenant of grace.

should interpret Scripture according to Scripture, that is, according to the analogy of faith. One might well affirm the infallible truth of every part of Scripture and even the accuracy of every individual Reformed doctrine, but without a system these truths are in danger of remaining unconnected and bearing no necessary relation to one another.

Another source of need for a theology that is self-consciously systematic is the proliferating of boutique theologies in contemporary conservative Reformed circles. The size of these circles is quite paltry, if the truth be told, yet the number of rather distinctive "schools" of Reformed theology may leave even the over-leisured somewhat baffled. Each school seems to have its own periodicals and even seminaries to publicize them. The proliferation of Reformed seminaries is perhaps the most remarkable product of this phenomenon. Though the number of confessional Reformed denominations has not grown substantially over the past couple of decades, the number of seminaries has burgeoned, and many of the new seminaries have been established around a few theological distinctives. As dissident Roman Catholic priests for centuries have founded new orders rather than leave the mother church, thus Reformed churchmen with distinctive theologies have been founding new seminaries while largely remaining—at least for the time being—in their denominations. That the current situation borders between humorous and perplexing is illustrated by a quick comparison to the Missouri Synod Lutheran Church, another confessional church of Reformation heritage. By my rough estimation, the LCMS has more than five times as many members as the NAPARC bodies combined, yet has about one-eighth the number of seminary campuses serving them. The decline of a generally understood Reformed *theology* in favor of a plethora of Reformed *theologies* does not seem to bode well for the future peace and unity of historically Reformed churches.

In the face of this timebomb, the renewal of a *systematic* theology is perhaps all the more crucial. One of the mechanisms that has traditionally kept Reformed churches in a certain degree of institutional unity, despite the inevitable and not entirely undesirable differences of judgment on various issues by thinking people, is its confessions and catechisms. Disagreement on a wide variety of matters, including even exegetical questions, has been permitted to ministers and elders, provided that they maintain allegiance to the confessions. Ecclesiastical unity, therefore, has been much more a matter of systematic consensus than exegetical consensus. Reformed ministers and elders of disparate background and perspective unite around a system of doctrine encapsulated in confessional statements, not around consensus about the precise exegesis of a certain list of passages. Whether or not a given denomination adheres to a concept of "system subscription," presbyters must make systematic sorts of judgments about its own number and about candidates to join their number: does candidate's view x fit within the teaching of the Westminster Standards / Three Forms of Unity? Without a concept of the coherence of ecclesiastical confession, such judgments become extremely difficult to make. Yet, the alternative to making such judgments would be reducing licensure/ordination exams to mere repetition of catechism answers. A robust confession by ministers and elders surely requires something much more than memorization of the right answers; it requires a grasp of the teaching of Scripture as summarized by the confessional standards in its coherent and beautiful harmony. In light of this ecclesiastical need, therefore, interest in a *systematic* theology is more rather than less important today. If competing theological agendas are not to divide Reformed churches hopelessly, renewed attention to the system of doctrine that unites is of compelling necessity.

One possible concern about renewed interest in the *system* of doctrine is whether such a system will come to control exegesis, so that Scripture no longer is allowed to speak for itself. Especially if a system of doctrine presupposes some idea or principle that unifies the whole of Scripture and theology, along the lines of Weber's suggestion, will theologians contort individual passages of Scripture in order to fit them into the neat box dictated by that idea? Does a robust system of doctrine inevitably turn into a Procrustean bed? This is a legitimate concern that deserves a serious

answer. Objectors to the concept of a system of doctrine might
well point to Martin Luther's famous criterion of canonicity, the
doctrine of justification by faith alone, which in turn caused Luther
to doubt the place of James in the biblical canon. One need not
question the truth or the vital importance of the doctrine of justification to doubt the propriety of demanding that every individual passage of Scripture teaches it. Presumably, proponents of a
system of doctrine will not attempt further refinements of the biblical canon, but any particular unifying idea might seem to pose
an inordinate temptation to interpret each text to express that idea,
even when it does not. Can this danger be sufficiently mitigated
to justify a renewed attempt to think systematically?

The answer is probably negative in regard to just about every
possible unifying, system-central idea one might propose—and
this itself may display the ultimate unacceptability of a "systematic" theology as Weber defines it. Imagining the doctrine of justification by faith alone as the unifying idea illustrates the reason
for this. Though one can make a defensible case that this is the
most important individual doctrine in the whole spectrum of theological truth, it probably would serve as a poor system center.
The doctrine of justification by faith alone cannot itself unify all
of doctrine because there are other points of doctrine that can
only be defined in *contrast* to justification or even without reference of justification at all. The Reformed doctrine of sanctification, though not opposed to justification in any ultimate sense,
exists in sharp distinction from it. Only with great difficulty, and
perhaps tortuous intellectual definition, can theology explain
sanctification *in terms of* justification. Or, to borrow Weber's language, sanctification is not "already present" in justification. The
same is true in regard to the doctrine of creation, which is certainly also not contained in the doctrine of justification. Since
justification is all about the gospel, and since the gospel is central to the entire Scriptures, a systematician who arranges the
structure of biblical truth around the idea of justification is likely
to shed much helpful light on things and go a long way toward
unifying the message of Scripture. Nevertheless, both the require-

ment and sufficiency of such an approach probably cannot be established. Something is needed other than an individual doctrine such as justification or sanctification serving as center of the system. The need is for a way of expressing the unity and coherence of the whole of Reformed doctrine, an architectonic structure that undergirds all of the various threads of revealed truth. Reformed systematic theology is looking for a theological idea that *centers* the system, even if it is not *the center* of the system in the stark Weberian sense.

Centering the System: The Covenants

Such a centering idea is found in the idea of the covenants. The doctrine of the covenants can itself unite the various strands of theology into a unified, coherent, and harmonious whole. Before defending this claim at some length, two collateral benefits of centering Reformed systematics around the covenants are worth mentioning. First, the covenant theme is indisputably a recurring and prominent theme throughout the Scriptures. Not only the explicit language of "covenant," but the associated oaths and promises pervade the revealed account of redemptive history. The covenant, then, is not an idea distinctly affiliated with only certain biblical books or authors, and therefore is not liable to being used as a tool for pitting one part of Scripture against another. In light of this, emphasis on the covenant theme happily allows and even demands that systematic theology be in close dialogue with the kind of exegetical and biblical theology that has marked the Westminster tradition.[22] Second, the doctrine of the

22. The importance of covenant theology as an organizing principle for biblical theology in the Princeton-Westminster tradition is illustrated, for example, in the comments of Geerhardus Vos: "The importance of this aspect of revelation has found its clearest expression in the idea of the covenant as the form of God's progressive self-communication to Israel. God has not revealed Himself in a school, but in the covenant; and the covenant as a communion of life is all-comprehensive, embracing all the conditions and interests of those contracting it" ("The Idea of Biblical Theology," in *Redemptive History*, 10); and Meredith G. Kline: "*Kingdom Prologue* engages in a biblico-theological analysis of the foundational revelation contained in the book Genesis. Taking the kingdom of God as our

covenant is a subject that not only has been of great interest to Reformed theology through its history, but has also been of rather distinctively Reformed interest. Reformed theologians developed the idea of the covenant as a unifying theme in Scripture in a way that theologians from no other mainstream Christian tradition have. Therefore, an attempt to develop the Reformed system of doctrine around the covenant cannot provoke any initial objection that fidelity to either the biblical record or the Reformed theological heritage is compromised.

However, the question still lingers whether the doctrine of the covenants can really unite the disparate mass of theology into a unified whole. The answer is affirmative only in regard to certain forms in which Reformed covenant theology has grown. The distinctive covenant ideas taught by John Murray do not seem a likely candidate for centering the system, and proponents of Murray's covenant theology probably must look elsewhere, if they are interested in looking at all, for a centering doctrine. The deficiencies of Murray's covenant theology in this regard do not depend on *critique* of it, but on simple observation of its structure. For example, Murray did not believe that God's pre-lasparian dealings with Adam constituted a covenantal relationship, nor did Murray ascribe covenantal significance to the eternal Trinitarian life and counsel.[23] Whether Murray is correct or incorrect in his conclusions, he effectively eliminates creation and the creation order from the covenantal sphere, with its concomitant features such as the nature of man, the image of God, and the eschatological promise of life. Likewise, he takes election and the Trinitarian divine life out of the realm of the covenant. In constricting consideration of the covenant to the outworking of redemptive grace in history, Murray makes the covenant only one

---

central, organizing theme, we inevitably find ourselves fully involved with the subject of the divine covenants of Scripture; for to follow the course of the kingdom is to trace the series of covenants by which the Lord administers his kingdom." See *Kingdom Prologue* (Overland Park, Kans: Two Age Press, 2000), 1.

23. See Murray, "The Adamic Administration," in *Collected Writings*, 2:49; and "The Plan of Salvation," in *Collected Writings*, 2:130.

aspect of Christian doctrine, not an idea that unifies the whole, for while redemption may be the most important theme of biblical revelation, it is not the only theme.

Though Murray's covenant theology does not lend itself to unifying a theological system, a more traditional structuring of Reformed covenant theology in fact does, or at least might.[24] The traditional structure identifies God's three-fold covenantal dealings: the covenant of works (or life) with Adam; the covenant of redemption (*pactum salutis*, or counsel of peace) in eternity among the Father, Son, and Holy Spirit; and the covenant of grace, made in time between God and his people. In this way of organizing covenant theology, the covenant of works with Adam is the first covenant administration revealed in Scripture. It posits a promise of eschatological life to Adam and his posterity upon the condition of perfect obedience to God, as well as a threat of death upon disobedience. This covenant is one of "works" because Adam's righteous work would have earned or merited him life. The covenant of redemption concerns the counsel of the divine Trinity from eternity. In view of the breaking of the covenant with Adam, the Godhead purposed salvation for a chosen people. The Father willed that the Son become incarnate, come under the law and fulfill all of its righteous requirements, and suffer and die. The Father also promised that upon completion of these tasks he would raise up the Son by the power of the Holy Spirit, exalt him with all glory and honor, and bestow upon him a kingdom and inheritance, including a people of his own who would receive all the redemptive benefits of his work. The Son, on his part, sub-

24. In regard to this contrasting of Murray with the broader Reformed tradition, Murray himself openly acknowledged that he differed from his predecessors on various points, such as the covenantal identity of the Adamic administration and of the eternal divine counsel. See Murray, "The Adamic Administration," in *Collected Writings*, 2:49; and "The Plan of Salvation," in *Collected Writings*, 2:130–31. At one point, Murray claims to seek "a revised definition of the biblical concept of covenant." See "Covenant Theology," 217. He does not interact with his predecessors in implicitly rejecting the view of a great number of Reformed theologians concerning a republication of the covenant of works in the Mosaic covenant. See Murray, *The Covenant of Grace: A Biblico-Theological Study* (1953; reprint, Phillipsburg, N.J.: Presbyterian and Reformed, 1988), 20–22.

mitted himself to this plan and purposed to enter the world and fulfill his Father's will. The covenant of grace, then, concerns the application of the benefits of Christ's covenant obedience.

In this arrangement, God covenants with his people for their salvation, and Christ the God-Man stands as Mediator. In various administrations of this one covenant through redemptive history, God graciously bestows salvation upon sinners who could in no way merit it. In this basic form, Reformed theologians have developed the covenant idea. I am convinced that careful exegesis of Scripture confirms the truth of this theological construct, and I spend considerable lecture time in my courses defending and expounding it. Unfortunately, space does not permit the sort of detailed arguments that hours of lectures seek to unfold. I must ask the reader, without hearing my own argumentation, to assume momentarily the biblical fidelity of these ideas and to reflect with me on its implications for the principal question before us: Could such a covenant theology itself unify and center the Reformed system of doctrine?

My answer is yes. The very way that this traditional Reformed covenant theology has been structured makes it all-encompassing in nature. It takes into its purview not only the relationship of God to man but also the relationship of God to himself. It accounts not only for the relationship of God to sinful man for salvation but also for the relationship of God to upright man in the original creation. Its reach spans eternity, the history of this world, and the eschatological future. What is more, if one considers the covenant with Noah as a distinct covenant of preserving, common grace, as articulated by some Reformed theologians,[25] then this covenant theology also encompasses God's dealings with the fallen world as a whole as well as with his redeemed community. All of the basic realms that systematic theology investigates are defined in covenantal terms. This conclusion is bolstered and developed by consideration of the major

25. Among older Reformed theologians, see Witsius, *The Economy of the Covenants*, 2:239. More recently, see Kline, *Kingdom Prologue*, 244–62.

loci of systematic theology and their distinctly covenantal hue: prolegomenon, theology proper, anthropology, harmatiology, Christology, soteriology, sacraments, ecclesiology, eschatology, and ethics.

First, prolegomenon. This theological sub-discipline is where theologians ordinarily expect systematics to begin. Prolegomenon defines the nature of theology, the nature and means of knowing truth in general and God in particular, and the character of God's revelation. Theologians have not always duly appreciated the reciprocal relationship between prolegomenon and the rest of theology: not only does prolegomenon define the forthcoming theological task, but this broader theology ought also to define the foundational material of prolegomenon. The Westminster Seminary theological tradition has perhaps been more sensitive to this reciprocity than other streams of the Reformed tradition. Van Til consciously grounded his understanding of apologetics in the broader truths of Reformed doctrine,[26] and Michael Horton has recently argued persuasively for a prolegomenon permeated by the truth of the larger system.[27] Horton's work is particularly relevant for present purposes in light of the fact that he identifies *covenant* as a controlling aspect of Reformed theology that must mold the task of prolegomenon. The covenantal nature of prolegomenon is quite clearly perceived once one is attentive to it. The Reformed tradition has in fact recognized the absolutely covenantal nature of all knowledge of God.

26. For example, Van Til writes: "Now the basic structure of my thought is very simple. I have never been called upon to work out any form of systematic theology. My business is to teach Apologetics. I therefore presuppose the Reformed system of doctrine. . . . An examination of my syllabus on Apologetics shows that the first chapter deals with the question *what* we are to believe and defend. We must defend Christian-theism as a unit." See Cornelius Van Til, *The Defense of the Faith* (Philadelphia: Presbyterian and Reformed, 1955), 23.

27. Michael S. Horton, *Covenant and Eschatology: The Divine Drama* (Louisville: Westminster John Knox, 2002), 1: "Although it is rather different in style and method from a traditional prolegomenon, this work represents an exercise in theology in which theological method is determined by the content of the system instead of being regarded as predogmatic reflection."

The Westminster Confession of Faith, 7.1, for example, speaks of the impossibility of finite man bridging the chasm between himself and an infinite God. He has no knowledge, no relationship with God by his own efforts or by any resource in nature, abstractly conceived. Man does enjoy knowledge of and relationship with God, however, because he never exists according to nature in the abstract; instead, God has been pleased to condescend to man "by way of covenant." From the very outset of history, God has relationship with man, and covenant is the way in which this relationship functions. Covenant defines all relationship with God, and thus all knowledge of God—which is precisely what "theology" is—is necessarily covenantal. The same can be said in regard to the revelation itself by which this knowledge comes. Once again, one need not leave the Reformed theological tradition, particularly not in its Westminster incarnation. Meredith G. Kline, for example, has argued extensively for the covenantal character of all of scriptural revelation.[28] The various biblical books are covenant documents, means for commemorating and regulating the sovereign administrations of God's kingship that Kline understands covenants to be.[29] Even general revelation must be seen in covenantal light. Jeremiah 31 and 33 speak of the original creation covenant as encompassing the natural realm,[30] through which general revelation communicates, according to Psalm 19 and Romans 1. Man's first contact with nature, both that within and outside of himself, confronts him with the powerful Deity who is none other than covenant Lord. The re-creation of this nature after its virtual destruction in the Noahic flood issues in a covenant of common grace that draws the entire created order within its lair. In this light, prolegomenon is thor-

28. For example, see Meredith G. Kline, *The Structure of Biblical Authority* (Grand Rapids: Eerdmans, 1972), especially Part 1.

29. On the relationship of covenant and kingdom in Kline's theology, see *Kingdom Prologue*, 4.

30. For a defense of the claim that Jer. 31:35–36 and 33:20–26 speak of the original creation covenant, see O. Palmer Robertson, *The Christ of the Covenants* (Phillipsburg, N.J.: Presbyterian and Reformed, 1980), 19–21.

oughly covenantal. Human beings know God in covenantal relationship by means of covenantal revelation.

How the covenant theme pertains to the doctrine of God, "theology proper," is perhaps not as obvious. In general, theologians must be especially cautious in venturing to speak of God's inner life and Trinitarian existence. Yet, tending to revelation in our speech about such things indeed compels theologians to reflect on such topics in a covenantal frame. The traditional Reformed doctrine of the covenant of redemption, for example, thrusts before us the portrait of eternal, intratrinitarian divine counsel transpiring covenantally. Father and Son, with the Holy Spirit actively present, covenantally purpose the salvation of a chosen people. In doing so, the Trinitarian persons manifest the very attributes that demand central attention in the doctrine of God: wisdom, power, holiness, justice, goodness, and truth. Indeed, Christians would know not one of these attributes as fully as they do were it not for their manifestation in the outworking of the covenant of redemption. The inner life of the Trinity consists in more than simply their counsel for our salvation, one might object. This is true, yet Scripture gives warrant for understanding this inner life—in as far as we might understand it at all—in covenantal terms. In the Upper Room Discourse, Christ speaks of our relationship with God as occurring along analogous lines to God's relationship with himself (e.g., John 17:21). If Scripture conceives of the former only by way of covenant, theologians properly conceive of the other in terms of the covenant too. If covenant governs the ectype, how much more the archetype.

Reformed theologians take the next locus of systematic theology, anthropology, in a covenantal manner more explicitly. Consistent with the teaching of Westminster Confession of Faith 7.1, that no relationship with God is possible apart from God's condescension by way of covenant, Reformed theology has confessed that man existed from the beginning in the covenant of works/life/nature/creation. This covenantal arrangement is best seen not as merely an apparatus for determining whether the human race would be granted life or death, but as also the defin-

ing factor of human nature itself. In other words, the covenant of
creation ought to control discussion not only of the requirement
of obedience and the promise/threat of life/death, but also of the
fundamental anthropological topics of the image of God and the
constitutive elements of the human person. Scripture first asserts
human creation in the image of God in the context of God's original commandments to the human race. God creates man in his
image *so that* he might have dominion over the earth.[31] Man is
the image of God so that he might image God, the God who himself has exercised absolute dominion over the world. Thus, man's
most basic responsibility in the covenant of creation, to exercise
dominion, is the direct result of and obedient expression of his
creation in the divine image. To put things in these terms is also
to draw discussion about the constitutive elements of the human
person into the covenantal framework. The image-bearer of God
is precisely man, body and soul, and this dichotomous nature,
unique in creation, can surely not be disconnected from his unique
image-bearing. At the very least, body-soul existence is the only
mode in which the image may be expressed.

The locus of sin in systematic theology, so closely bound with
anthropology, also necessarily enjoys a covenantal starting-point.
Insofar as the covenant of works established that disobedience to
God's commands would result in condemnation and death, the
theological exploration of this condemnation and death must view
them through the lens of this violated covenant. Human sin was
at its origin and essence unfaithfulness toward God's creation
covenant, and discussion begins with the imputation of the sin of
the covenant head, Adam, to his posterity. This covenantal imputation, then, was the font of all moral corruption and actual sins.

The locus of Christology returns theologians to the
covenant of redemption. This eternal, intratrinitarian covenant

---

31. On the indirect volative as expressing purpose, see, for example, Paul Jouon, S. J.,
A Grammar of Biblical Hebrew, trans. and rev. T. Muraoka (Rome: Editrice Pontificio Insti-
tuto Biblico, 1991), 2:381. The context of Gen. 1 supports this reading: the one who is created in the image of God is given a task—the exercise of dominion over the earth—that
precisely images the work that God has been doing in the first 25 verses of Gen 1.

is properly the grid through which all of the doctrine of the person and work of Christ emerges. The incarnation, the central theological affirmation concerning the person of Christ, was itself covenantal obedience on the part of the Son, who *came into this world* in order to do the will of his Father (Heb. 10:7–9). The Son became the God-man for the purposes of covenantal obligation. Likewise, the covenant of redemption looms over discussion of the central doctrine of the work of Christ, the atonement. Both Christ's active and passive obedience are nothing other than obedience that he rendered to fulfill his eternal, covenantal purpose to keep the law for his people and to bear their sins. The resurrection and ascension are rewards bestowed upon the Son by the Father for his perfect obedience to the covenant. Christ's continual intercession at his Father's right hand represents a perpetual reminder that the covenant conditions have been fulfilled. Here might also be the proper place for Reformed theologians to consider the locus of eschatology, which in many ways is simply Christology consummated. The promises bestowed upon Christ in the covenant of redemption—not only his own glory but a glorious kingdom and glorified people—remain inchoately fulfilled until the day of his return.

In soteriology the need for a covenantal perspective persists. Discussion of the application of salvation in Reformed theology has traditionally revolved around the *ordo salutis*, the way in which God bestows the various blessings earned by Christ to his elect. Neither the *ordo salutis* nor the complementary—or, to some lights, competing—idea of union with Christ, another central concept for Reformed soteriology, is explicitly covenantal. Yet, the very blessings comprising the *ordo salutis*, such as regeneration, justification, adoption, sanctification, and glorification, are applied to believers only as the result of Christ's perfect righteousness in the covenant of redemption. Likewise, the believer's union with Christ is at the very least a covenantal union with the Second Adam, the new federal head. The great promise of the union of God with believers is also the great promise of the covenant: "I will be your God and you will be my people."[32] Soteriology is perhaps the location in the systematics curriculum to explore the basics of the covenant of grace. One characteristic of the Reformed understanding of the covenant of grace is that the redemption purchased by Christ according to the covenant of redemption is the one way of salvation for God's people throughout history. Soteriology is the ideal forum for reflecting upon that claim and defending it from the Scriptures. The unity of the covenant of grace through history is precisely the tool for understanding the consistency and veracity of God's application of salvation to his people.

The doctrine of the sacraments, insofar as it comprises a distinct topic in the system, provides another example of the centrality of covenant. The sacraments are overtly covenantal rituals. This was true quite clearly of the Old Testament sacrament of circumcision, which God instituted in the very act of confirming his covenant with Abraham, in Genesis 17. The similar function to circumcision that baptism plays in the New Testament strongly implies its own role in the life of the covenant. In fact, the continuity of the covenants through redemptive history has served as the linchpin of Reformed arguments for the propriety of infant baptism: as Old Testament children received the sign of the covenant as heirs of the Abrahamic covenant, so New Testament children receive the sign of the covenant as heirs of that very same covenant. The Lord's Supper too is overtly covenantal. In ordaining this ritual for his church, Christ proclaimed the cup to be drunk as the "new covenant in my blood" (Matt. 26:28; Mark 14:24; Luke 22:20). As God swept up Moses and the elders to a covenant repast under the old covenant (Exod. 24:11), so he draws up his New Testament people to a greater covenant meal.

Two more topics draw this discussion to its close, ecclesiology and ethics. The covenantal nature of the church is not difficult to perceive. The church is the New Testament covenant com-

---

32. Gen. 17:7; Jer. 31:33; 32:38–40; Ezek. 34:23–25, 30–31; 36:25–28; 37:26–27; 2 Cor. 6:16–18; Heb. 8:10; Rev. 21:3.

munity. In the church the covenantal salvation is bestowed and the covenant rituals performed. As the Old Testament Scriptures addressed the old covenant community, Israel, so the New Testament Scriptures address the new covenant community—either the church directly or the church through one of its representatives. Precisely in the church does God announce that those who were once far off, alienated from the covenants of promise, have been brought near through the blood of Christ (Eph. 2:11–13; 3:8–11). Ethics, of course, does not ordinarily constitute a distinct locus in Reformed theology. However, it arguably belongs in the system somewhere, and any explanation of the Christian's moral life must again take account of its covenantal nature. At every point of redemptive history, God has delivered his word to his people and demanded the proper response—through his covenant. The Christian's moral life, marked by the freedom that the gospel brings, is comprehensible only as pursued by those who have received the salvific blessings of the covenant, abide in the covenant community, and await the covenant's consummation.[33]

Conclusion

The conclusion to which I come—which I offer not as the final word, but as a working proposal for myself and a suggestion and challenge for fellow Reformed theologians—is that a more systematic Westminster systematic theology is both a real possibility and a promising avenue for further development of this emerging tradition. In proposing that the covenant idea ought to center our systematics task, I aim to capture the best of multiple worlds. On the one hand, the pervasiveness of the covenant theme throughout the Scriptures allows and even demands a continuation of the exegetical and biblical-theological work that has marked

---

33. I might add, in concluding this section, the observation that Reformed systematic theology, structured in this way around the biblical covenants, meets Weber's criteria for dogmatics that he does not believe "systematic" theology is able to satisfy: it accounts for the historicity of the biblical revelation, the multiplicity of its witness, and the inchoate character of our present knowledge of theological truth. See Weber, *Foundations*, 1:60–62.

the Westminster systematics tradition to this point. On the other hand, the distinctiveness of the covenant idea as an organizing theme throughout the broader history of Reformed theology, as well as the Reformed tradition's historic presentation of the three-covenant view, means that my proposal stands in organic connection not only with Westminster systematics but also with the Reformed doctrinal tradition as a whole. Whatever the success of the details of my proposal, the goal, I hope, is noble: an exegetically grounded, biblical-theologically energized, historically faithful, and systematically rigorous theology. And only so noble a goal is worthy of those entrusted with the legacy of Robert B. Strimple and the Reformed theologians who preceded him.

Part Four

Westminster Systematic Theology and the Life of the Church

10

The Whole Counsel of God: Westminster Seminary and the Orthodox Presbyterian Church

John R. Muether

When J. Gresham Machen founded Westminster Theological Seminary in 1929, he conceded at its opening convocation that it was dedicated to an "unpopular cause." "It is devoted," he announced, "to the service of One who is despised and rejected by the world and increasingly belittled by the visible church."[1] Seven years later, Machen helped to found the Orthodox Presbyterian Church, describing its prospects in identical terms. Though he rejoiced that he and his colleagues were "members at last of a true Presbyterian church," he warned his friends that "a desperate struggle [lay] ahead, with a tiny little group facing the hostility of the world and the still more bitter hostility of the visible church."[2]

The similarity in the rhetoric may appear at first unremarkable, as the same spiritual father formed both institutions amid

1. J. Gresham Machen, "Westminster Theological Seminary: Its Purpose and Plan," in *What Is Christianity?* (Grand Rapids: Eerdmans, 1951), 224.

2. J. Gresham Machen, "A True Presbyterian Church at Last" *Presbyterian Guardian* 2 (June 22, 1936): 110. At the time of its founding, the church was named Presbyterian Church of America, and its name was changed to "Orthodox Presbyterian Church" in 1939. For convenience, I will refer to it by that name throughout.

the same ecclesiastical controversies. Still it should not go unnoticed. Westminster was always independent and it had from its founding an international constituency that extended beyond any single denomination. The burden of this essay is to explore the relationship between Machen's two institutions, and particularly the way in which the seminary shaped the theological identity of the church.

Without question Westminster played a vital role in the formation of the OPC. It is most likely that the OPC would never have come into existence had Westminster not been formed. A new denomination would have been futile were there not the reasonable hope that it could raise a future generation of faithful and godly ministers. Machen himself would not live to see what would unfold in the decades that followed the church's birth. What developed between the impoverished seminary and the small church became, in the words of Charles Dennison, "one of the most amazing relationships in Presbyterian history."[3]

From the start the OPC acknowledged its debt to Westminster. Early OPC General Assembly minutes record the consistent recommendation from the church's Committee on Christian Education that congregations support the seminary. This was most explicitly stated in the report to the sixth General Assembly: "In view of the great and central place of Westminster Theological Seminary in the educational work of our church, sessions and congregations be urged to place this Seminary in their respective church budgets."[4]

Westminster Seminary served the church in several ways. It raised the theological literacy of the laity of the church to impressive levels. Professors regularly wrote tracts for the church and contributed to the *Presbyterian Guardian*. (The second half of John Murray's book *Redemption Accomplished and Applied* was originally serialized in the *Guardian*.) They served on General Assem-

3. Charles G. Dennison, *The Orthodox Presbyterian Church 1936–1986* (Philadelphia: Committee for the Historian of the OPC, 1986), 11.
4. Minutes of the Sixth General Assembly of the Orthodox Presbyterian Church (1939), 19.

bly study committees and were the chief authors of some of the most important reports. The *Guardian* followed the seminary closely, reporting on annual enrollments, and the speaking itineraries of faculty, and publishing the texts of convocation and commencement addresses.

Above all, Westminster was committed to the training of Presbyterian ministers, and it is here that Westminster had its greatest effect on the Orthodox Presbyterian Church. In 1962, 77 percent of the ministers in the Orthodox Presbyterian Church were trained at Westminster Seminary. This high percentage continued for another two decades: in 1984, 78 percent were trained at Westminster.[5] What is more, these figures do not simply represent Westminster's training of Orthodox Presbyterian students. Surveys of the student body have consistently revealed that Westminster produced Orthodox Presbyterian ministers from students with non-Orthodox Presbyterian backgrounds.[6]

Perhaps even more remarkable are the ways in which Westminster provided the theological leadership for the OPC. Of the 63 ministers who have served as moderator of the OPC General Assembly from 1936 to 2003, only two (J. Oliver Buswell in the second Assembly in 1936 and Ross Graham in the sixty-fifth Assembly in 1998) were not alumni either of Princeton Seminary or Westminster Seminary. On twelve occasions, Westminster professors themselves served the General Assembly as moderators.

The long-standing influence of the seminary upon the church owes to the unusually long tenure of the founding faculty of Westminster Seminary. Professors Murray, Stonehouse, Van Til, Woolley, and Young co-labored at Westminster for over 25 years. All of these men were active ministerial members of the Orthodox Presbyterian Church, but two of them were particularly influential, John Murray (in systematics) and Cornelius Van Til (systematics and apologetics). Westminster alumni consistently identified the two as their most influential instructors, and the link between the

5. Ibid., 321.
6. John R. Muether, "Has Orthodoxy Changed? A Survey of Westminster Alumni." Unpublished paper presented at Westminster Seminary (Philadelphia), May 1989.

school and the church was particularly established by their labors.[7]

The particular influence of the systematics faculty was consistent with Machen's founding vision for the school, which identified systematics as the heart of its curriculum. In Machen's words, "Systematic theology, on the basis of Holy Scripture, is the very center of what we have to teach; every other theological department is contributory to that; that department gives a man the message that he has to proclaim."[8]

In 1966 the General Assembly paid tribute to Murray at the last Assembly he attended with a testimonial scroll that read in part, "You have been a faithful presbyter, spending untold days in the service of our beloved church, both in its assembly services and as a member of its committees."[9] Murray was far from an ivory tower theologian; his service for the church was astounding. He served on the Foreign Missions Committee for 25 years and on many special committees, including the Westminster Confession of Faith with Proof Texts, Revisions to the Form of Government, Local Evangelism, Theological Education, Guidance, and Song in Worship (where he authored his well-known minority report against the use of uninspired hymns). In addition, he was very active on the Committee for the Propagation of the Reformed Faith in New England and in the Presbytery of New York and New England.

Although only 41 years old at the time of Machen's death, Van Til was quickly thrust into the capacity of the seminary's senior faculty. John Frame rightly described Van Til as "the chief consolidator of the Machen reformation,"[10] and he served that role both within the church and the seminary. Van Til extended Machen's argument against liberalism to later threats to Reformed orthodoxy, especially Barthianism. Van Til's leadership in the

---

7. Ibid.

8. Machen, "Westminster Theological Seminary," 229.

9. "Testimonial Scroll to John Murray," *Presbyterian Guardian* 35 (December 1949): 149.

10. John M. Frame, *Cornelius Van Til: An Analysis of His Thought* (Phillipsburg, N.J.: P&R, 1995), 40.

church and the seminary became especially evident on two occasions when Calvin Seminary courted him to join its faculty, first in 1943 (as Louis Berkhof's successor in theology) and then in 1951. Former students flooded Van Til with letters despairing of the future of the church if it lost its second Machen, and appealing that he stay and continue to prosecute Machen's cause. As with Murray, when Van Til retired there was a massive outpouring of appreciation in the church.

The Whole Counsel of God

A Westminster education from Professors Murray and Van Til was, one would expect, Reformed. However, in promoting its theological distinctiveness, Westminster tended not to refer to itself in that way. Instead, it described its instruction by claiming the language of Paul, asserting its commitment to "declare the whole counsel of God" (Acts 20:27). John Murray's words to entering students at Westminster in 1966 employed this popular phrase in a characteristic way:

> Many of the positions maintained [at Westminster] are unpopular and we lose support. Sometimes we are tempted to stand for things which the counsel of God does not warrant. But we may not succumb. The whole counsel of God and nothing more! The whole counsel of God and nothing less! We must not presume to tone up this counsel and be better than God. We most not tone it down and prove unfaithful to our commission.[11]

The predominance of this language over more conspicuously Reformed terminology raises the question of the function that the Westminster Confession of Faith served in the curriculum. In reflecting upon his Westminster education and his experience as an Orthodox Presbyterian minister, John Frame has suggested that

11. John Murray, "Greeting to Entering Students, 1966," in *Collected Writings of John Murray*, 4 vols. (Edinburgh: Banner of Truth, 1976), 1:111–12.

the Westminster Standards had a diminished role in the seminary curriculum. Frame recalls two features of his student life: first, it lacked an overt "confessional or traditional focus" and, second, there was a spirit of creativity and openness in theological reflection. Frame then goes on to make a startling admission:

> After graduation I became ordained in the Orthodox Presbyterian Church, and I confess I was rather surprised at the seriousness with which my fellow ministers took the confessional standards and the Presbyterian tradition. Eventually I became more like my fellow Orthodox Presbyterian . . . elders, but not without some nostalgia for the openness of theological discussion during my seminary years.

Frame goes on to attribute this difference to Westminster's understanding of *sola Scriptura*, which unburdened the school from the constraints of confessionalism.[12]

If Frame is right, then he has identified a departure at Westminster from the past. For if this tension existed at Westminster, it was unknown to previous generations of Reformed theologians. Richard Muller's extensive work in Reformed scholasticism reminds us that confessional integrity never impeded theological creativity. For the scholastic mindset, Muller writes, "Once a churchly confession is accepted as a doctrinal norm, it provides boundaries for theological and religious expression, but it also offers considerable latitude for the development of *varied* theological and religious expressions within those boundaries."[13]

Machen himself imagined no conflict between biblical authority and confessional boundaries. His opening address at the founding of Westminster tied them closely together:

12. John M. Frame, "*Sola Scriptura* in Theological Method," found as an appendix in his *Contemporary Worship Music: A Biblical Defense* (Phillipsburg, N.J.: P&R, 1997), 183–86.

13. Richard Muller, "Confessing the Reformed Faith: Our Identity in Unity and Diversity," *New Horizons* 15 (March 1994): 10.

That system of theology, that body of truth, which we find in the Bible, is the Reformed Faith, the Faith commonly called Calvinistic, which is set forth so gloriously in the Confession and Catechisms of the Presbyterian Church. It is sometimes referred to as a "man-made creed." But we do not regard it as such. We regard it, in accordance with our ordination pledge as ministers in the Presbyterian Church, as the creed which God has taught us in his Word. If it is contrary to the Bible, it is false. But we hold that it is not contrary to the Bible, but in accordance with the Bible, and true. We rejoice in the approximations to that body of truth which other systems of theology contain; we rejoice in our Christian fellowship with other evangelical churches; we hope that members of other churches, despite our Calvinism, may be willing to enter into Westminster Seminary as students and to listen to what we have to say. But we cannot consent to impoverish our message by setting forth less than what we find Scriptures to contain; and we believe that we shall best serve our fellow-Christians, from whatever church they may come, if we set forth not some vague greatest common measure among various creeds, but that great historic Faith that has come through Augustine and Calvin to our own Presbyterian Church. Glorious is the heritage of the Reformed Faith. God grant that it may go forth to new triumphs even in the present time of unbelief![14]

Subsequent reflection by Westminster on biblical and confessional authority also appears to dismiss the tension that Frame imagines, particularly in the 1973 faculty symposium, *Scripture and Confession*. In his contribution to that anthology, John Murray, while acknowledging some deficiencies in the Westminster Standards, defended them as peerless in their fidelity to Scripture. He went on to describe them as "singularly relevant and up to date on the great issues of faith in contemporary life," concluding that "creedal expression when faithful to the revealed counsel of God never becomes obsolete." For Murray, the whole

14. Machen, "Westminster Theological Seminary," 229.

counsel found its ablest summary in the Westminster Confession. Thus "the *doctrine* of the Confession is the doctrine which the church needs to confess and hold aloft today as much as in the seventeenth century."[15]

Frame's analysis owes more to his idiosyncratic view of *sola Scriptura*. Earlier Westminster faculty, especially Murray, never imagined that confessionalism would eclipse the doctrine of *sola Scriptura*. Rather, they upheld the subordinate standards as a necessary means for the church to submit to its primary standard, the Confession and Catechisms being the way in which the church has agreed to interpret the Scriptures. The confessional consciousness that surprised Frame when he joined the OPC is a testimony to the effectiveness that Murray and others had in instructing the church in both biblical authority and confessional integrity.[16]

Non-American Theology

"The whole counsel of God" may have sounded simple and appealing. But Westminster's understanding of the counsel of God would often prove unpopular, and the distinctiveness of Westminster's teaching would land it and the church into shared controversies. In 1937 the seminary and the church both suffered from divisions from within their ranks. In April of that year, Professor Allan MacRae suddenly resigned from the faculty of Westminster, charging that the seminary had fallen under the control of "a small alien group without American Presbyterian background."[17] MacRae elaborated in his letter of resignation:

15. John Murray, "The Theology of the Westminster Confession," in *Scripture and Confession: A Book About Confessions Old and New*, ed. John H. Skilton (Nutley, N.J.: Presbyterian and Reformed, 1973), 145, 146.

16. For an analysis of the confessional consciousness in the OPC see John R. Muether, "Confidence in Our Brethren: Creedal Subscription in the Orthodox Presbyterian Church," 301–10 in *The Practice of Confessional Subscription*, ed. David W. Hall (Lanham, Md.: University Press of America, 1995).

17. "Professor MacRae Leaves Westminster Seminary," *Presbyterian Guardian* 4 (May 15, 1937): 50.

This alien group to which I have referred considers no one to be truly Presbyterian unless he agrees with them in everything which they choose to call essential to being "Reformed"—much of which is derived from their own non-Presbyterian background. They have evidenced an inflexible determination to enforce their own peculiar notions by crushing the broad evangelical point of view which in its earlier years made the Presbyterian Church in the U.S.A. a great Reformed Church, and not a mere sect. All this is far from the real purpose for which the Seminary was founded.

MacRae's charge was that Westminster was turning non-American after Machen's death, and it was departing from the broad fundamentalist consensus that had previously characterized it. What particularly provoked him was a series of articles that John Murray had written in the *Presbyterian Guardian* on "The Reformed Faith and Modern Substitutes." In exposing contemporary departures from historic Presbyterianism, Murray did not limit himself to exposing the modernism of the Auburn Affirmation. The Reformed system of doctrine "is to be carefully distinguished from, as well as set over against, not only non-Christian systems of thought but also systems of belief that in general terms may be called Christian or even Evangelical."[18] For Murray, this included Arminianism and dispensational premillennialism.[19]

A few months later, Carl McIntire led an exodus of 14 ministers (including MacRae) out of the OPC to form the Bible Presbyterian Synod. McIntire's claim was similar to MacRae's: the denomination had departed from the "historic position of American Presbyterianism." At issue was the one-year-old church's claim that it was the spiritual successor of the church it had separated from, the Presbyterian Church in the U.S.A. That claim was fraudulent, McIntire contended, because the church failed

18. John Murray, "The Reformed Faith and Modern Substitutes," *Presbyterian Guardian* 1 (February 3, 1936): 143.

19. Another work by Murray that incurred McRae's wrath was "Dr. Buswell's Premillennialism," *Presbyterian Guardian* 3 (February 27, 1937): 206–9, a review article of J. O. Buswell's *Unfulfilled Prophecies*.

to embrace fundamentalist teaching on dispensational premillennialism and abstinence from alcoholic beverages.

And so the church, following the seminary, was assuming a perilously non-American character. The language directed attention to the immigrant Americans on the Westminster faculty, especially Cornelius Van Til, a Dutch-American and John Murray, a Scotsman.[20] One can only imagine how this charge played out within the church on the eve of the Second World War.

The battle for the identity of the church soon focused on its confessional standard. The second General Assembly in 1936 marked a victory for the Westminster faculty over the Americanists when the Assembly rejected the 1903 revisions to the Westminster Confession of Faith. For McIntire, the rejection of these American revisions further damaged the OPC's claim of spiritual succession, because it was no longer confessionally an *American* Presbyterian church.

Both sides had a point. American Presbyterianism had historically been represented by two parties, one more confessionally oriented, with a restrained view of the social witness of the church, and the other less concerned with confessional subscription and more oriented toward the cultural influence of the church. The Old School–New School split in 1837 saw these two part ways. The reunion of 1869 did little to solve the differences. Each side was operating with a different conception of American Presbyterian tradition, and each saw the other as abandoning the task of spiritual succession.

When he left the OPC, Carl McIntire went on to predict that "all that will be left" of the OPC, so out of touch with the fundamentalist mainstream, would be a "little group around Philadelphia." In defending the OPC against McIntire's charges, Edwin Rian enthusiastically predicted that the church would continue to experience significant growth despite the high-profile departures of McIntire and MacRae.

20. Also falling under this indictment, but playing a secondary role, were two other Dutch-Americans, Ned B. Stonehouse and R. B. Kuiper.

As it would turn out, both McIntire and Rian would prove wrong.

Reformed versus Evangelical

Soon after the McIntire-led departure of fundamentalists, Westminster and the OPC were caught in another controversy. When Gordon Clark was dismissed by Wheaton College in 1943, he sought ordination in the Orthodox Presbyterian Church. The ensuing examination of his theology launched the "Clark Controversy" in the OPC.[21]

This controversy is often described as an esoteric philosophical debate between Clark and Van Til on the incomprehensibility of God and the Creator-creature distinction. But to reduce the debate in that way is to profoundly misunderstand the matters that were at stake. When the entire faculty of Westminster joined in signing a complaint against Clark's ordination, they objected not only to Clark's theological formulations but to the plan of his supporters to take over the denomination, and to cooperate more fully with American evangelicals. The Westminster faculty warned that this agenda would usurp the church's allegiance to the Reformed faith.

Clark's evangelical supporters saw a debate between ecumenical Calvinism and narrow Calvinism. Frustrated with the failure of the OPC to grow to a large and influential size, the evangelicals such as Edwin Rian sought to establish the church's priorities in fighting modernism and promoting evangelism. Their opponents, they claimed, were mired in extra-confessional causes such as exclusive psalmody and closed communion. In a telling comment, Clark supporter Floyd Hamilton asserted that "the Orthodox Presbyterian Church should follow the American tra-

---

21. For a careful analysis of this controversy see Michael A. Hakkenberg, "The Battle Over the Ordination of Gordon H. Clark," in *Pressing Toward the Mark: Essays Commemorating Fifty Years of the Orthodox Presbyterian Church*, ed. Charles G. Dennison and Richard C. Gamble (Philadelphia: Committee for the Historian of the OPC, 1986), 329–50.

dition in Presbyterianism, rather than the traditions of churches holding to the Reformed Faith in other lands."[22] Once again, the nativist card was being played, and Westminster's immigrant faculty was accused of being out of touch with American culture.

Eventually, the complaint against Clark's ordination was denied. But the agenda of the evangelicals failed in other ways, including their efforts to gain control of Westminster Seminary. Within a few years, Gordon Clark, Edwin Rian, Floyd Hamilton, and their sympathizers would leave the OPC. The church would remain Reformed and not evangelical in identity, and it was Reformed as defined by the Westminster faculty.

The Clark controversy and its related debates took place in the church during the rise of the neo-evangelical movement in the 1940s. Led by Harold Ockenga, himself a graduate of Westminster and a disciple of Machen, neo-evangelicalism sought to shed itself of the separatism and anti-intellectualism of fundamentalism. In order to mobilize conservative Protestants for evangelism and social action, several key evangelical organizations were established, including the National Association of Evangelicals, Fuller Theological Seminary, and the Billy Graham Evangelistic Association.

Westminster Seminary and the OPC watched with particular interest the formation of Fuller Theological Seminary. Ockenga, Fuller's first President, articulated the mission of Fuller as carrying out the tradition of Old Princeton, evidence that he denied Westminster's claim to that role. For its part, the *Presbyterian Guardian*, under the editorial pen of two Westminster professors (Stonehouse and Woolley) at the time, looked with astonishment at the effort to start a school without a clear doctrinal standard. While Westminster and Fuller were both seminaries independent of ecclesiastical control, there is where the similarities ended. "The doctrinal standards of Fuller Seminary have not yet, to our knowledge, been published. . . . Westminster Seminary has stood like a rock throughout its history on the propositions

22. Quoted in ibid., 344.

that a system of doctrine is taught by the Bible, that that system is what is generally known as the Reformed Faith."

Fuller's doctrine-less foundation doomed it to failure, the editorial went on to suggest. "American fundamentalism has preached a far more limited creed. It has, characteristically, stood on a platform of discrete points, elements taken out of systems of doctrine, rather than elements making up such a system. . . . [Such a platform] is not good as a foundation for solid, hard, systematic thinking, learning, and teaching."

Stonehouse and Woolley conceded that Fuller was attracting an impressive faculty. But they urged *Guardian* readers not to be seduced by names. "The faculty of Fuller Seminary represents the idea of aggregating a collection of loosely related points. The Westminster faculty represents a carefully integrated system. It is for this reason that we are convinced that Westminster Seminary promises to be superior to the newer Fuller. Fuller is attempting to gather a galaxy of stars, Westminster has a team."

What emerges, then, is a clear difference between Westminster and the OPC on the one hand, and the nascent evangelical movement on the other: the former has a "carefully integrated system of doctrine" and is committed to the theological maximalism of the whole counsel of God. The latter is a movement incoherently defined by a vague list of fundamentals. Fuller Seminary's catalog described its doctrinal position as "the fundamentals of the faith believed by Christians through the ages and as taught in the Holy Scriptures." Doubtless with Westminster in mind, Fuller's catalog explained the folly of going beyond the fundamentals: "Independent seminaries are too often associated with a particular doctrinal emphasis which limits their appeal and usefulness."[23]

Stonehouse and Woolley warned readers about a movement mentality within the American neo-evangelical circles.[24] Their antidote was more precision in theological formulation: "A sys-

23. The Fuller catalog was quoted in Arthur W. Kuschke, "Fuller Seminary," *Presbyterian Guardian* 18 (October 1949): 183.
24. For a discussion of evangelicalism as a "movement" see D. G. Hart, *Deconstructing Evangelicalism* (Grand Rapids: Baker, 2003).

tem of truth is itself a guard" against theological "fads" and "hobbies."[25] The language here is important because it contrasts sharply with John Frame's analysis of what he calls the "Machen movement" in twentieth-century American evangelicalism. As Frame sees it, the "Machen movement was born in the controversy over liberal theology," but "once the Machenites found themselves in a 'true Presbyterian church' they were unable to moderate their martial impulses. Being in a church without liberals to fight, they turned on each other." Frame's provocatively titled article, "Machen's Warrior Children," goes on to describe no less than 21 battles that have been fought by the "Machen movement." Many of these were unwisely chosen battles that have rendered Machen's cause badly fragmented, and the moral of Frame's story is a greater toleration of theological differences.[26]

Surely Stonehouse and Woolley would have challenged the language of a "Machen movement." Machen started a church. It was Ockenga who launched a movement, and the history of his neo-evangelical cause, especially the seminary he helped to found, hardly provides confidence for Frame's theological diversity.

Moreover, a careful reading of Machen's *Christianity and Liberalism* would reveal how faithfully Westminster and the OPC were following in the direction of Machen's teaching. Machen wrote his book to warn conservative Protestants that the ultimate danger in liberalism lay not in false doctrine but in doctrinal indifference, which is the source and carrier of doctrinal deviation. "The church," Machen insisted, was to be "a doctrinally strict company of believers." Not for him was a coalition loosely gathered around a set of fundamentals. Ockenga, despite his claims of allegiance to Machen, abandoned Machen's churchly and doctrinally precise vision when he launched the neo-evangelical crusade. Machen made clear in his book how he would have assessed

25. "Stars or a Team?" *Presbyterian Guardian* 16 (July 10, 1947): 199. Although the editorial is unsigned, it was likely written by either or both of the editors at the time, Ned B. Stonehouse and Paul Woolley.

26. John M. Frame, "Machen's Warrior Children," in *Alister McGrath and Evangelical Theology*, ed. Sung Wook Chung (Grand Rapids: Baker, 2003).

Ockenga's ambition: "Indifference to doctrine makes no heroes of the faith."[27]

This context helps to explain why Westminster claimed to teach "the whole counsel of God." The phrase was a response to theological minimalism that generated the evangelical cause. (The Evangelical Theological Society, founded in 1949, had one doctrinal affirmation for membership: biblical inerrancy.) Far from seeing a renaissance in orthodoxy with the rise of the neo-evangelical movement, the Westminster faculty saw in the movement's doctrinal diversity the very conditions that permitted liberalism to triumph in the Presbyterian church. "May the day come," the *Guardian* editorial on Fuller Seminary concluded, "and come soon, when American fundamentalists will stop being content with the minimum of God's truth and start proclaiming the maximum."

Ultimately, Westminster proved unwilling to teach less than the whole counsel of God and thus link arms with fellow evangelicals. Westminster was a recovery of a Reformed and Presbyterian consciousness, and in its distance from evangelicalism it bred distinct features in Orthodox Presbyterian ministers. In Charles Dennison's words, the OPC emerged as a unique denomination in twentieth-century American Protestantism because it "refused to denigrate doctrine. From the beginning it has worked to communicate the fullness of the Reformed faith and retain the ministry of the Word for men who are neither weak nor ignorant."[28]

The struggle that Westminster waged here was not merely between theological maximalism and theological minimalism. The lines were also drawn between the unpopularity of its confessional cause on the one hand and the "appeal and usefulness" of Ockenga's, on the other. As the evangelical movement blossomed in the 1940s, Orthodox Presbyterians were tempted to find it attractive and abandon their small denomination. For that reason, West-

27. For an analysis of Machen's book and its application to neo-evangelicalism, see Carl R. Trueman, *Christianity, Liberalism, and the New Evangelicalism: Lessons from J. Gresham Machen* (Bristol: Onesimus Books, 2002).

28. Dennison, "The Orthodox Presbyterian Church 1936–1986," 10–11.

minster's church historian Paul Woolley penned the brief article, "Discontent!" in the *Presbyterian Guardian.* Woolley contrasted two forms of discontent within the eight-year-old denomination. An unhealthy discontent was a yearning for large numbers and cultural influence. Healthy discontent was a concern for "progress in the completeness with which the faith is preached in [OPC] pulpits." Woolley put the matter directly before his readers:

> The question is really a very simple one. Does the Orthodox Presbyterian Church want to have a growing revival in the preaching and application of the Reformed Faith in these United States in the year 1944? Or does the Orthodox Presbyterian Church want to have many members and much money and read about itself often in the newspapers? It can have one, but it cannot have both.

Woolley urged his OPC readers not to lose heart. If the church would cultivate a healthy discontent, "God's blessing is awaiting us." Characteristically, he concluded by quoting Acts 20:27.

This distance from the emerging evangelical consensus had two effects. First, it consigned both institutions, in the minds of their broader evangelical opponents, to a sectarian status. Gordon Clark, for example, labeled the OPC a "sectarian oddity," and Westminster alumnus E. J. Carnell of Fuller Seminary came eventually to describe Machen's defense of orthodoxy as cultic.[29] In response, Westminster and the OPC turned that argument on its head. It was evangelicalism that was steeped in American provincialism. Sensing themselves liberated from an American agenda, they claimed an expression of the Reformed faith that was ultimately more genuinely international. The non-Americanism of the founding faculty helped steer the OPC into a far greater appreciation for the catholicity of the church. Westminster was more cosmopolitan than Fuller, and the OPC more

29. Gordon H. Clark, "Blessed River of Salvation," *Presbyterian Guardian* 14 (January 10, 1945): 14; Edward John Carnell, *The Case for Orthodox Theology* (Philadelphia: Westminster, 1959), 115.

ecumenical (in a churchly sense) than the National Association of Evangelicals.[30]

This distance from evangelicalism kept both institutions small. But it also provided for both institutions a firmer and more coherent theological identity. For their part, the Westminster faculty looked at the emerging evangelical movement, with its collapse of doctrinal identity and rise of parachurch cooperation, not as a sign of renewed health, but as a manifestation of theological weakness. In subsequent decades, Westminster Seminary and the Orthodox Presbyterian Church continued to define themselves in distinction from their surrounding American evangelical subculture. In debates that followed, such as the Peniel controversy[31] and discussions on Sabbath observance,[32] the OPC continued the task of boundary-maintenance, sustaining an identity that was self-consciously Reformed and not evangelical. In all of these episodes the voice of Westminster Seminary was prominent in defining that identity.

Under Westminster's theological leadership, the OPC thus became, in Charles Dennison's words, "a Presbyterian anomaly."

30. To be sure, the OPC was not fully spared the trappings of Americanism. In an unpublished paper, "Reconciling Two Kingdoms and One Lord: Conservative Presbyterians and Political Liberalism in the United States," D. G. Hart finds a nationalist agenda within the OPC rhetoric, especially during times of war. Hart identifies two traditions at Westminster, and ironically, the more Americanist one was sponsored by the non-Americans (Murray and Van Til). Contrary to the assessment of Westminster's fundamentalist and evangelical critics, it was the native-born Americans on the faculty (Machen and Woolley), whose politics were least pro–"Christian America." Hart's analysis offers important qualifications to the case for Westminster and Orthodox Presbyterian exceptionalism. Still, the nationalist argument tended to be muted at Westminster, even where it seemed most likely to be found. For example, while the Westminster Confession's discussion of the Sabbath may have theocratic leanings, a strict sabbatarian such as John Murray rarely made a nationalist argument for Sabbath-keeping, focusing instead on the importance of the Sabbath for the welfare not of the state but of the church.

31. For a fuller treatment of the Peniel controversy in the OPC, see chapter 8 in D. G. Hart and John R. Muether, *Fighting the Good Fight: A Brief History of the Orthodox Presbyterian Church* (Philadelphia: Committee for the Historian of the OPC, 1995).

32. On the OPC and Sabbath see John R. Muether, "The Sabbath and Orthodox Presbyterian Identity," in *Perspectives: A Pre-Assembly Conference Commemorating the 60th Anniversary of the OPC* (Coraopolis, Pa.: Committee for the Historian of the OPC, 1997), 55–57.

In a sense beyond the way it was intended, the accusation that Westminster Seminary was promoting within the OPC a non-American theology was true. The theology of Westminster cultivated within the church a sense of cultural homelessness.

OPC estrangement from both establishment mainline Presbyterianism and social-crusading evangelicalism was reinforced by the prevailing amillennialism of the Westminster faculty. If the earlier challenge came from premillennialism, discussions of late have focused on postmillennialism. Recent studies by Robert Strimple and Richard Gaffin have likened the setting of the church today to the wilderness experience of the old covenant people of God. In Strimple's words, "Christ's church today remains in the wilderness, and gradual world-wide dominion does not occur in the desert."[33] Gaffin has criticized both premillennials and postmillennials for "de-eschatologizing" the present, and for an "eschatological impatience" that looks to a golden age in the future, failing to appreciate the church's present eschatological victory, even in its wilderness suffering, in union with Christ.[34]

The anti-postmillennial writings of Strimple and Gaffin bear strong resemblance to the anti-premillennial efforts of John Murray and R. B. Kuiper: exegetically grounded, pointing the church to her eschatological character, and restraining the church from the social agenda of competing eschatologies. Not surprisingly, some contemporary postmillennialists have dismissed Westminster and OPC as narrow and irrelevant in much the same way that McIntire and MacRae did in the 1930s.

Behind Westminster's rigorous amillennialism lay the fingerprints of Geerhardus Vos. "In a very real sense, what Van Til and Murray learned from Vos provided the theological tone and underpinning for the OPC," according to Charles Dennison.[35] Vos's

33. Robert B. Strimple, "Amillennialism," in *Three Views of the Millennium and Beyond*, ed. Darrell L. Bock (Grand Rapids: Zondervan, 1999), 63.

34. Richard B. Gaffin Jr., "Theonomy and Eschatology: Reflections on Postmillennialism," in *Theonomy: A Reformed Critique*, ed. William S. Barker and W. Robert Godfrey (Grand Rapids: Zondervan, 1989), 223–24.

35. Charles Dennison, *History for a Pilgrim People: The Historical Writings of Charles G. Dennison*, ed. Danny E. Olinger and David K. Thompson (Willow Grove, Pa.: Com-

teaching has made an indelible impression on Orthodox Presbyterian spirituality. In maintaining a Vossian sense of the eschatological location of the church, the OPC has insisted that the church is not for hire, neither by the state nor by any other cause short of the hope to which it is called to testify. Consequently, Orthodox Presbyterians have been "pilgrim people," with a corporate identity of a disenfranchised and counter-cultural character.

Westminster and the OPC: A Thing of the Past?

The OPC was careful never to take its dependence on Westminster for granted. At several points in its history it debated the wisdom of relying upon an independent seminary for the education of its ministers. From time to time the church considered the establishment of a denominational seminary. The most significant of these discussions took place with the creation of a special General Assembly Committee on Theological Education in 1944. That committee reported to the thirteenth General Assembly that it did not judge it "necessary as a matter of principle for the church to provide comprehensive theological education for training of its ministerial members" and further that under the prevailing circumstances the church did not have to conduct such a seminary.[36]

As this survey has demonstrated, the preeminent "prevailing circumstance" was Westminster Seminary, which functioned as a denominational seminary. Though independent of ecclesiastical control, Westminster's Orthodox Presbyterian churchmen and scholars inducted Orthodox Presbyterian ministerial candidates into a Reformed and Presbyterian culture of interpretation. Westminster performed that function ably, and for a long time: from

---

mittee for the Historian of the OPC, 2002), 77. Dennison goes on to write: "In fact, it could be that the most important theologian to the OPC in its early days was Geerhardus Vos. Even though he never joined the new church or even sought to influence it, Vos could be as much the OPC's fundamental counselor and as essential to OPC identity as any of the people usually mentioned."

36. Minutes of the 13th General Assembly of the Orthodox Presbyterian Church (1946), 91–94.

June 11, 1936, to November 18, 1962. Ned B. Stonehouse's unexpected death on that date triggered the rapid passing from the scene of the original faculty in the next decade: Murray retired in 1967, Young died in 1968, Van Til retired in 1972, Woolley retired in 1977.

With the passing of that first generation of faculty, Westminster began to expand ambitiously beyond a primarily Orthodox Presbyterian constituency. It aggressively recruited larger numbers of students, and it added faculty from a wider diversity of denominations. As a result, Westminster's "nearly exclusive bond with the OPC was a thing of the past."[37] Statistics bear this out. By 2002 the number of ministers in the OPC trained by both Westminster Seminaries was down to 60 percent (48 percent from Philadelphia and 12 percent from Escondido). Even more dramatically, in the decades of the 1990s, Westminster Seminary, for the first time, was producing a minority of the younger ministers becoming ordained in the church.

The seminary's decision to expand to a West Coast campus in 1979 may have unintentionally abetted this trend, especially by stripping the Philadelphia campus of its systematic theology department with the departures of Professors Frame and Strimple. Moreover, the formation of the Escondido campus began the recent trend in the pluralization and regionalization of theological education within conservative Reformed circles. But it is also worth noting that the Escondido campus, though smaller than the Philadelphia campus, is presently producing more ministers for the OPC than Philadelphia. While it is too early to tell, Westminster in California may eventually reverse the trend of seeing fewer OPC ministers with Westminster degrees.

To their credit, both Westminster and the OPC have made recent efforts to rekindle their relationship. In 1975 the OPC Committee on Ministerial Training reported to the General Assembly that members of its committee were meeting with seminary administration "to explore ways in which the Orthodox Presby-

37. Dennison, *The Orthodox Presbyterian Church 1936–1986*, 12.

terian Church and the seminary may assist each other in the preparation of men for the Gospel ministry."[38] One fruit of those discussions was an elective course in Presbyterian polity. In 1990 Westminster in Philadelphia communicated to the General Assembly that the "faculty was seeking to express its desire to continue building and nourishing its relationship with the Orthodox Presbyterian Church."[39] Further, in 1991 Westminster sent an invitation to the OPC to send an observer to seminary meetings of the board of trustees. The OPC accepted the invitation, and its observer reported to the 1993 Assembly on the cordial reception he received. However, it appears that those efforts were sporadic and not ongoing. Instead, the seminary and church continued to grow apart.

Perhaps the greatest indication of the split was the termination of Norman Shepherd in 1982. Shepherd's dismissal did not represent the defeat of Shepherd's continental Reformed formulations by his nativist American theological opponents, as some of Shepherd's supporters have argued (although the rhetoric of some of Shepherd's critics might lend plausibility to that claim). Nor was it a battle between OPC and non-OPC factions in the seminary. (The church itself was strongly divided over Shepherd's views.) Still, the Shepherd case revealed how distant the Philadelphia campus and the church had become because the outcome of the controversy revealed how little the seminary saw itself answerable to anything but public opinion. In the end, Shepherd was terminated "for the good of the seminary." In taking this step Westminster seemed to join other schools in establishing themselves as accountable to the educational marketplace and not to the church.

But Westminster is not entirely to blame for its severance from the church. Over the past quarter century, Reformed seminaries have proliferated, and the OPC is receiving ministerial can-

38. Minutes of the 42nd General Assembly of the Orthodox Presbyterian Church (1975), 181.

39. Minutes of the 57th General Assembly of the Orthodox Presbyterian Church (1990), 104.

didates from a wide range of sources. Some of these schools, in
a effort to compete in the competitive marketplace of theological
education, have highlighted their extra-confessional distinctiveness (such as teaching on the days of creation or theories of
preaching).

The loss of Westminster as the nearly exclusive training
ground for the OPC has profoundly affected the church. Within
the past generation the OPC has witnessed the disappearance of
its sense as a community of interpretation. Presbytery meetings
and General Assemblies, which were formerly, in effect, meetings
of the Westminster alumni association, have become gatherings
of strangers. (At the 2003 General Assembly, for example, the ministerial commissioners came from 25 different seminaries or Bible
schools.) Suspicion and distrust have entered where confidence
and charity formerly reigned. (One indication is the sharp rise in
appeals and complaints before the General Assembly. A rarity in
the early history of the OPC, the General Assemblies in the 1990s
have averaged more than 3 appeals or complaints per year.)

Machen founded the OPC with the confidence that Westminster Seminary could produce her ministers. Can the OPC preserve the Reformed tradition in America after its intimate relationship with Westminster has been severed? The answer depends,
once again, on how one defines the American Presbyterian tradition. Some observers see Carl McIntire's vision finally tri-
umphing in the OPC: it is becoming an activist church increasingly embroiled in the culture wars. Stated clerk Donald J. Duff
has gone so far as to suggest that a reformed fundamentalism
may now characterize the church.[40]

In an effort to reestablish the corporate culture of its earlier
history, the Orthodox Presbyterian Church established the Ministerial Training Institute (MTIOPC). At present, the goal of the
MTIOPC is modest, and is designed to supplement the education
Orthodox Presbyterian ministerial candidates receive, from West-

---

40. Donald J. Duff, "Reflections on the Last Ten Years of the OPC," *New Horizons* 17
(June 1996): 6.

minster east and west and elsewhere, with specific courses related to ministry in the Orthodox Presbyterian Church. Whether MTIOPC strengthens OPC relationships with Westminster or expands eventually into a denominational seminary remains to be seen.

Whatever shape MTIOPC eventually takes, its success will not be measured by the numbers of ministers it produces or the ways in which it might contribute to the numerical growth of the church. Rather, it will prove effective to the extent that it serves the church as Westminster so ably did in the past: proclaiming the whole counsel of God, maintaining the church's confessional integrity, and asserting her eschatological identity.

11

Reflections on Westminster Theology and the Seminary Constituency

Derke P. Bergsma

In 1980 Westminster Seminary expanded from its long-term center in Philadelphia to a second campus site in Escondido, California. Robert Strimple served as founding president of this emerging seminary and discovered challenges for which his previous experience as professor of systematic theology and academic dean in Philadelphia had not prepared him. High among those challenges stood the issues relating to the churches and individuals who constituted the broad company of supporters of the seminary. His prior academic experience had orientated his institutional perspective to the academic and administrative matters related to the internal environment of the seminary's on-campus life. Now, thrust into the role of president, he became conscious of the crucial need for an extended company of people who would identify with the cause and mission that the seminary represented. Such an identifiable community was certainly one of the indispensable needs, along with students, faculty, and library resources, without which the prospects for a "Westminster in the West" would be slim indeed. The lack of a supporting constituency for this new venture would assure its failure.

Bob engaged me, in those early years, in serious dialogue reflecting on the ideal relationship that the seminary should sustain with its supporters. From the outset we agreed that the seminary bears a responsibility of service or ministry beyond the immediate, on-campus life of the institution. That dispersed company of congregations and individuals who together help to make the work of the seminary possible is also a part of the seminary family. The resources of the seminary should be used beneficially with their welfare in mind too. But what forms of ministry would be appropriate for them? Would the seminary be in danger of duplicating, or, worse, intruding upon the work that is being done by other Christian institutions? And what motivational perspective should inform that relationship? In this essay we will emphasize that a wholesome, God-glorifying, and believer-enriching relationship between the seminary community and its broader constituency requires the discipline and motivation of consciously recognized attitudes. These include a broad kingdom vision, a clear recognition of who we are as a seminary, a humble attitude of servanthood, and a willingness to minister to people where they are in their varied circumstances of life.[1]

A Kingdom Vision

The opposite of a kingdom vision is one in which narrow institutional concerns dominate and shape all of our efforts to "sell" ourselves to those who we hope will provide financial support for the seminary. The typical approach is for a seminary to follow the prevailing techniques of the advertising industry to advance the seminary's institutional interests. Whether through personal contact or

1. The observations that follow are not positions drawn from scientific analysis of research questionnaires submitted to present or potential supporters of a seminary to determine their expectations from their relationship with it. Rather, what follows are conclusions that are the result of personal observations made during successful degree programs at four theological schools and while teaching at two seminaries.

through publicity brochures, the best qualities of the institution are highlighted. These include the professional quality of the staff, the reliability of the convictions of the teaching faculty who can be trusted to transmit faithfully its theological heritage, the high caliber and diversity of the student body and their leadership potential, and whatever other qualities that may serve to influence people to become or continue to be generous with their support. And, of course, the need for a continuing supply of competent and committed pastoral leadership, which the seminary is uniquely qualified to provide, is always emphasized. The prevailing sentiment underlining such a stance toward those outside her formal institutional life is to convince enough people to provide enough financial resources to assure the institution's survival. While emphasizing its qualities to its public constituency is certainly legitimate, there must be a better way for a seminary to relate to a wider audience. A servant role vis-a-vis its broader community of supporters is far more worthy of an institution that names the name of Jesus as Lord. If the primary motive is service, ardently devoted to others for Jesus's sake, can we doubt that all other needs will be supplied?

The seminary's supporting constituency is also in danger of being motivated by self-interest in its relationship with the seminary community. The tendency is to evaluate the appropriateness and effectiveness of their investment in terms of two criteria. For one, the theological positions of faculty members are carefully scrutinized to assure that they meet the test of orthodoxy, especially in terms of one or another pet doctrine. And another, very obviously closely related to the first, graduates as potential pastors are expected to conform to the esoteric interpretations of disputed Scripture portions as understood by a particular ecclesiastical body. Often if just one faculty member fails to meet just one of these criteria, the loss of support, in terms of both finances and student recruitment, is threatened.[2]

2. I was present at a denominational Synod meeting that debated whether to continue supporting a particular seminary. The issue involved the interpretation of the Genesis creation account by one faculty member. Without a hearing, the professor involved was judged to be in error, and financial support of the seminary was discontinued.

If we are brutally honest, relations between the seminary and the company of people we identify as "supporters" are too often characterized by the two unworthy attitudes mentioned above. Institutions cautiously position themselves in a favorable light before supporters who are viewed primarily as the source of donations, and supporters assure themselves of a consistent supply of the properly indoctrinated religious leadership. Only a shared kingdom vision pursued together in very concrete participatory action will provide the needed corrective to these unworthy attitudes. Later we will flesh out how a "shared kingdom vision" can be championed together in united "participatory action." By way of anticipation let me just observe that a seminary should have as much in common with the model of a medical school as it has in common with, for instance, a graduate school of philosophy. The former requires both the academics and the medical practice of the faculty, while the latter moves between library, classroom, and personal study chamber to engage in disciplined theoretical reflection. Among seminaries, the latter most often is typical. The challenge for a seminary is to be both.[3] A seminary should be as scholarly as a graduate school of philosophy and as practice-oriented as a medical school. What we will contend for is real, comprehensive, and in-depth involvement of the teaching faculty in pastoral work shoulder-to-shoulder with churches, missions, and related kingdom ventures. This involvement may sometimes be part-time in nature but also ought to include periods of full-time immersion in ministry service.

The study and teaching of theology should never be separated from the practice of the Christian faith by rank-and-file believers who constitute the body of Christ in the world. While some disciplines are less tempted toward scholarly abstraction by virtue of their subject matter—the pastoral subjects, for instance, because of their focus on the theology of the practice of

---

3. The term "seminary" itself implies a union of theology and practice as distinguished from a graduate school of theology associated with a university, with its purely academic focus.

ministry—all theological teaching is vulnerable to the lure of intellectual abstraction and, with it, the real danger of irrelevance in relation to the ministry of the Church[4] in the world. The seminary community—that is, board, faculty, staff, and broader constituency—should be recognized as a company of believers united in a common undertaking to advance the cause of Christ in the world as he gives us opportunity to do so. Or, to use a biblical figure, our calling is to seek together God's kingdom and righteousness, assured that all needs will be supplied—financial, staff, and trained leadership for the Church's ministry in the world.

This kingdom vision, which should inform our common task, will prevent us from the tendency toward distinguishing parties or groups on the basis of self-interest, each looking to the other as a means of advancing its own agenda. Those most closely identified with the cause of Christ as represented by Westminster Seminary, faculty and administrative staff particularly, ought to have a vision of a united company of believers with a common task most clearly defined. On them, therefore, rests the greater responsibility to articulate and demonstrate actively what it means to be a part of a company of believers committed to advancing the work of the kingdom. It is they who should be expected to take the initiative in offering themselves in a variety of service roles in ministry.

But how shall we serve? In what shall our service consist? The answer to these questions requires an answer to a prior question, namely, who are we, or how do we identify ourselves as a seminary? The reason why these questions must be addressed is that all of our service must flow consistently from our understanding of who and what we are. Our involvement in ministry must be consistent with our nature.[5] To this matter we now turn.

4. In this chapter the word *Church* is capitalized whenever the reference intended is to the church universal or the faithful believers in Christ throughout the world. The lower case is used whenever the reference is to an unnamed local congregation or to congregations.

5. The temptation is to do anything that encourages fund raising even if the activity has nothing to do with a seminary's character and mission.

What Is Westminster Seminary?

First, Westminster Seminary is a *Christian* institution.[6] This
means that we exist in the name and for the sake of Jesus who is
the Christ. Jesus is the reason for our being. As an institution we
are committed to Christ and to the thesis that in him alone the
fullness of the Godhead dwells and in him alone is the truth attain-
able and life meaningful. Whatever else there may be in our program or even in our constitution and by-laws that may be subject
to alteration, this is unalterable and unchangeable. We stand
unshaken in the conviction that Christ, and only Christ, is the
Way, that is, the Truth and the Life. It is in Christ's name that the
seminary stands, and all its efforts must be directed toward win-
ning and confirming people's allegiance to him as the only Lord
and Savior of the world.

Second, Westminster is a *Reformed* institution. There are
those who profess commitment to Christ who contemplate and
understand him in ways that are alien to our seminary because
we believe them to be unfaithful to the Scriptures. Therefore a
second observation must be made to properly identify who we
are. Our nature as an institution requires an identity with a specific theological heritage that bears the name Reformed. Basically it is the understanding of God, of the Fall and redemption,
and of sin and grace that was recovered in the Reformation and
articulated in a systematic way by John Calvin on the basis of the
Scriptures and *only* the Scriptures. Others since the Reformation
have contributed to the broadening and deepening of our understanding of the gospel of grace, and we acknowledge their contributions with thanksgiving. Creeds and catechisms have been
written as abiding testimonies to a Reformed and, therefore, God-
glorifying understanding of the biblical faith. These together pro-

6. "Westminster Seminary" is referred to here in the singular for ease of reference. The
author of this essay has had a long association with Westminster in California, and these
remarks are made particularly with this institution in mind. But the proposals made here
are certainly applicable also to Westminster in Philadelphia as well as to other Reformed
seminaries.

vide the truth that we hold in common and upon which we stand and which serves as the core of our teaching and witness. We are a *Reformed* institution.

We are also a *seminary*. The term immediately implies scholarship, since it identifies us as an educational institution. It is a place where one has the right to expect learning and the development of clear thinking, judging capacities, and competence in making disciplined conclusions. To do so requires academic effort as faculty and students work together to master the great movements in church history, the biblical Hebrew and Greek to be able to open up the Scriptures, systematic theology to grasp the biblical truth in its coherent wholeness, and the theology of the practice of ministry to make possible the effective communication of the gospel from the pulpit, in classroom teaching, and in the full range of joyful and sorrowful experiences of life. As a seminary, we are part of the church, Christ's body in the world at work reflecting upon and systematizing God's gracious revelation of himself and his will, and training leadership to proclaim that revelation to his everlasting glory.

A Seminary as Servant to the Church

Seminary communities are customarily identified as institutions of disciplined theological reflection whose primary purpose is to prepare students for leadership positions in the Church and outreach ministries of the churches. For Westminster Seminary, this reflection is pursued consciously in obedience to the Scriptures as understood and affirmed in the Westminster Confession and Catechisms. Convinced that the honor of the Lord is best promoted within the framework of such an understanding, it invites faculty and students to join together to share and promote that theological heritage. This community or company of theological scholars is not so much one of teachers and students as it is one consisting of more mature and less mature students of the Word, focusing on ministry in the name of Christ for a lost

world. The impact of the seminary, its calling to reach the world
with the Good News, is primarily met through well-prepared graduates. Its preeminent purpose and reason for existence is viewed
as a preparatory environment for future ministers and teachers,
specialists in the Word, who will serve as messengers of the grace
of God to the nations. This is all well and good, and one could
argue that it adequately describes the *primary* role of the seminary followed by theological writing and professional conference
speaking. But such a point of view is too limited. It assumes that
a seminary has fulfilled its mission if it provides well-trained graduates who are dispatched (deployed, to use military terminology)
to do battle for the Lord in hostile environments. Its "outreach"
is by way of extension through its student graduates. In this view,
seminaries are part of the essential logistical support for the ministry of the Church through the training of leaders and by providing them with the ammunition they need for spiritual warfare.

The seminary's servant role as part of the Church requires
much more direct involvement in the active ministry than is traditionally recognized. Academic theology is too often separated
from the practice of the Christian faith in real world situations of
life. Like professors of medical schools who are expected to practice medicine as patient care, so professors of theology should be
practitioners within their field of learning. The biblical example
is that of the apostle Paul. Unequaled theologian that he was, he
ministered from house to house, to individuals, families, and small
groups, and so demonstrated the relevance of his theology in the
context of life's relationships. We should expect no less of professors of theology today. The question of a Westminster theology and the seminary's responsibility outside its own lecture halls
and study centers to its broader family and beyond is really a question of identifying and engaging in active ministry opportunities.
These must be consistent with the seminary's nature as a
Reformed, Christian, graduate institution of theological learning.
Ministry involvement of its personnel must be in harmony with
its nature.

People-Centered Pastoral Ministry

Traditionally, "study leaves" are used for academic research projects and theological writing, which, of course, is fine. Both purposes are theologically valid and in the interest of further productive contributions to the mission of the seminary. But faculty personnel should also be required to serve a "leave of absence for ministry" on an alternating schedule with "study leaves." Some of the best theological thinking is done in the context of the practice of ministry. Theoretical issues take on a vital, life-impacting reality when one is engaged daily and over a protracted period of time with real people who are called to live out their faith in a world unfriendly to the faith. As a volunteer member of the staff of a church or mission, a professor would be part of a frontier unit working shoulder-to-shoulder with local office bearers and missionaries. Covenant theology will take on fresh urgency when ministering to parents grieving over a wayward child from whom they may not have heard for years. Imagine studying the biblical teaching on the work of the Holy Spirit with a young father who has come, deeply troubled that his faith may not be genuine, since his sister in a nearby Pentecostal church has assured him that she has been "baptized by the Spirit, signified unto her by the speaking in tongues." Or the doctrine of Providence when you are called to a home where a six-year-old boy's body is still lying dead on the kitchen floor, brought in from the backyard where he fell off of a swing and broke his neck—and then you have to go directly to an anniversary celebration to recount God's providential goodness for forty years.[7] Face-to-face, people-to-people ministry is the perfect antidote for theology divorced from life. At the very least, it will serve as a needed reminder that the clarification of Christian

---

7. The three examples listed are not hypothetical. Each was taken from my own personal ministry experience. While I was theologically educated, I do not think I was pastorally educated. I suspected that it was partly because few of my seminary professors had ever been pastors. True or not, this explains the urgency I feel toward the issue being addressed.

doctrine and the exposure of heretical threats to it are not ends in themselves.

The benefits would be mutual for both the permanent church and mission personnel and the short-term seminary teacher volunteer. Imagine wrestling with a local pastor with the increasingly strident demands of people for change. Or how do we develop leadership that is both thoroughly grounded in historical Reformed doctrine and equally alert to the subtle contemporary cultural values that contradict it? How should church life be ordered in an increasingly diverse, postmodern culture? How can the church grow as a multigenerational body when the generational divide seems to be growing. How do we minister to the increasing numbers of divorced persons and their families? Imagine the mutual stimulation that would result from reflecting together on the theological and pastoral dimensions of such issues and many more. The benefits to the ministry of the pastors of the churches involved and for seminary classroom teaching are immeasurable as both experience the confirmation of the truth that the Word of God is sufficient for ministry in all circumstances of life.

Graduates of the seminary are foremost among the broader company of supporters for whom the seminary should evidence a vital interest. A continuing dialogue with graduates well beyond occasional correspondence and periodic newsletters would serve to enrich the work of the Lord of both the seminary and its graduates. Presumably, several years of intimate association of students and seminary faculty resulted in a shared vision of the kingdom of our Lord and an intense urgency to see it advanced. That relationship deserves to be preserved and strengthened. What if graduates had been informed while they were students that the seminary expects them to spend one week every ten years back on the campus reporting on how Westminster theology shaped their ministry? In the case of Westminster Seminary California, seventy persons per year would tell us how they were fortified and equipped for service and where the program needs strengthening. If just one half of that number responded, imagine a week set aside each year (during the January interim?) for thirty-five graduates, active in ministry, to sift through the joys and struggles of their calling while the faculty listened. Listening to them and learning from them could only enrich the education offered. A stronger bond between the seminary and this extremely important segment of its supporting constituency, increasing with every graduating class, would be a significant additional benefit.

It may be difficult for some graduates to be present on campus one week every ten years. Perhaps the seminary could dispatch representatives to meet them where they are. Alumni in specific locales with specific expertise could be encouraged to host and/or lead local events with seminary faculty input. In this era of convenient travel, professors could provide workshops, discussion opportunities, and mini-conferences in those areas where a cluster of graduates and other interested pastors are present. Concerned about the impact on faculty loads? One or preferably two such responsibilities per year on the part of each faculty member is hardly too much to expect, particularly if scheduled in the summer months. Besides, so important is this continuing relationship between graduates and seminary that other speaking and writing opportunities can be assigned a lower priority. And it is simply irresponsible for professors to pursue their personal speaking and writing agendas while pastors need help in presenting the gospel in a compelling, contemporary fashion. While maintaining their roots and grounding in the theology of Westminster, pastors are confronted with a needs-based, consumer-driven culture that places a premium on numbers as the mark of success. And when our eyes are on numbers, questions of theology, in particular ecclesiology, quickly become subordinate.

The emphasis of this essay on "participatory involvement" in the form of periods of total immersion in face-to-face ministry on the part of seminary faculty members is not suggested as a replacement or substitution for professional writing and speaking. These forms of service to the broader Christian community are so necessary as means of both clarifying the essentials of Westminster theology and exposing contemporary movements whose teachings are contradictory to it. Westminster has an enviable tradition of vigorous defense of the historic Christian faith and the responsibility now rests upon us to extend that worthy heritage.

We are beneficiaries of nineteenth- and early twentieth-century Reformed theology that affirmed the truth in contrast with liberalism, for which J. Gresham Machen stands as an abiding example. Then followed the Barthian reconstruction of theology, which Cornelius Van Til assumed a prominent role in exposing. During the second half of the twentieth century a variety of departures from the historic Christian faith arose. In the 1960s the specter of so-called radical theology appeared on the scene. It not only rejected the Bible as authoritative revelation, as liberal theology had done, but also discarded the belief in a transcendent, personal, sovereign, Creator God. Closely allied to this "theology of Christian atheism," and sharing its spirit, was the rise of "situation ethics." It claimed that no fixed standard for the moral life of mankind could be normative for any specific situation. The self-realization movement subtly continued a kindred spirit with its emphasis upon the sufficiency of individual human potential to effect positive change in its moral and spiritual life. Whether identified under the rubric of "self-affirmation," "self-esteem," or "self-realization," a common theme lurked: human beings have the inherent capacity to achieve spiritual fulfillment apart from repentance and the transforming work of the grace of God. And then came the "new spirituality" movement that was essentially an appeal to self-deification, urging everyone to affirm the divine within each one of them. It has no need of a "god" or reduces *it* to an impersonal creative force, available on demand, to be tapped when needed.

Through its theological writing and speaking, Westminster serves its broader community well to "test the spirits to see whether they are from God, because many false prophets have gone out into the world" (1 John 4:1–2). But, even when exposing error, the governing motivation must be to witness faithfully to the biblical truth, to hold high the Cross, and to win the lost for the Lord.

To reach a broader audience, the seminary's service will be both centrifugal and centripetal in nature, both moving out from the seminary center and attracting participants to the seminary's facilities. Some programs may be adaptable for both directions, others for just one. Consider the following possibilities:

- Weekend training sessions for elders, deacons, Sunday school teachers, and Bible study leaders on campus or elsewhere.
- Serving as a clearing house for services available through Westminster's board members, alumni, and friends. These represent a repository of great talent. Churches need advice on budget matters and building plans as well as resource persons to advise on Christian educational programs.
- Preparing a booklet indicating the availability of faculty members for lectures on topics they would like to be invited to give. Expect each faculty member to contribute two or more topics.
- Preparing video and audio tapes of special lecture programs and study series with accompanying printed material to guide discussion on the material presented.
- Committing the seminary to include on its Web site, in addition to the information about the seminary, regularly offered studies adapted for a general audience. All faculty members should be expected to participate.[8]

It is important to think creatively about a seminary's ministry to those beyond the immediate on-campus faculty and staff to all who will identify with its cause. The motive for it all must be service for and in obedience to Christ. In his name we serve the Church so that, through the Church we may reach the world. By faithfully doing the Lord's work as he gives us opportunity, we

---

8. The point is that such an effective service opportunity ought not to be left as an optional activity. Each faculty member has so much to offer.

can expect a broadening of the community that stands with us and a deepening of their commitment to the Lord. We want more people to know who we are. Especially do we want them to know about our loyalty to Jesus Christ and our commitment to the Reformed faith as the faithful expression of God's Word.

12

Reflections on Westminster Theology and Homiletics

Jay E. Adams

I have known Bob Strimple over the years as a good friend. I am personally aware of his devotion to the Lord and to his work. If there is one word that rightly characterizes his ministry during his tenures as professor of systematic theology at both Westminster Theological Seminary in Philadelphia, and then in Escondido, it is *faithfulness*.[1] It is a pleasure, therefore, to share in the composition of this *festschrift*. Indeed, I consider it a distinct honor to do so.

Bob's retirement from the seminary marks the end of an era. Beginning his work as a teacher in Westminster Seminary in Philadelphia, he served as second to John Murray. It was from Murray as his teacher and colleague that Strimple acquired the concern to teach from an exegetical base. Philosophical and confessional theological teaching had long been the rule in many other institutions, but Westminster soon became known for its fidelity to the text of the Scriptures. Under Murray students

---

1. Something might be said of his highly successful presidency of Westminster in California during its formative stages and how well he carried its ministry forward to establish it as a solidly viable institution in leaner times. But since that is not my topic in this chapter I must forego the privilege of doing so.

learned their theology as the fruit of careful biblical exposition and systematic treatment of the results. Strimple carried on the work that Murray had begun in a competent and forceful manner. What Murray had done exceedingly well, Strimple did even better. His unsung dedication to equipping men properly for the ministry produced a host of preachers, missionaries, and Bible teachers who carried the method of exegesis that was so central a part of the Westminster training into their various professions, so that today throughout the country and all over the world, men rightly taught to turn to the Bible as their only standard of faith and practice faithfully carry on their ministries. Bob Strimple's faithfulness has been greatly multiplied in the work of these men.

I said that Strimple had carried Murray's vision and work a stage further. That is true. While Murray was a brilliant exegetical theologian, students commented that his teaching in the classroom left much to be desired. From the old Scottish school, he inherited and used methods that not only failed to communicate but also often left students cold. Strimple brought a different and more vital teaching method to classes that gave new life to and love for the study of theology (and of even more importance—for the study of the Bible). But my assignment is to discuss the importance of theology for preaching as it has been taught at the Westminsters. I must turn, then, to this task. However, since Strimple was intimately involved, I cannot wholly divorce him from it.

When I went to Westminster to teach practical theology, with an emphasis upon preaching, I expected to find that students would spend the lion's share of their efforts to learn to preach by doing exegesis. To my surprise, and chagrin, that was not the case. Students were regularly engaged in preaching the big picture rather than settling down on a passage of Scripture or two in careful exposition and application. I discovered that the theology inherent in their sermons for the most part was precise and correct, but that their sermons lacked biblical support. Exposition was largely absent. Unlike Christ on the road to Emmaus, they failed to "open" the Scriptures for their listeners. At length, I found it necessary in their homiletic courses to teach many of the principles of exegesis that they lacked. This astounded me, and I sought an explanation for this unexpected situation.

Eventually, I came upon what I believe was the crux of the matter. The problem was that enthusiasm for exegesis and exposition of the sort that was being taught in systematics courses was being undermined and eclipsed by an overwhelming emphasis upon biblical theology. The importance of biblical theology, ever since Geerhardus Vos rescued it from the liberal theologians, had been gaining ground so surely that it had all but overcome other disciplines taught at the seminary. Some students even spoke of biblical-theological preaching, as if exposition and application of the Scriptures were to be replaced by this new approach. Vos's *Grace and Glory* is an interesting and helpful volume, but what you find there are not sermons but excellent essays.[2] Yet, there were students who took this book as exemplary of what preaching ought to be. The book, however, lacks the obvious exegetical base and the personal application that every sermon ought to have. It was a model for writing helpful essays, but not for preaching.

Strimple, I believe, understood that the overemphasis upon biblical theology that was gaining ascendancy among Westminster's students could only do harm if carried to excess. Biblical theology, of course, is necessary in the preparation of sermons so as to demonstrate that sanctification is by the Spirit of Christ and not by one's own unaided efforts. This is definitely needed in a day in which there are so many who moralize rather than teach the Word christologically. To that extent the study of the history of redemption taught by biblical theologians is salutary.

But as important as it was to assure that ministers of the gospel did not fail to present the gospel, biblical theological teaching was not a proper mold into which to cast preaching. The death and resurrection of the Lord Jesus Christ is central to all else; of that there should be no serious doubt. To see Jesus Christ as the

2. Geerhardus Vos, *Grace and Glory: Sermons Preached in the Chapel of Princeton Theological Seminary* (Grand Rapids: Reformed, 1922).

One who saves, and then by his Spirit sanctifies, is also essential to faithful preaching. I am sure that Strimple believed and taught that at Westminster as fully as any of us. But I do not doubt that he also saw that these facts were being so emphasized that other truths of the Bible were often lost in the process. That he went on teaching in a balanced fashion was of great comfort to me as a professor of practical theology. It was readily apparent that to be prepared for ministry men must go forth with more than the gospel to proclaim—as crucial as that is. And there was insufficient teaching to this effect.

To bring the congregation to say at the end of every sermon, "Well, I see even more clearly how wonderful Jesus is," is commendable. Certainly, the need to help Christians come to the realization that it is Christ who brings about all change is essential. Moralizing ("I can pull myself up by my own bootstraps") should be taboo. But, many men who became immersed in the flood of biblical theology that eventually overwhelmed both seminaries seemed to lose track of what the ministry is all about. It is not the writing of fine essays; it is preaching to people about their lives from the Bible in order to help them honor and serve Christ better.

Biblical-theological emphases that resist using application in sermons, for instance, fail to meet people where they are. The many homes facing problems of children caught in drugs, husbands struggling with pornography, and marriages breaking up need to hear more than essays. And that is true even when these essays present the great and wonderful news of redemption in Christ. They need to hear the Bible directly applied to their life situations. That Strimple believed this was clearly revealed by his practical preaching. He taught it in his systematic classes, as I did in homiletic and counseling classes, but I am sure he found that it was an uphill job to convince students to prepare for the real world where they would be facing these things in their ministries. I doubt that he believed fine essays that failed to show the relevance of Scripture to everyday life would do. Systematic theology should prepare men for preaching by helping them to formulate in an orderly fashion the truths that are gleaned from

Scripture. Its purpose ought not be merely to make theologians out of students. The systematic formulation of God's truth must be known and used in ministry to those in need. That is the sort of systematic theology that Strimple taught. It was immediately available for men to preach. The same could not be said for the wrong use of biblical theology, which, because it emphasized the indicative over (or to the exclusion of) the imperative, often clashed with homiletical training. Strimple's theological instruction, in contrast, fit snugly with good homiletical instruction; the two were of a piece. And those students who understood this and profited from it have had successful pastoral ministries.

The exclusively biblical-theological approach to ministry is often vague, generalized to the point of abstraction, and leaves congregations wondering whether there is anything to Christianity other than the history of redemption. Hearing the same emphasis over and over again may ingrain it in their thinking, but few know what to do with the facts that they have learned. The question is, "How does the history of redemption solve my problems so that I can please and honor God?" After a while, the facts themselves, repeated excessively, tend to become old hat—the very opposite of what those who preach this way want to happen.

While systematics once was the strong suit of seminaries, over the years its influence waned, probably because its teaching had become more philosophical than exegetical. As a consequence, it became sterile to many, viewed as "mere doctrine." Biblical doctrine should never be thought of that way. Doctrine is not antithetical, on the one hand, to exalting Christ or, on the other, to vital Christian living. Strimple's teaching provided, in biblical balance, instruction for students that was at the same time both Christ-honoring and practical for Christian living. This ability to buck the trend was, doubtless, due to his own lifestyle that exemplified each. The man was personally affected by the theology, just as all theologians should be. And, in turn, he taught that which affected him for good in such a way that others might profit from it.

So, we have seen that in the two Westminsters there came to be an ascendancy of biblical theology over systematic theology that was detrimental to good, solid preaching. In part, this was countered by the homiletical and theological instruction given, but even together, these did not always prevail. If there is anything to be learned from the progress of theological training that the two schools offered during the last thirty years, it is that an overemphasis in any one discipline is unhealthy and becomes a detriment to the training of ministers for the pastorate. Young men, preparing for the ministry of the Word, must not become sidetracked from *that* goal by anything else, no matter how attractive or interesting it may be. Yet, in a number of incidents, that is what happened during that period.

One thing that may be blamed for the tendency to value biblical-theological training above all others was the number of students who swelled the seminary in the East during the Vietnam War. How many of these students genuinely intended to enter the gospel ministry and how many were escaping service in the armed forces is difficult to say. But they were clearly a different breed of student from those who attended in other periods. There was a decided interest by many of them in the now bankrupt Dooyeweerdian philosophy that stressed the theoretical over the practical. There was little interest on their part in theology and in homiletics. In class, one day, such a student said, "There is more revelation in that thermometer on the wall than there is in the Bible." Men like this, whose thinking pervades a student body, can decidedly influence—if not determine—the direction that a school takes. Some of us were anxious to eliminate them from the ranks, but being newcomers on the block we were hindered by the highly academic approach of faculty chairman Paul Wooley and the theoretical apologetical approach of Bob Knudson. So, the seminary's previously more balanced approach took a turn away from exegetical theology only to emerge after the war—with the exodus of those students (many of whom I am convinced were avoiding the draft)—greatly weakened, especially in the field of systematic theology. Into the gap stepped the biblical theologians, to take over the vacant ground. They were ready when others, exhausted from the fight with the Amsterdam philosophical theology, were not.

Now, I don't want to claim that the problem that I have been chasing all over this article was wholly due to the influx of wartime students. But I am convinced that, more than some may realize, this factor was strongly involved in the weakening of the emphasis upon systematic theology, and as a result, of the failure of students to take homiletic and pastoral ministry as seriously as they might have. These war-time "students" cared little for systematics and homiletics alike.

Exactly what relationship do preaching and systematics have to each other? Both share the same source from which they draw their disciplines: the Bible. Instructors of both, as good householders, seek to bring from the treasury of the Scriptures things both old and new (Matt. 13:52). The one (systematic theology) serves by providing those good things, systematically formulated, that the other (practical theology) puts to work in preaching and other sorts of ministry to God's people. Systematics helps preachers to take into consideration all of the Scriptures that pertain to any given subject rather than so focusing upon one text that the larger picture is forgotten. When one preaches from a passage in John's Gospel that seems to teach that he may obtain anything that he wishes through prayer, he must keep in mind the whole doctrine of prayer, and not only the text immediately before him. Otherwise, failing to take into consideration passages that present qualifications to that promise (prayer must be fervent; the man praying must be righteous; he must pray according to God's will, in Christ's name, not to consume what he prays for upon his own desires, etc.), he might go off half-cocked in some wrong direction. Systematics, then, helps the preacher keep in the back of his head what James said when preaching from John. He does not preach one thing from John, then, later, when he comes to the book of James, preach something different. The two are laid out side-by-side in his thinking—if not always in his sermons—affording a more complete understanding of all that God has to say about prayer. Conversely, systematics taught in a manner that is divorced from its practical use in ministry is sterile. This natural relationship of systematics to practical theology should never be broken by anything that threatens to sever it. In the Westminsters, under Strimple's teaching, it was never severed.

So what is the upshot of all this? In my opinion, the proper balance between systematics and the rest of the seminary disciplines must be restored. When that happens, the natural relationship between homiletics and systematics will be seen even more clearly. While the affinity of the one to the other was never lost in either school, it was severely hampered by factors I have mentioned in this article. My hope is that these reflections will be instructive to both present and future teachers and students at the Westminsters.

13

Reflections on Westminster Systematics, Spirituality, and the Christian Life

D. Clair Davis

The way the Christian life is understood at Westminster Theological Seminary has a history. (Much of that history has been the teaching ministry of Robert Strimple!) Westminster has been very much aware of its heritage, as at the same time it has sought to move ahead in its understanding of the Bible. We know the wheels that already exist, and do not want to be caught reinventing any of them. That consciousness has been of vast importance as the context of the theological progress it has been able to achieve.

So continuity and development characterize our understanding of the Christian life. No element of theology exists in an ecclesiological vacuum, and that is especially true when the issues of sanctification and Christian living, the heart of the church's life, are at stake. What does a Reformed view of sanctification look like? How does it interface with other aspects of gospel truth? What does it mean that the Spirit who works in our hearts is the Spirit of the One who died for us to take away our sins? How is sanctification covenantal, within that context of reward and blessing, of punishment and curse? How is sanctification an expression of the Lord's election of his people, within the setting of eternal infallible purpose and promise?

There are many possible contexts, but the most significant setting of sanctification must be within the Reformation context of the application of redemption. If the center of the Reformation is the doctrine of justification, "the hinge of the gospel," what is the place of sanctification? Is it primarily in terms of our response of gratitude? Is it an add-on, something that "completes the Reformation," as in English Puritanism or the Dutch Second Reformation? Does biblical sanctification enjoy a vital or only secondary connection with the gospel? Is the gospel about forgiveness, or about change? To ask such questions betrays their foolishness. Any reductionism is bad, but a reductionism of the work of Jesus Christ or of his Spirit is absurd and intolerable. The whole Jesus Christ, in all his offices, Savior and Lord, has saved us from all our sins and all the curses of our sins. We worship him, not some divine provision or tool for spiritual growth.

Nevertheless, reductionism was often the way early Protestant theology went. We honor our fathers because they recognized that salvation is of the Lord alone, ours only because of his grace; but the questions kept coming up. Just what is the connection between forgiveness and change? Both are at the very heart of the Christian faith. But just how they connect often turned out to be a question frequently more puzzling than helpful.

The medieval background was the setting. Much Roman Catholicism had suggested that being forgiven depended upon your own heart-attitude. Grace was a divine fudge-factor, the giving of more credit for a little change than it really deserved. Grace could be thought of as, while not quite deserved, still something appropriate, congruous, fitting for God to give. If you did the best you could, would it not be appropriate for God to respond halfway? However obvious that may have first sounded, it soon became a confusing message, leading only to despair and cynicism. How could you ever know you were doing the best you could? Whatever the right answer is, it was still always about what *you* did, *your* heart-attitude. To be even a bit worthy of God's favor—how much would that take? Always much more than you could ever produce! For Martin Luther, that meant more and more activity, deeper and deeper searching confession of sin—so much so, that finally his monastic confessor had to accuse him of the great sin of overscrupulosity!

Forgiveness had been about me, barely about Christ. While his death had made the sacramental system possible, by giving the sacraments their power, they still had to be received properly! While grace made that possible, it was another kind of grace, not coming through Jesus Christ at all. It was something mysterious that came, or did not come, directly, unmediated, from God's naked will. A far-off God, with far-off grace, a mysterious, threatening God—that was all that the old church could give.

No wonder that the Reformation of Luther and Calvin was so liberating, so life-changing. No wonder that it was not just about theological reform, but was instead a whole theological paradigm-shift: the only grace there is always comes through Jesus Christ and his work on the cross. Faith is not ever about my own heart, but always about the power and completeness of what Jesus Christ did for me. The gospel is not about what I do, but always about what he has done. I stop looking at myself, and look only and always to him. It is not introspective, but extraspective.

But when I say that, what do I mean? Am I talking just about my forgiveness "out there," my legal justification only—or am I also talking about a real change in my heart, within myself? When I say *alien* righteousness, the righteousness of Jesus Christ, am I saying anything about my own righteousness, my own character? Since looking within to find some little spark of righteousness is what generated introspective confusion, should that not be avoided at all costs? Is it not wise to ignore totally all questions about my own personal change and focus completely on the alien righteousness of Jesus Christ, solely upon my legal righteousness? Understandably that was a common tendency, particularly within Lutheran orthodoxy. Making justification and forgiveness the hinge of my own salvation is just much clearer, much more

straightforward. The question of what am I really like, what change
I can see in my actions and in my heart—isn't that always a threatening, deadly thing to ask? Who can fathom the deviousness of his
own heart? Or, who can look at the progress in his life without
immediately being proud of himself, instead of Christ? Everyone
who has ever thought about his own character struggles with questions and doubts like that, but Lutherans more. That is partly
because of the old medieval background, but also partly because
of their understanding of the Reformed alternative.

That was especially true within eighteenth-century Pietism.
Pietism was just Reformed piety, manifest earlier in English Puritanism and Dutch second-Reformation Precisionism, and now
being transplanted into Lutheran Germany. If you are already
convinced as a Lutheran that there is something inherently extra-
biblical and rationalistic about the Reformed way of looking at
things, then you will have similar suspicions about the Reformed
understanding of the Christian life. Reformed theological rationalism had seemed obvious to Lutherans. If Jesus said, "This is
my body," and the Reformed say, "Well, not literally, but spiritually," then that reeks of rationalism. While the Bible clearly teaches
election, the Reformed addition of God's rejection too (reprobation) just goes beyond the Bible. That is rationalism too. With
that Reformed track-record, when Puritans tell us to look at the
condition of our hearts, *in addition to* the righteousness of Jesus
Christ, then is that not again the Reformed thing, of adding something speculative to the gospel? Does not considering the ebb and
flow of our faith inevitably compete with and minimize our joy
in the complete and finished righteousness of Christ? Does not
such a subjective, inward approach threaten our trust in *God's*
saving grace?

Worse yet, the Reformed had made the assurance of salvation, which the Reformation had seen as the greatest of all com-
forts and blessings, into a problem. While the Heidelberg Catechism had earlier included assurance within its understanding of
saving faith, saying that faith in Jesus Christ is faith in him as my
Savior, the later Westminster Confession defined assurance in a

much more involved and complex way. It spoke of the great gift of assurance and how we must seek after it, but went on to say that assurance was not of the *essence* of saving faith. It made a fine distinction between the seed of assurance and full assurance. While the seed was always there (basic confidence of belonging to Christ forever), full assurance (deep joy and delight in Christ right now) was difficult to attain and easily lost.[1] While this could be of some pastoral value in assuring those whose joy had grown cold that they did indeed still belong to Christ, to send the Reformed message that this assurance is an extra, an add-on, something *not of the essence of faith*, was just too much.

Lutherans saw their own faith as simply biblical, and the Reformed as complex, biblical plus rationalistic. Such a theology, they thought, was bound to influence the Reformed understanding of the Christian life. The Reformed, of course, wanted to put their faith and their lives together. William Ames had even defined theology as "the *art* of living unto God." Because of the perceived coldness of later Lutheranism, Reformed devotion of that practical, Puritan sort had become increasingly appealing to many orthodox Lutherans. They even felt the need to supplement an orthodox sermon with the practical piety of a mixed Reformed/Lutheran conventicle. They seemed to be pulling apart orthodox doctrine and issues of Christian living! Pietists, faced with the incongruity of learning devotion from Reformed "heretics," had come to believe that the points of difference between the two churches were after all unimportant. They observed that while the Reformed did not accept the physical presence of Jesus Christ in the Supper on earth, still they were enthusiastic about the fellowship they enjoyed with the incarnate Savior in heaven. Does it matter if Christ is here, or whether we are in heaven? Is the point not that we have true fellowship and communion with him? Was it not only reasonable that Pietists saw that kind of difference as less than at the heart of their faith? Also, Reformed people do speak of reprobation—but they offer

1. Westminster Confession of Faith, chapter 28.

the gospel to everyone. They follow the teaching of Calvin that it is impossible to distinguish between the nonelect unbeliever and the elect unbeliever until he dies—when finally he dies as a believer, or not. Can there be not only devotional fellowship between Lutheran and Reformed, but also a deep theological unity too—if it is not really about what doctrines say logically, but about how they function practically and devotionally?

To the orthodox Lutheran, however, Pietists appeared to be anti-theological, anti-doctrinal—because they kept looking for the *devotional* value of doctrine. Whatever you think of the locale of the presence of Christ, is not the important thing that we are there with him? Whatever you think of reprobation, is not the important thing that we are totally unable to determine who the reprobates are? From a Reformed point of view, this Pietist conclusion is just the triumph of ecumenical common sense, the recognition that the lines between Lutheran and Reformed are inconsequential and do not constitute a serious barrier to a common fellowship and devotion (as the Reformed had always said). But from a Lutheran perspective, Pietism was a sellout of the great theology of the Reformation.

This latter perspective is what has given Pietism (Reformed devotion!) a bad name to this day. Experiential devotion (how much do you love Jesus Christ right now? Is God's glory more important to you than your own happiness?) can be perceived as undermining not only the grand objectivity of the gospel (my faith has its value not from its own strength, but only from Jesus Christ, its object), but also the objectivity of *everything* in the Christian faith. It is not hard to see the Pietistic roots of Immanuel Kant ("a Moravian of a higher kind," he said) and Friedrich Schleiermacher, and hence all of modern liberalism. American liberalism's disparaging of any doctrine without a "cash-value" can be blamed on Pietism!

We still ask those questions today. Is it possible to recognize that a *few* doctrines really are essentially meaningless, or at least comparatively unimportant, and not an obstacle to Christian fellowship, without immediately jumping to the liberal conclusion that *all* theology is irrelevant and only practical living counts? Ecumenical confusion is deplorable, but intramural imbalance within the Reformed community is just as bad. Do Reformed people have a uniform position on the role of Christian experience? Do some see the Christian life as "slow and steady wins the race"? Do others seek more immediate changes in "revival"? Where is the line between revival and revivalism? Do differences like that threaten to splinter the Reformed community?

Particularly, why have the lives of our churches been characterized by the boom/bust cycle of revival and moralism, moralism and revival? While that cycle may not be rooted in theological reflection, it certainly has been characteristic of the emphases pastors have believed necessary to make. Are the people lazy, uncommitted, indifferent? Should they not be urged to be more motivated, should they not be warned about the danger of falling away? Is the grace of God not the last thing they should hear? As zeal in Puritan New England grew colder and colder, "legal preaching" seemed to be the right dose, breaking up the fallow ground for a deeper understanding of the gospel. It seemed that way to everyone—except to Jonathan Edwards, who dared to declare in Calvinist New England itself that legalism was Arminian and that the biblical doctrine for the hour was the old orthodoxy of gracious election and justification by grace through faith. For him, that was the only antidote to legalistic works-righteousness.

While the Great Awakening was truly global, with roots in the Moravians, the Wesleys, and Whitefield, the theological issues and implications were scrutinized and resolved by American Congregationalists and Presbyterians under the leadership of Edwards. Once more it became obvious that the preaching of Christian obedience and commitment *deliberately outside of a gospel context* was not just a tactical error but simply a denial of the gospel itself.[2] The Awakening was a "narrative of surprising conversions"—but the real surprise was that the church had

---

2. See Christopher F. Allison, *The Rise of Moralism: The Proclamation of the Gospel from Hooker to Baxter* (London: Society for Promoting Christian Knowledge, 1966).

thought it did not need to talk about the gospel very much. They presupposed church people would keep on understanding God's grace indefinitely without need of any reminder. What was truly startling was that the church had focused so much on the need for greater commitment that the gospel itself had been obscured and forgotten.

There had been serious theological misunderstandings. Believing that conversions ordinarily followed a certain pattern was confusing. While pastors and theologians had taught that no inevitable pattern exists, that the Holy Spirit is able to bring unbelievers to Christ "when and where and how he chooses," still, when people recited their conversion experiences, they all tended to sound the same. An initial period of spiritual insensitivity was followed by a period of recognition of sin and need, followed by attempts to make spiritual change in order to attain to a genuine faith in Christ, followed by failure and despair, followed by resolution to allow God to bring conversion in his own time, with earnest prayer that he would do it, followed by true conversion, followed by doubts, followed by assurance. Or even after that: assurance, recognition of false assurance, deeper despair than ever, deeper seeking for the regeneration that only God could give, a more startling conversion experience, and finally true assurance. Communion Sunday was when that pattern became most obvious, when hundreds of "seekers" thought about the perfect sacrifice of Christ—but only a few, with the right kind of conversion, dared come to the Table.

Reformed Christians had agreed that in conversion, spiritual change had to *precede* faith in Christ. The idea of something *preceding* faith had derived from the Reformed "plan of salvation," the *ordo salutis*. It taught that regeneration preceded faith, a way of saying that God's grace alone can open our hearts to enable us to believe. But what did that really mean? Did it intend to say there was a chronological, temporal sequence through which people coming to Christ ordinarily passed? Did it intend to say that people could be regenerate unbelievers, in the sense that they became regenerate years *before* becoming believers? It sounded that way. What was an unsatisfying and ultimately ridiculous conclusion (John Murray called it a "theological monstrosity") had become the pastors' consensus.

But when theologians had discussed the *ordo*, they were thinking of logical or causal sequence, not a temporal, experiential one. That is, if one is truly dead in sin, of course he must first be brought to life (regeneration) before anything else can happen. That did not mean that new life could be present before faith was exercised. It definitely was not intending to send the message that before you even think about trusting Christ, you need to first determine that you are able to. But good theological intentions were of little value against the long tradition of stereotyped conversion experiences. The *ordo*, which in its original form in Romans 8 was intended to provide encouragement during persecution, suffering, and struggle with sin, had been entirely turned on its head, warped and twisted, and had become a threatening word: don't you dare try to trust Christ until you're sure you have a transformed heart!

Within what should be a new universe of Reformed experience, the old medieval threat of congruent grace had come back again from its well-deserved death![3] Focus had been shifted from the revealed gospel of the cross back to the unrevealed, the hidden, the shadowy search for a change of heart. When the certainty of possessing a new heart was missing, then the gospel of faith in Jesus Christ had no relevance. It was time for the new Reformation of the Great Awakening to remind God's people again that the gospel is never about my heart, but always about the good news of Christ's righteousness. Where theological foolishness had abounded, once again the gospel abounded!

The words had changed, but the issues remained the same. The issue is always: How do the two sides of salvation, forgiveness and change, relate to each other? That once meant, how do justification and sanctification relate to each other? Now it meant,

---

3. Herman Bavinck, *Gereformeerde Dogmatiek*, 4 vols. (Kampen: Bos, 1895–1901), 4:1–16, 433–36.

how do justification and regeneration connect? The meaning of justification stayed the same, the objective or "legal" relationship a believer has to God, without taking his own ethical character in account. While sanctification and regeneration are different words, the first Pauline and the second Johannine, they both mean "change," the new transformed character that God gives his people. Through the debates of the Reformation, Protestants had come to understand that never could sanctification ("infused righteousness") be understood as something that needed to be present before justification could happen. That would be Roman Catholic, that would confuse the righteousness of Jesus Christ with our own righteousness. But when the words changed, and regeneration became the subject, then suddenly the fixed truths of the Reformation became problematic again—or worse, since the "priority" of regeneration to faith had become a badge of Reformed orthodoxy. The necessary distinction between temporal and causal priority had become hopelessly blurred.

What should the sinner do? Should he come in faith to Christ? Is it better to tell him to pray for a new heart? That was the perplexing question. The answer was complicated. What does faith look like now, placed between regeneration and justification? As far as justification is concerned, faith is "passive," extraspective, not looking to itself but only to Jesus Christ. From the direction of regeneration faith is "lively," made alive, transformed. Can faith be both passive and lively? Not if ordinary definitions are used. Properly understood, faith expresses such a radical heart transformation that it no longer looks to itself at all, but only and always to Christ. Faith is so lively that it is passive!

While the goal of this article is to consider the Reformed heritage of the Christian life, and then the Westminster contribution building upon it, we first needed to see it within its perplexing and controversial relation with justification. While the Awakening placed it high on the agenda, the issue has always been with us. Remember the Puritan master Walter Marshall and his *Gospel Mystery of Sanctification*. In spite of the title, that book is heavily about justification! Its theme is: Do not ever forget what you have learned about justification, that it is completely by grace through faith, for that is the main thing you will need to remember when you think about sanctification. The lesson of both Marshall and the Awakening is very simple: it is easier to understand that nothing we can do contributes to our forgiveness. Because living the Christian life is so much about what we do and how and why we do it, it seems more difficult to remember the old lesson, that we also live for the Lord only by grace through faith. Salvation is always of the Lord, whether it concerns forgiveness or change.

But the Christian life is a life of unremitting struggle, of battle, of hardship and trouble. How should we understand that? Reformed people see the universe lying in the bondage and corruption of sin. They know humanity as *totally* depraved, with every aspect of the personality twisted and poisoned by sin. However many aspects there are, biblical teaching is abundantly clear: all have been created good by God, all have fallen in sin, all are being renewed in Christ. The rational side of people is just as likely to be misdirected by unbelief and temptation as the emotional side (Calvin and Van Til!). The emotional or volitional sides are not inherently less stable or less sinful than the rational. No aspect of the personality is more susceptible to sin than any other, nor is any a better bridgehead for the gospel, more open to the truth of the Lord.

That has needed to be said many times. Rationalism is part of our ongoing Western Greek heritage. To find stability and order in reason seems natural, particularly in a static and flat world. The biblical orientation of sin and salvation as the context of human life may be obscured and forgotten in that artificial "rational" world. But it is not obscured in the world of sinful reality, where the Fall has perverted the human race; but also not in the world of God's salvation, where the Lord has made all things new, where those who were once far off have been brought home again, where death has been swallowed up in victory. In that world, not of cruel determinism, but of the Lord's good pleasure, what the living God has done is what is real, not what is theoretically possible. The world of probability, which goes on the way it always has, is an artificial world, but the Lord's covenant story of promise and faithful fulfillment is the real world. Within the climate of unbelief around him, the believer does not lose time on the foolish question of whether resurrection is possible, but always proclaims with joy that Christ is risen indeed!

God's story is reality, especially within his redemptive history, but also within the history of his church. In a time of Awakening, the issue is not whether a return to God in this corrupt age is still possible, but rather whether we serve the living God. Nor is it enough to evaluate a minister's ability in terms of his measurable academic qualifications; the basic question is whether he preaches with power, authority, the anointing of the Holy Spirit. Can solemnity guarantee that a worship service honors Christ? Can an unusual display of emotion dishonor him? Should the preacher speak to the mind, or learn from Edwards to speak to the whole person, to the heart? All those questions speak to the issues of the human personality: should we evaluate people descriptively, by what we see, or should we see them through the lens of Scripture? The biblical answer is, we see ourselves and each other not by sight, but by faith. We have the same expectations for believers as the Lord has. We look at God's people in hope. Depravity, failure, frustration are not the last word; the Lord's liberating, persevering salvation is.

What the Lord does in salvation is much more than Satan did in the Fall.[4] While we need to see the implications of total depravity, there is more benefit and encouragement in grasping the realities of total redemption! Where sin abounded, and it did, grace abounded more, and it does. The side of the Reformed faith which appears so denigrating, so pessimistic about the character of humanity, is not at all its last word. Reformed optimism (biblical *hope*) is rooted and grounded not in some residual, peripheral dignity of man, but rather in the unfailing love and power of

4. See Jay Adams, *A Theology of Christian Counseling: More Than Redemption* (Grand Rapids: Zondervan, 1986).

the Lord himself.[5] The more uniquely Westminster expression of that powerful and vital direction within the Reformed doctrine of humanity should be seen in several of its foci: apologetics, biblical theology, and counseling. The apological method of Cornelius Van Til has been from Westminster's beginning one of its foundational distinctives. He and his many disciples were committed to declaring as clearly as they could that God himself in his revelation is the only criterion we can ever have for the way we understand him, worship him, and love him. No alleged inherent ability or strength of man can take the place of that criterion, including the reason. That Westminster fine-tuning of the Reformed grasp of the nature of the creature's relation to his Creator is of vast and enduring value. But perhaps too much attention has been given to the fine distinctives between Van Til and the other Reformed apologists of his day. By now, contemporary postmodernism, with its radical relativism and fatal consistency, has made much clearer than it was in Van Til's day what the implications of unbelief really are. The sickness unto death of unbelief has caught up with Van Til's diagnosis, and much more of the Reformed world has caught up to him.

Biblical theology comes to the reality of redemption from a different beginning. Is the Bible timeless doctrinal truth, or is it the story of the Lord's unchanging love to his people? How is the eternal promise of God seen in the unfolding, surprising, amazing story? How do we see God's eternal election expressed in the history of the Lord's dealing with his people, in their weakness and unbelief as well as in their faithfulness? Is Jesus Christ yet another illustration of the eternal love of God, or is his story the heart of the Bible? Is the way a Christian preaches, especially from the Old Testament, significantly different from the way the rabbis or mullahs do?

When those questions are truly understood, then Reformed people quickly and vigorously recognize that something has been

---

5. See Jürgen Moltmann, *Prädestination und Perseveranz* (Neukirchen, 1961). There he traces interaction between Reformed theologians, some of whom saw the believer's new nature as the primary cause of his persevering in faith, and others who saw the source in Christ's faithful intercession and care.

missing in the way they have looked at the Bible. If the uniqueness of redemption in Christ is not understood as the foundation
for everything the Bible says, then the Bible has not been really
understood at all. If the Christian faith is not always about Jesus
and what he has *accomplished*, then it is no more than an empty,
frustrating, dead moralism. The biblical theologian is emphatic
that being a Christian is not just about listening carefully to God's
imperatives, but also about doing them always within the context
of the triumphant *indicative* of the gospel of the risen Christ. That
insight is the beating heart of the Christian life. The "not yet" of
the believer's daily battle with sin may not be allowed to swallow
up the "already" of the victory of the Lord Christ—and our victory too in our union with him!

The enthusiasm with which the giants of old Princeton recognized the biblical-theological paradigm-shift in the work of
Geerhardus Vos led to his being also a great guiding spirit at Westminster. The further insights of Herman Ridderbos in the Netherlands were also gratefully accepted there. Richard Gaffin Jr. has
given his academic life to greater and deeper clarification.
Edmund Clowney taught a generation how to preach in a Christ-
glorifying way. Westminster students received a training contin-
ually being reinforced by a rigorous and devout focus on Jesus
Christ, the one offered to us in the (biblical-theological) gospel.[6]

Jay Adams, the perfect wingman for Clowney, trained preachers. Clowney's gospel indicative was superbly flawless, but what
were his imperatives? They could seem at times to be simply, isn't
Jesus just marvelous? Isn't what he has done for us amazing?
Shouldn't our hearts overflow with joy because of him? Certainly,
if that glorious application is missing, we know immediately that
everything is missing. Jesus Christ is indeed not only the grand
indicative, but our worship of him the grand imperative too.[7] But
Adams was eager to add other imperatives, those specific to the
sin and need addressed by the biblical passage. He stressed the

6. Westminster Shorter Catechism, Q. 86.
7. Edmund P. Clowney, *The Unfolding Mystery: Discovering Christ in the Old Testament*
(1988; reprint, Phillipsburg, N.J.: P&R, 1991).

specificity of the passage and the concreteness of its application.[8] Illustrating the Clowney and Adams team-play through the star players of the Calvinism of the seventeenth-century Netherlands, I suggest that while Clowney was the German Reformed covenant theologian Koch (Coccejus), Adams was the Voetius of the English Puritan tradition. He wanted to ask not just the "what is new" question of the biblical theology, but also the "how" question, of how *specifically* the gospel is relevant with this temptation in your life today. Of course, applicatory preaching also expresses a theology of sanctification. How to preach about the Christian life is the same in content as how to live it. Perhaps these two differing homiletical/pastoral/biblical-theological approaches have yet to be resolved and coordinated at Westminster, or anywhere else. But the germs of their resolution are there. Adams is so biblical that he could not be a moralizer. Clowney is so Christ-centered that he honors the Christ of the Bible, the Jesus who is true God and also true man, who wrestled with real temptations in order to do the will of his Father. Westminster students have been putting them both together: it is always about Christ and it is always about being specific. It is not really that hard, is it, to know that our message must express both the newness of the gospel and also its specificity (precision, method) in our lives? The "new" and the "specific" are coming together at Westminster, something like this: just *how* is it right now that the *startling gospel* makes a difference? This is the age of gospel fulfillment, certainly and definitively. Any theologically accurate or pastorally helpful understanding of the Christian life must embrace that reality completely and enthusiastically. Westminster has spelled that out in at least those three ways.

Christians live now in the age of victory. What a grand message that is indeed! But is that really so new? Déjà vu suggests nineteenth-century Perfectionism, Higher Life, Keswick teaching, and the like. Generations of Reformed people were convinced that they had been taught that the only meaningful progress in

8. Jay Adams, *Truth Applied: Application in Preaching* (Grand Rapids: Zondervan, 1990).

Christian living they would ever accomplish would be at death.[9]
They were sure that all they had ever heard about the Christian
life was fruitless struggle, and that for them too nothing more
could be said than the frustration in obedience described in
Romans 7. So when they heard from the perfectionists of the parallel between justification and sanctification, that sanctification
too is by grace through faith, their lives of frustration turned into
lives of joy and victory—until they discovered that there was still
unmistakable sin in their lives, even after they were confident that
they had trusted God completely for deliverance. What did that
mean? Could it be that they were mistaken about their faith after
all? Or could it be that they had been trusting Christ in their own
strength, instead of "letting him do the trusting for them"? If those
are correct explanations for continuing sin and defeat, the practical conclusion is depressing indeed. Only two options were left.
Either you could try again and again to get the right kind of faith
that would really give victory over sin. Or you could decide that
you could not do anything anyway except wait longer for the Lord
to do for you what you could not do for yourself. That is, trying
to get the right kind of sanctification-faith turned out to be a replay
of trying to get the right kind of saving-faith. Preparationist
trauma resurfaced all over again. Faith turned into something
very introspective, mysterious, and threatening, something not
at all the way of approach to Christ, but rather that which separates from Christ—until and if we ever get it right.

Warfield wrote many articles[10] on this phenomenon, and as
his series progressed, became more and more testy with those
who claimed that they had come to understand that sanctification was by grace through faith. He became shriller and shriller,
saying: but that is what the Reformed churches had always taught!
What they had always taught—but what so many people were
sure they had never heard. Déjà vu: what we have heard before,

9. Steven Barabas, *So Great Salvation: The History and Message of the Keswick Con-
vention* (Westwood, N.J.: Fleming H. Revell, 1952).
10. Benjamin B. Warfield, *Perfectionism* (Philadelphia: Presbyterian and Reformed,
1971).

that of course Presbyterian ministers believed in justification of the ungodly by grace alone—but no one had ever heard them say it. Does the falling tree in the forest make a sound if no one is there to hear it? Do Presbyterian churches teach sanctification by grace through faith when no one thinks he ever heard it?

The parallel with justification can be somewhat misleading. Justification is ordinarily understood as instantaneous, at the moment of saving faith. Does "by grace through faith" always mean immediately? Since sanctification is a life-long process, does "by grace through faith" then not apply? Do you have to choose between "grace and faith" and "process"? That confusion results in massive misunderstanding. If sanctification is a process, a battle—then how can the language of grace and faith apply?

When Barabas's *So Great Salvation* (the history of Keswick) had appeared, John Murray's review, though dissenting, was very sympathetic.[11] Thus, it was not that surprising when Murray later came to speak of "definitive sanctification," his recognition that sanctification is not just life-long struggle, but also the definitive break with sin that the believer enjoys as soon as he is united with Christ by faith.[12] Murray thereby gave much clearer expression, in his own careful way, to many venerable Reformed themes that had regrettably fallen into disuse (the reason for Warfield's complaint). That was especially the case in terms of the doctrine of union with Christ. The older, even medieval, sequence within the *ordo* had generally been to regard union as the last in the series, the climax, reflecting final eschatological fulfillment of final and complete union with the Savior. While Murray himself followed that sequence, with the union chapter at the end in *Redemption Accomplished and Applied*, he made very clear that union belongs at the beginning, as the source of all the other blessings we receive through Christ and his work for us. Further, Gaffin and Sinclair Ferguson have expressed their indebtedness to Calvin, in Book Three of the *Institutes*, where union is so prominent. While Calvin

---

11. John Murray, *The Collected Writings of John Murray*, 4 vols. (Carlisle: Banner of Truth, 1982) 4:281–86.
12. Ibid., 2:277–93.

there develops justification at much greater length than union, clearly his structure is that of both justification and sanctification being coordinate blessings under union.

That broader view of the theology surrounding sanctification is a clear advance. It means that its gracious, faith-derived character remains prominent, but without undermining the reality of the ongoing battle against sin that is also so crucial to a biblical balance. The biblical-theological already/not yet seems particularly useful. Christ's definitive triumph is the "already," while the ongoing battle is the "not yet." To use more biblical and pastoral language, the triumph is the source of "hope," while the battle demands "patience." That balance, especially considering the sad history of perfectionism (as well as the initial need for perfectionism!), gives enormous encouragement for the way ahead. Are we not all coming to see the Christian life as an ongoing interaction of repentance and faith, and to recognize that we have not arrived but at the same time continue to trust in the power of the Spirit? Is not this biblical balance already bearing much fruit? We now see that both faith and repentance are based on Christ's definitive, eschatological "already" victory over sin, and that both require ongoing trust and obedience from the believer.

But from within this balance, further tensions around theologies of the Christian life have arisen, with two Westminster professors, Jack Miller and Norman Shepherd, articulating the differences. For many years Miller taught practical theology at Westminster, notably in evangelism and in two electives in "Christianity in American literature," which became a major seminary evangelistic thrust to the community. Partly out of discouragement with his own ministry, partly from the desire to give encouragement to missionaries and pastors in difficult situations, Miller spoke of what it meant to live as a child of God, and not as an orphan. Is not the discontent and worry in our lives a clear indication of our practical denial of the love of God and of the gospel that has brought us into the Father's family? Is it not imperative that our repentance go much deeper, that we be much more focused on the quality of our faith as it relates to the foundation of the gospel, what Jesus Christ has really done for us? While "Sonship" is clearly an appeal to the neglected doctrine of adoption, for Miller its tight linkage with justification was very important (in much the same way that the immediacy of justification and sanctification had been linked by the Perfectionists). Trusting solely in God's grace for justification must be relearned and recycled as the key to trusting the grace of God for one's adoption. Only when unbelievers come to understand and to receive grace can they be freed from thinking they can find their forgiveness in their works-righteousness. Only when believers understand grace, that they as God's children have solid claim on his blessings, can they live lives of faith and joy and effective ministry.[13]

Sonship has been helpful. Seeing God's grace in this comprehensive way has been startling and life-changing to many. It always helps to remind believers that there is a right way and a wrong way to deal with doubt and discouragement. Is there a practical connect between great difficulty and trouble in one's life and the way we understand the gospel? Miller helped us see a bigger gospel and a bigger Jesus Christ. But is there in Sonship a reductionism, an oversimplification of the Christian life, perhaps even with mystical tendencies?[14] Is its focus too exclusively on heart-motivation and not sufficiently on the structure of obedience? Sonship advocate Neil Williams and others have been alert to such criticisms and have sought to correct misconceptions and to preserve the heart of its teachings while removing confusing language.[15] It is notable that the PCA's Mission to the World, which also saw the need for a biblical focus for the encouragement of its missionaries, for many years made use of Sonship materials, but has since gone on to develop its own "grace-oriented" direction, with, I believe, much of the same emphases.[16]

13. C. John Miller, *A Faith Worth Sharing: A Lifetime of Conversations about Christ* (Phillipsburg, N.J.: P&R, 1999).

14. See Jay Adams, *Biblical Sonship: An Evaluation of the Sonship Discipleship Course* (Huntersville, N.C.: Timeless Texts, 1999).

15. Neil H. Williams, *The Theology of Sonship* (Jenkintown, Pa.: World Harvest Mission, 2002).

16. Paul Kooistra, *Thirty-one Days of Grace* (n.p.: Mission to the World, n.d.).

The Norman Shepherd emphases have been more controversial and difficult to analyze. In Miller, the up-front issue was adoption, but clearly within the context of justification. In Shepherd it was about justification, but within the broader context of sanctification, perseverance, and the Christian life. Shepherd said that sanctification and perseverance were not add-ons, but were vitally connected with justification. He sought to focus the discussion on the immediate covenantal interaction between God and the sinner, not the more remote context of election and regeneration. He desired a much tighter connection of the aspects of the *ordo* than had frequently been the case. He sought a straightforward presentation of Christ without the encumbrances of alleged elements of Calvinism that inevitably qualify or minimize the gospel.[17] Shepherd had a good nose for the previous complexities associated with the gospel, and hoped to limit their impact and to proclaim a clearer, simpler message. If he succeeded, then there would be much less of the "yes, but" theology that affirmed a biblical truth but then immediately weakened it by many qualifications. If he succeeded, then we could look at the trends of theology earlier in this article and say a relieved farewell to them all. Without question, Shepherd's attempt was well worth making.

Unfortunately, it met with limited success. While his views seemed to some to be a significant new beginning in theology, to others they were deeply puzzling, to yet others a clear threat to the heart of the gospel. All desired a tighter linkage of faith and obedience, of justification and sanctification, of forgiveness and change. The whole history of Reformed theology had shown that necessity. To that interest in theological tidiness had been added a new urgency in the church's need for theological clarity. Radical dispensationalism had pushed its message of grace to the ultimate in its rejection of "lordship salvation." It taught a saving faith as bare intellectual assent, and was perceived as giving com-

17. Norman Shepherd, *The Call of Grace: How the Covenant Illuminates Salvation and Evangelism* (Phillipsburg, N.J.: P&R, 2000).

fort to the endemic moral collapse of the contemporary church. The knee-jerk response appeared legalistic, neonomian. The hour demanded a pastorally clear and ringing expression of faith in the Christ of the Bible, the Savior and the Lord. Both justification and sanctification, and their covenantal union-with-Christ unity, needed to be vigorously affirmed without compromise.

Shepherd's covenantal way of thinking was very congenial. Is it not refreshing for us to follow along the biblical story of God's people enjoying his favor, obeying and enjoying his favor further? Or, disobeying and being given up to exile—as the Lord's loving goad to bring us back? Does that not resemble our lives today, as we struggle with unbelief, needing the Lord to intervene in our lives to get our attention? The track record of the older theology of a mysterious God and a mysterious regeneration, swallowing up the proclaimed gospel with its the imperative call to repentance, should teach us that we need a theological fresh start. Shepherd expressed biblical creativity and a heart-desire for a Reformed faith that would be not just described, but vigorously proclaimed.

But many struggled to understand and still could not recognize in his teaching the heart of the gospel, the justification of sinners. Did he not say that obedience was within faith right from the beginning? Did his stress on union with Christ leave room for the alien, imputed righteousness of Christ? What do these statements mean: "His was a living, active, and obedient faith that took him all the way to the cross. This faith was credited to him as righteousness." "But just as Jesus was faithful in order to guarantee the blessing, so his followers must be faithful in order to inherit the blessing."[18] Union with Christ is a grand key to the gospel—but has Shepherd left room for the uniqueness of Christ's work, for the reality of the Savior who is rewarded by the Father, but in no sense saved by him?

For many, those questions remained without answers. The Westminster board determined to dismiss Shepherd for the good

18. Ibid., 16, 19.

of the institution, though they had not specified error in his teaching. Though not a satisfactory resolution for anyone, it did provide a response, however ambiguous, to an apparently ambiguous theology. The lengthy theological reflection carried on throughout the Westminster community on these issues may yet be of help to the church. Further confusion can be diminished, we hope. Many agenda questions could be put more clearly. Is the need of the hour innovative theological progression, or is it a clearer understanding of the Reformed theological heritage? That is, do we need to replace or supplement other views? Could that be done within more conventional expressions of justification, with supplemental insights grafted in? Could the target audience be more closely identified? For Miller, the audience is clearly discouraged, anxious, worried Christians who needed radical reminder of the Lord's grace (as in the old "antinomian" Marrow agenda?). Would closer targeting of that audience mitigate against apparent imbalance? Perhaps, but right now, as long as Shepherd's views have not been placed within the broader context of the biblical gospel (including its "for sinners" aspects), in isolation they seem imbalanced and misleading.

Did I speak too soon when I spoke of "resolution" of views of the Christian life, especially as attained by "Westminster theology"? I continue to believe its contributions have moved doctrine further along than ever before in the history of the church. I think that the Clowney-Adams synthesis is alive and well, and gloriously salutary—that biblical theology can also show us the *how* of Christian living. Both Miller and Shepherd in their desires to move ahead exaggerated their agendas. Miller's oversimplifications are being corrected, best by Williams, and remain a substantial work in process; that is not yet happening with Shepherd's—but that may still occur.

Forgiveness and change are momentous issues, not to be limited to in-house discussions. Westminster theology can be more easily understood within its own context, but its concerns are vitally important to everyone. Any believer, whoever he is, needs to put grace and obedience together. Westminster's biblical theology, with its focus on grace and on Jesus Christ, has been obscure (Vos is hardly a page-turner!). But its *Doppelgänger*, British and American dispensationalism, has been ubiquitous, as the simultaneous rustle of turning Scofield Bible pages attests. This popular outlook on interpreting the Bible has been so close, so almost right! In the face of legalism it vigorously affirmed grace. While Paul's attitude to God's law is almost too complicated, dispensationalism shouted that the church is "not under law but under grace." The Old Testament is not legalistic or irrelevant, but vital to the church today (charts help!). The collapse of postmillennialism, when Christian triumphs over slavery and Demon Rum turned into the Gilded Age and the Mafia, did not mean the end of eschatology and its Old Testament foundation. Rather, eschatology was revitalized into premillennialism, where it became clearer than ever that the eschatological significance of this age is world-wide evangelism (50 years before Cullmann). This was core Fundamentalist theology—but Scofield was, after all, a Presbyterian minister and Dallas Seminary existed to train Presbyterian ministers.

Dispensationalism had made many things clearer—but the price was much too high. The earliest version claimed that the Sermon on the Mount was not for the church, that the Lord's Prayer with its "forgive us our debts as we forgive our debtors" was also "legal ground" and not for the church, and that the Sabbath was Jewish. In earlier days it had suggested that Jews were saved by keeping the law. It made of eschatology a *description* of the future state of affairs in the world—after all of us have been raptured out if it. It suggested that since the church at the end will by definition be apostate, attempts at church discipline, or indeed at any kind of church structure that went beyond independency, were all futile and a waste of time. The kingdom became a Jewish thing, not at all the foundation of Christian witness and effort within a corrupt world—why polish the brass on a sinking ship?

It opened the way for the radical dispensationalist conviction that it was legalistic to ask sinners to come to Jesus Christ as their Lord. For some dispensationalists it was possible to think that "grace" and the "lordship of Christ" could not co-exist. To those issues Reformed scholars responded with the volume *Christ the Lord*,[19] with notable contributions from Westminster Seminary in California. Robert Godfrey summarized Calvin's response to the Catholic Council of Trent, pointing out its merely intellectualistic understanding of faith and how closely that approaches the anti-lordship wing of dispensationalism. Calvin's careful distinction between justification and sanctification, coupled with their vital relationship, is a compelling lesson from church history that would give much greater cohesion and balance to the entire lordship discussion; without that distinction Christianity collapses into either neo- or antinomianism. Godfrey brought Reformation and present-day issues tightly together, providing useful context for the discussion. In the face of contemporary oversimplifications, Godfrey reminds us how we've all been there before, and we should know better.[20]

Robert Strimple's contribution was exegetical in character, a careful discussion of repentance in the sixth chapter of Romans. His writing expresses the essence of the foundational already/not yet—while avoiding its jargon. Strimple tells us that Paul does not describe what *should* be true of believers—but informs us what *is* true! We are to consider that sin does not rule over us—because that expresses a gospel reality! And, because we have been set free, we are called to live that way![21] The multiplicity of (my) exclamation points underlines the practical doxology gloriously proclaimed in Strimple's display of the biblical freedom we enjoy by Christ's gift.

Can we understand the Christian life by the hard work of exegesis and theology? Certainly. But how do we live that life? Reformed labor in theology is a commitment to connecting with the Reformed style of life.

19. Michael Horton, ed., *Christ the Lord: The Reformation and Lordship Salvation* (Grand Rapids: Baker, 1992).
20. W. Robert Godfrey, "Calvin and the Council of Trent," in *Christ the Lord*, 119–28.
21. Robert B. Strimple, "Repentance in Romans," in *Christ the Lord*, 61–68.

The Reformed and Westminster perspective on sanctification is a rich and profitable one. It builds upon a grand heritage, and goes on to improve the good beginning. It recognizes the terribleness of sin, and does not at all want to explain it away. But the more it sees the need, how much more does it see the surpassing grace of the Lord. Where sin abounded, how much more does grace abound.

Strimple expresses that compellingly: "Sanctification, deliverance from sin's dominion over your life, is not merely the purpose of justification. Purposes, by definition, can fail. Sanctification, being set free from sin's dominion, is God's gift to you, along with justification; it is the inevitable partner of justification."[22]

22. Ibid., 66.

Bibliography of Robert B. Strimple

1965

Anselm and the Theology of Atonement: A Study of the Man and His Message. Th.M. thesis, Westminster Theological Seminary, Philadelphia, PA.

"What is Your Starting Point?" *Evangelical Recorder* 71 (June 1965): 9.

"Give Attendance . . . to Doctrine." *Evangelical Recorder* 71 (December 1965): 4–5.

1966

"Our College's Philosophy of Education." *Evangelical Recorder* 72 (September 1966): 7.

"Accreditation: What Does It Mean?" *Evangelical Recorder* 72 (December 1966): 5–6.

1968

"Needed: A New Authorized Version!" *Evangelical Baptist* 16, no.1 (1968): 12–13.

1971

"Theological Education in a Revolutionary Age," Westminster Theological Seminary, no date. Reprinted as "Theology for Revolution," in *The Presbyterian Guardian* (March 1971): 34, 42; and in *Presbyterian Journal* 30 (May 5, 1971): 9–10.

1972

Jesus and the Church: A Critical Study of the Christology of John Knox. Th.D. dissertation, Trinity College, University of Toronto, Ontario, Canada.
"Jesus and the Church: A Critical Study of the Christology of John Knox." *Westminster Theological Journal* 35 (Fall 1972): 36–64.

1974

"Introduction and First Chapter of 'Jesus and the Church: A Critical Study of the Christology of John Knox.'" In *Studying the New Testament Today*, ed. John H. Skilton. Nutley, N.J.: Presbyterian and Reformed, 76–96.
"Do Not Lie to One Another." *The Presbyterian Guardian* 43 (October 1974): 125.

1975

"All Things in Common." *The Presbyterian Guardian* 44 (June 1975): 88–89.

1976

"Jubilee!—Gospel Command." *The Presbyterian Guardian* 45 (August-September 1976): 4–6.

"The Lord's Servant," printed Morning Devotions message, Westminster Theological Seminary, October 4, 1976. Reprinted in *Nouthetic Confrontation* (Summer 1977): 3–4.

1977

"The Healing Touch of Christ." *Bulletin of Westminster Theological Seminary* 16 (Fall 1977): 6–7.
"The Relationship Between Scripture and Tradition in Contemporary Roman Catholic Theology." *Westminster Theological Journal* 40 (Fall 1977): 22–38.
"Learning Christ." *The Presbyterian Guardian* 46 (November 1977): 3, 13.

1979

"The Lord's Servant." In *Conflict: A Moment for Ministry*, ed. Wesley M. Pinkham and William C. Hill. Wheaton: Wheaton Graduate School, 53–54.
"Philippians 2:5–11 in Recent Studies: Some Exegetical Conclusions." *Westminster Theological Journal* 41 (Spring 1979): 247–68.

1982

"Our Reformation Heritage." *Bulletin of Westminster Theological Seminary* 21 (Spring 1982): 1–3.
"The Glory of the New Covenant." *Bulletin of Westminster Theological Seminary* 21 (Fall 1982): 1–2.

1983

"How Christians Can Rejoice Despite Sufferings." *Escondido Times-Advocate* (December 31, 1983): B4.

1985

"Be Shepherds of God's Flock," printed Morning Devotions message, Westminster Theological Seminary in California, September 5 and 6, 1985.

1987

"Bernard Ramm and the Theology of Sin." *Westminster Theological Journal* 49 (Spring 1987): 143–52.
"Remember the Risen Christ." *Kerux: A Journal of Biblical-Theological Preaching* 2 (December 1987): 31–41.

1988

"Report of the Minority of the Committee on Women in Church Office." In *Minutes of the Fifty-fifth General Assembly of the OPC, 1988*. Philadelphia: Orthodox Presbyterian Church, 356–73.
"Phoebe Was a Deacon: Other Women Should Be, Too." *New Horizons* 9 (June-July 1988): 17–18.

1989

"Was Adam an Historical Person? And What Difference Does It Make?" In *Christian Renewal*, June 20, 1989. Reprinted in *The Outlook* 40 (May 1991): 21–24; and in *New Horizons* 14 (February 1993): 6–8.

1990

"For All People—One Christ, One Gospel, One Mandate," message presented at the Tenth Anniversary of Westminster Theological Seminary in California, September 7, 1990.

"Christian Perfection and Academic Freedom," printed Morning Devotions message, Westminster Theological Seminary in California, November 20, 1990.

1991

"No-Lordship Salvation: Romans 6 and the 'Lordship Salvation' Debate." *Modern Reformation* (November/December 1991): 5–9.

1992

"Systematic Theology at Westminster." *Update* 10 (Winter 1992): 2–3.

"Roman Catholic Theology: Thirty Years after Vatican II." *New Horizons* 13 (October 1992): 3–6. Reprinted in *The Outlook* 43 (February 1993): 3–5.

1993

"God's Sovereignty and Man's Free Will." *Modern Reformation* (January-February 1993): 3–7.

"Repentance in Romans." In *Christ the Lord*, ed. Michael Horton. Grand Rapids: Baker (1992), 61–68.

1994

"The 'Lordship Salvation' Debate—and Romans 6." *The Elders' Forum* 5 (Spring 1994): 1–2, 7–8.

"Roman Catholic Theology Today." In *Roman Catholicism: Evangelical Protestants Analyze What Divides and Unites Us*, ed. John Armstrong. Chicago: Moody Press, 85–117.

1995

---

*The Modern Search for the Real Jesus: An Introductory Survey of
   the Historical Roots of Gospels Criticism.* Phillipsburg, N.J.:
   P&R Publishing, 1995.
"What Is the Jesus Seminar? An Interview with Dr. Robert Strimple." *Modern Reformation* 4/6 (Nov/Dec): 13–15.
"Why We Believe the Bible Is God's Written Word," In *Insight* (Fall
   1995).

1996

"What Does God Know?" In *The Coming Evangelical Crisis*, ed.
   John H. Armstrong. Chicago: Moody Press, 1996, 139–53.
"St Anselm's Cur Deus Homo and John Calvin's Doctrine of the
   Atonement." In *Anselm: Aosta, Bec and Canterbury*, ed.
   D. E. Luscombe and G. R. Evans. Sheffield: Sheffield Aca-
   demic Press, 348–60.
"The Awe of New Covenant Worship," printed Morning Devotions
   message, Westminster Theological Seminary in California,
   May 2, 1996.

1999

"Amillennialism." In *Three Views on the Millennium and Beyond*,
   ed. Darrell Bock. Grand Rapids: Zondervan, 83–129.
Responses to Kenneth Gentry and Craig Blaising. In *Three Views
   on the Millennium and Beyond*. Grand Rapids: Zondervan,
   58–71, 256–76.
Review: Jacob van Bruggen, *Christ on Earth: The Gospel Narra-
   tives as History. Themelios* 25 (November 1999): 92–93.

2000

"Cur *Cur Deus Homo*," In *Tabletalk* 24 (October 2000): 11–13, 57.

2001

"The Fear of the Lord," In *New Horizons* (March 2001): 3–4.
"I Don't Want to Join the Church!" In *New Horizons* (May 2001):
    8, 21.

2002

"Do You Believe This?" In *New Horizons* (March 2002): 3–4.

2004

"The Hyper-Preterist Doctrine of the Resurrection of the Body,"
    in *When Shall These Things Be? A Reformed Response to
    Hyper-Preterism*, ed. Keith Mathison. Phillipsburg, N.J.: P&R
    Publishing, 2004, 287–352.

Contributors

All of the contributors to this volume have held faculty positions in at least one of the Westminsters—and in several cases both. All of us have been colleagues of Dr. Strimple in various capacities, and a number of us his students. As such, we must acknowledge that ours is an insider's view of Westminster and its theology, with both the advantages and the limitations that this entails.

Jay E. Adams (Ph.D., University of Missouri) is a retired pastor. For many years he was a professor of practical theology and held various administrative positions at Westminster Theological Seminary and Westminster Seminary California.

Derke P. Bergsma (Rel.D., Chicago Theological Seminary) is professor emeritus of practical theology at Westminster Seminary California.

R. Scott Clark (D.Phil., University of Oxford) is associate professor of historical and systematic theology at Westminster Seminary California.

Edmund P. Clowney (S.T.M., Yale Divinity School) is president and professor emeritus of practical theology at Westminster Theological Seminary. He also taught in semi-retirement at Westminster Seminary California for many years.

D. Clair Davis (Dr. theol., Georg-August Universität, Göttingen) is professor of church history at Westminster Theological Seminary.

John M. Frame (M.Phil., Yale University) is professor of systematic theology and philosophy at Reformed Theological Seminary, Orlando. He was formerly a professor of apologetics and systematic theology at both Westminster Theological Seminary and Westminster Seminary California.

Richard B. Gaffin Jr. (Th.D., Westminster Theological Seminary) is professor of biblical and systematic theology at Westminster Theological Seminary.

W. Robert Godfrey (Ph.D., Stanford University) is president and professor of church history at Westminster Seminary California. He formerly served as a professor of church history at Westminster Theological Seminary.

D. G. Hart (Ph.D., Johns Hopkins University) is director for honors programs and faculty development at the Intercollegiate Studies Institute in Wilmington, Delaware. He was a professor of church history and held various administrative positions at both Westminster Theological Seminary and Westminster Seminary California.

Michael S. Horton (Ph.D., University of Coventry and Wycliffe Hall, Oxford) is professor of theology and apologetics at Westminster Seminary California.

Dennis E. Johnson (Ph.D., Fuller Theological Seminary) is professor of practical theology and academic dean at Westminster Seminary California.

John R. Muether (M.A.R., Westminster Theological Seminary; M.L.S., Simmons College) is librarian and associate professor of church history at Reformed Theological Seminary, Orlando. He was formerly the librarian at Westminster Theological Seminary.

David VanDrunen (J.D., Northwestern University; Ph.D., Loyola University Chicago) is associate professor of systematic theology and Christian ethics and Robert B. Strimple chair in systematic theology at Westminster Seminary California.

Index